RESEARCH TO PRACTICE

Other books published by Learning Disabilities Worldwide

Bound and Determined: To Help Children with Learning Disabilities
  written by Mark Cooper

Best Practices for the Inclusionary Classroom: Leading Researchers Talk Directly to Teachers
  edited by Maureen K. Riley & Teresa Allissa Citro

Many Shades of Success: Other Views of Post-Secondary Options
  edited by Teresa Allissa Citro

Transitional Skills for Post-Secondary Success: Reflections for High School Students with Learning Disabilities
  edited by Teresa Allissa Citro

Successful Lifetime Management: Adults with Learning Disabilities
  edited by Teresa Allissa Citro

The Experts Speak: Parenting the Child with Learning Disabilities
  edited by Teresa Allissa Citro

Los Especialistas Aconsejan: Ser Padres de Ninos con Problemas de Aprendizaje
  edited by Teresa Allissa Citro

RESEARCH TO PRACTICE:

Effective Interventions in Learning Disabilities

Learning Disabilities
Worldwide

To my parents Demetrios and Athena, thank you for your constant support and inspiration.

Georgios D. Sideridis

To my wonderful sisters-in-law . . . Annette, Tina, and Gina your encouragement and support have been a blessing. You are my sisters!

Teresa Allissa Citro

Contents

FOREWORD

How do children learn to read? How does a small child who's only been on Earth five or six years learn so quickly to manage 26 letters and 44 phonemes to produce meaning? Before we take up the problem of children who do not learn to read well enough, we should reflect on the almost miraculous fact that so many children do become proficient readers. The ancients understood the connection between reading and sorcery, and we still speak of witches "casting spells" and fortune-tellers "reading palms" or "reading tea-leaves." Even teachers themselves have long seen the reading process as mysterious. There is an old saying that "math is taught, but reading is caught," expressing teachers' beliefs that their own teaching efforts in reading do not account in a direct way for children's reading successes (or lack of them).

It's not only reading that is a mysterious process. As much as we have learned in recent years about how the brain operates, it is still astonishing how much complex knowledge and skill children normally acquire in and out of school.

The children who seem to learn so effortlessly are not the concern of this volume, however. Instead, the focus is on the children who do not learn so easily, those with learning disabilities. If reading were truly caught, not taught, then there would be little to do with children who do not read well. Yet in recent years, we've learned that reading can be taught to those who do not acquire it easily. This is of enormous importance. If we know how to teach a far greater proportion of children how to read, this knowledge places a great responsibility on educators and policymakers to use what we know. Although we know much less about the teaching of subjects other than beginning reading, we know far more than is in regular use in schools.

The stakes involved in solving the problem of learning disabilities are very high. Every year, hundreds of thousands of children in our schools experience failure in learning, and begin a declining spiral of frustration, anxiety, and more failure. This is bad enough, but made worse by the fact that school failure is more common among African-American, Hispanic, and Native American students, and children living in poverty, than among other students. The deep divisions in our society are maintained and exacerbated by the school failure of disadvantaged and minority children, and this in turn is substantially determined by success or failure in early education.

The greatest hope we have to reverse the longstanding problem of school failure, well represented in this volume, is the move toward a science of learning and toward policies based on this science. In the U.S., the No Child Left Behind Act of 2001 famously mentions practices "based on scientifically-based evidence" more than 100 times, mostly in the context of reading instruction. Despite some criticism, the substantial consensus around the findings of the National Reading Panel has provided a base for policies and practices that are at least consistent with evidence about how children learn to read. Research on how to create programs based on these principles of good practice is under way, and within a few years we should have many programs known to be capable of ensuring reading success for a much larger number of children. Hopefully, a similar process will take place in subjects other than reading, and with other children as well.

This volume plays an important part in the progression from the principles of good practice in No Child Left Behind to actual practice in real classrooms. It contains a broad set of chapters focusing on effective teaching strategies to prevent learning disabilities in the first place or to remedy them when they are detected. The term "learning disabilities" appears in the book's title and in all the chapters, but this book is really about effective teaching designed to meet the diverse needs of all children. The best solution we have for children with learning disabilities is effective instruction and the creation of supportive environments for all.

I hope this book will be widely read by educators committed to the idea that we cannot rest until we find effective strategies capable of ensuring the success of every child.

Robert Slavin, Ph.D.
Johns Hopkins University

INTRODUCTION

R esearch findings highlighting the functional roles of neuropsychology, motivation, emotion, and cognition have been catalytic in our understanding of the etiology and treatment of learning disabilities (Blair, 2003; Botsas & Padeliadu, 2003; Pintrich, Anderman, & Klobucar, 1994; Sideridis, Morgan, Botsas, Padeliadu, & Fuchs, in press; Troia, 2003). That body of knowledge has had implications on how students are identified, placed, and treated in our elementary school classrooms. Several recent studies demonstrated that interventions, which included advances based in the neurosciences and social sciences, when embedded in the instruction for students with LD, were substantially more effective compared to traditional instruction (e.g., Garcia & de Caso, 2004; Ruban, McCoach, McGuire, & Reis, 2003). An important challenge for the field of learning disabilities is whether or not all the knowledge produced in research labs, or in the field, is actually transferred to our elementary school classrooms (Greenwood & Abbot, 2001). Most major research journals in learning disabilities require that each study include a section on "Implications for Practice." Providing this information allows teachers, parents, and professionals to take with them the gist of each study's contribution to the literature. It is highly unlikely, however, that a paragraph or two on "implications for practice" would be useful enough for practitioners. It is equally unlikely that the sketchy and technical description of an intervention in a Methods section would be sufficient to implement the intervention with accuracy in our classrooms.

Several researchers and policy makers have argued that research findings are not readily available to the public (e.g., King-Sears, Boudah, Goodwin, Raskind, & Swanson, 2004). For example, Deshler (2003) described some of the reasons why it takes years for research findings to make their way to the classrooms. One possible barrier is our inability to translate research findings into a language that is "accessible" and easily understood by teachers and practitioners or in other words to "bring interventions to scale." Our purpose with this first volume on effective interventions in learning disabilities is to provide one vehicle to assist in bridging the gap between research and practice. From the conception of this project we faced two significant challenges: (a) how do we determine which practices are effective? and, (b) what is the best way to present this information to teachers and practitioners? The answers to these questions are reflected by the manner in which the chapters in this volume are structured. Each chapter contains two sections: (a) the research synthesis section, and, (b) the applied or "description of the intervention" section. The first section is intended to furnish justification that an intervention is effective. This section includes a thorough review of the literature where authors must provide empirical studies in support of their proposed practice. In that sense, interventions with limited empirical support are excluded. Although this criterion may seem harsh, in the end we want to say with confidence that the practices proposed herein are indeed effective. The second section is even more challenging than the first. In this section researchers describe the interventions in such detail that practitioners will be able to apply them immediately. Thus, we ask our authors to be as "graphic" and "pictorial" as possible by including relevant forms and visual aids that will assist in the understanding and the implementation of those practices by teachers. This requirement substantially lengthens the chapters, but is imperative in order to suggest "meaningful" interventions. Another goal is to include interventions and practices that will affect different domains such as academic, social, emotional, and behavioral. For example, the use of curriculum based measures (CBM, Lembke & Espin, this volume) can enhance our understanding of the effectiveness of an intervention such as the PALS (Morgan, Young, & Fuchs, this volume). The suggestions by Brooks (this volume) can be embedded within an instructional program (e.g., the PALS, Morgan et al., this volume) and the progress of this program can be monitored using CBMs (Lembke & Espin, this volume) or other monitoring practices (e.g., Mouzaki, Foorman, & Santi, this volume). Thus, the chapters can be used interchangeably and their suggestions can be implemented in multiple ways and in an enriched fashion, by incorporating the suggestions of other practices.

The present chapters describe interventions that can be grouped along four axes: practices that (a) evaluate assessment to intervention effectiveness (Lembke & Espin; Mouzaki, Foorman, & Santi), (b) alter classroom environments to be conducive for learning purposes (Brooks; Morgan, Young, & Fuchs; Sideridis), (c) enhance student skills and motivation to collaterally affect social-emotional and behavioral functioning (Michaels, Lodato Wilson, & Margolis; Tankersley, Cowan, & Cook), and (d) move beyond the typical elementary school classroom (Hughes; Peterson).

In the first chapter, Brooks describes how teacher and student's *mindsets, assumptions,* and *expectations* contribute to the creation of the classroom environment. His primary message is summarized in the following statement: I am convinced. . . that: "strengthening a student's sense of self-esteem is not an 'extra' curriculum; if anything, a student's sense of belonging, security, and self-confidence in a classroom provides the scaffolding that supports the foundation for enhanced learning, motivation, self-discipline, responsibility and the ability to deal more effectively with obstacles and mistakes" (p. 5). In essence Brooks argues that teachers should not just apply instructional practices. There is much more to instruction than the mere application of an intervention. The supportive or non-supportive instructional, motivational, and organizational discourse of teachers are important elements in the classroom. Brooks's ideas parallel recent advances in motivation and achievement which suggest that how teachers establish the psychological environment at school has implications for student achievement, well-being, and adjustment. He suggests empowering the student's social-emotional-motivational sphere by emphasizing empathy, autonomy, belongingness and connectedness, competence, self-discipline, self-regulation (monitoring), and positive affect (enthusiasm) in the classroom. Another important component in his contribution is his call for the creation of a partnership between parents and teachers for the well-being of the students.

Mouzaki, Foorman, and Santi (Chapter 2) describe an innovative prevention model that has been applied in the Texas schools. This model is based on the assessment of student skills. They stress that phonological awareness, letter-sound knowledge, and word identification are significant predictors of students' subsequent reading abilities. The authors base the development of their intervention on those predictive findings. Their suggestions for effective intervention include (a) instruction tailored to student needs, (b) application of systematic lessons, delivered by knowledgeable teachers using explicit direct and/or small group instruction, (c) use of continuous and systematic assessment, (d) application of classroom management strategies, and (e) emphasis on the creation of supportive environments that are conducive to students' emotional and social functioning. The authors go on to describe excellent practices, using real-class examples of how applying the early screening findings enhances student learning. Among other things, a significant contribution of their work is the authors' emphasis on prevention. Early assessments provide predictions for student achievement; if those predictions are unfavorable, teachers and parents can focus on intervening so that those predictions will prove false.

Tankersley, Cowan, and Cook (Chapter 3) propose self-monitoring as a way to improve both the academic performance and behavior of students with and without LD. The basis of this model lies in *cognitive training*. It is proposed that when students are taught how to use specific instructions, cognitions, and problem-solving strategies, they will successfully manage their behavior and achieve positive academic outcomes. The goal of this training then is to enhance self-management skills, which will in turn promote student independence, self-reliance, personal responsibility, and personal control. The authors then describe the elements of self-monitoring, after demonstrating its effectiveness in numerous previous studies across populations, settings, and behaviors. In their highly significant contribution, the authors include student training procedures and schedules on how to improve student behavior. Also, the use of this intervention for academic and non-academic behaviors is of tremendous importance because it enhances the application and generalization of self-monitoring.

Peterson (Chapter 4) redirects our attention to an intervention that has its basis in students' natural tendencies, interests, and desires. By describing a very rich knowledge base (empirical literature), Peterson explains how "incidental teaching" (i.e., naturally occurring learning) can facilitate language acquisition. The author cites several studies by Hart and Risley stating that this approach involves "the interaction between an adult and a single child, which arises naturally in an unstructured situation such as free-play and which is used by an adult to transmit information or give the child practice in developing a skill. . . . The situation or activity is 'child-selected' with the teacher or caregiver following the child's lead or interest" (pp. 73–74). This intervention has ample elements of reinforcement during the caregiver-child interaction and has its origins in the behavioral tradition. The value and contribution of incidental learning lie in the fact that this intervention can be implemented both at school and at home. Thus, parents and caregivers can enhance student learning by applying the careful monitoring principles described in this chapter.

Michaels, Lodato Wilson, and Margolis (Chapter 5) stress the importance of motivation. In particular the authors draw from social-cognitive theory and the role of self-efficacy beliefs in subsequent learning and achievement. As the authors describe, this personal and oftentimes private belief has enormous consequences on how students view achievement situations, failures, and on how they regulate their behavior for school tasks. In their view, "to achieve this with learners who doubt their competence, teachers must work to systematically strengthen struggling learners self-efficacy by creating emotionally and psychologically safe classes in which sound pedagogy is practiced" (p. 93). The authors go on to propose an elegant combination of research-based practices that enhance student motivation and achievement. The direction this work brings to the field of learning disabilities is very important given how under studied motivation is. Research evidence suggests that its inclusion is valuable and important for both the well-being and achievement of students with learning problems.

Morgan, Young, and Fuchs (Chapter 6) describe one of the most validated interventions to date in the elementary school classrooms (i.e., the use of peer-assisted learning strategies). The authors present rich evidence in favor of the PALS, some of which comes from their own systematic line of research during the last 25 years. The authors describe in great depth and detail how teachers apply the PALS to enhance reading. Besides the rich description of the PALS as a reading intervention, teachers can use the method as a "template" on which to build interventions in other subject matter (e.g., spelling, math, social studies). Thus, the application of the intervention is not limited to reading and with some alterations can improve students' skills in multiple content areas. Another advantage of the method is the attitude of acceptance and equality students exhibit toward their peers when engaged in cooperative learning experiences. Lastly, with modifications, the method can also be utilized by parents at home, to provide additional practice for students who need it.

Lembke and Espin (Chapter 7) propose the use of curriculum based measures as a means to develop effective interventions. Through repeated measurement teachers can monitor the progress of short-term or long-term goals and adjust instruction accordingly. This method has several advantages including the close monitoring of performance using graphs, the examination of student behavior using inspection of means and slopes, the ease of applying it, and the use of the method in multiple areas (in fact in as many behaviors as are in the student's repertoire). The authors emphasize the issues of reliability and validity in measurement and apply the method in both reading and math. The detailed presentation of case studies in reading and math, specifying when to apply or change an intervention, is extremely useful in describing how the CBM-based method works. Furthermore, because application of the method is so easy, the authors propose the possibility of its use on a school-wide level.

Hughes (Chapter 8) transfers our focus from the classroom to home. This is a very important focus given its developmental nature. The author directs our attention to the very early years and suggests that the application of family-centered practices provides natural and meaningful learning opportunities for students across disabilities. The author describes in detail the proposed model and highlights the importance of empowering families so that children will grow and develop across all domains. This work relates to the work of Peterson who proposes naturalistic learning but extends it with generalization to the home setting. The value of the program and the author's enthusiasm for this interactionist perspective are reflected in the following statement: "As a provider of early intervention services to infants and toddlers, you have a wonderful opportunity to directly impact the lives of families. Promoting caregiver-child interactions that are positive, that facilitate the child's developmental goals, and that produce competencies in parents that otherwise may never be known is an incredibly rewarding experience!" (p. 180). We too, believe that structuring those early experiences can be both rewarding and extremely beneficial for the natural development of children.

Lastly, Sideridis (Chapter 9) proposes the creation of classroom environments that may accelerate learning for students with and without learning problems. The creation of such environments is guided by achievement goal theory (Dweck & Leggett, 1988) and places an emphasis on student motivation. Two such environments are described, one with an emphasis on cooperation and intrinsic motivation (mastery) and one with an emphasis on competition and extrinsic rewards (performance). Both environments may be adaptive for different outcomes although recent research evidence favors the creation of "mastery" classroom goal structures. The chapter provides an analytic account of the elements of each goal structure that, if manipulated, can create the environments of interest. The author's recent data also indicate the superiority of mastery goal structures. Thus, teachers can follow the proposed suggestions to create non-competitive structures that will enhance student achievement through the use of interest and cooperative learning.

We are grateful to the generous contributions of our authors who enrich our understanding of how to identify and treat struggling learners. We believe there is a great deal to be discovered about how to educate students who have difficulties learning. One path involves transferring our research knowledge base to our classrooms. This first volume is one such attempt. By making the evidence-based practices compiled here accessible to practitioners, we hope teachers will be able to implement these methods in their classrooms. This will move us closer to achieving our ultimate goal of improving the educational experiences of individuals with learning disabilities. We intend to produce a series of "Research to Practice" volumes in order to assist teachers in their efforts to increase the academic opportunities and social-emotional functioning of individuals with learning problems. Your feedback and suggestions are appreciated as we work together as agents of change.

Georgios D. Sideridis
Teresa A. Citro

REFERENCES

Blair, C. (2003). Learning disability, intelligence, and fluid cognitive functions of the pre-frontal cortex: A developmental neuroscience approach. *Learning Disabilities: A Contemporary Journal, 2,* 22–29.

Botsas, G., & Padeliadu, S. (2003). Goal orientation and reading comprehension strategy use among students with and without reading difficulties. *International Journal of Educational Research, 39,* 477–495.

Deshler, D. D. (2003). Intervention research and bridging the gap between research and practice. *Learning Disabilities: A Contemporary Journal, 1,* 1–7.

Dweck, C. S., & Leggett, E. L. (1988). A social-cognitive approach to motivation and personality. *Psychological Review, 95,* 256–273.

Garcia, J. N., & de Caso, A. M. (2004). Effects of a motivational intervention for improving the writing of children with learning disabilities. *Learning Disability Quarterly, 27,* 141–160.

Greenwood, C. R., & Abbot, M. (2001). The research to practice gap in special education. *Teacher Education and Special Education, 24,* 276–289.

King-Sears, M. E., Boudah, D. J., Goodwin, M. W., Raskind, M. H., Swanson, L. H. (2004). Timely and compelling research for the field of learning disabilities: Implications for the future. *Learning Disability Quarterly, 27,* 141–160.

Pintrich, P. R., Anderman, E. M., & Klobucar, C. (1994). Intraindividual differences in motivation and cognition in students with and without learning disabilities. *Journal of Learning Disabilities, 27,* 360–370.

Ruban, L. M., McCoach, B. D., McGuire, J. M., & Reis, S., M. (2003). The differential impact of academic self-regulatory methods on academic achievement among university students with and without learning disabilities. *Journal of Learning Disabilities, 36,* 270–286.

Sideridis, G. D., Morgan, P., Botsas, G., Padeliadu, S., & Fuchs, D. (in press). Prediction of students with LD based on metacognition, motivation, emotions, and psychopathology: A ROC analysis. *Journal of Learning Disabilities.*

Troia, G. A. (2003). Auditory perceptual impairments and learning disabilities: Theoretical and empirical considerations. *Learning Disabilities: A Contemporary Journal, 1,* 27–36.

ACKNOWLEGMENT

As Learning Disabilities Worldwide becomes a global voice of hope for individuals with learning disabilities, their families, and the professionals who work with them and on their behalf, we would like to thank the dedicated people who share our commitment. We appreciate the support of Commonwealth Learning Centers for their history of awards to our organization, and for their most recent grant providing funds for the publication of this book; Moira Munns for her substantive editing, copyediting and attention to detail; Lauren Brownstein for proofreading the first draft; Susan Mcdonald for her magnificent design and layout; Sonia Foster for attending to all the unexpected, extra little things that were required to ensure this book was published on schedule; and every contributing author for translating research on effective interventions into classroom practice. Finally, we would like to thank the members of the governing and advisory boards of Learning Disabilities Worldwide for their enthusiasm and support of this project to bring help to teachers and hope to students.

Chapter One

Creating a Positive School Climate for Students with Learning Disabilities: The Power of Mindsets

Robert B. Brooks, Ph.D.
Harvard Medical School

I was asked to consult about Lisa, an eight-year-old girl with learning and attentional problems. Lisa's parents were not only concerned about her struggles learning to read and her difficulties attending and remaining organized, but were equally distressed by the sadness and feelings of hopelessness that were becoming prominent features of her life. Lisa told them that she was "dumb and stupid" and added, "I don't think I'll ever be smart."

Lisa's mother noted sadly, "Lisa is such a young child and already seems to have the problems of the world on her shoulders."

We scheduled a meeting with Lisa's teacher. While the teacher was aware of Lisa's learning disabilities, she observed, "The problem with Lisa is that she is inconsistent. I know she has learning disabilities, but she can do the work if she puts her mind to it. If she buckles down and tries harder she wouldn't have some of the problems she has. She just doesn't seem to have the motivation to finish her work, especially when things become more challenging. I tried offering her an award, some stickies with smiling faces, but I guess they didn't matter to her since she still gave up. I just don't know what else I can do to motivate her. She has to begin to take more responsibility and not be so lazy."

The teacher's frustration with Lisa was very apparent. In turn, Lisa's parents felt frustrated by the accusatory tone housed in her teacher's remarks.

Bret, a nine-year-old boy burdened with learning and attentional problems similar to those of Lisa, also questioned whether he was intelligent and capable of learning. He told his parents, "No matter what I do, I can't remember a lot of things I knew yesterday." In the conference we had with Bret's teacher, she offered a remarkable statement. "I think Bret uses every ounce of energy he has to learn. When he seems to give up, it's a sign for me that he's feeling defeated and I try to figure out what I can do to help him feel less defeated. Sometimes it's just an encouraging word, letting him know that I realize learning certain things is not easy for him. I tell him that together we can try to figure out what will help him to learn. I know he still gets discouraged and wonders if he will be able to learn, but I'm going to be very supportive and persistent with him. I don't give up easily."

Bret's mother responded, "I think Bret knows how much you care. Just yesterday, he told us, 'My teacher told me I am smart and she could help me to learn.'"

MINDSETS, ASSUMPTIONS, AND EXPECTATIONS

The contrasting comments offered by Lisa and Bret's teachers illustrate what may seem obvious but in many ways are not, namely, that we all possess different mindsets or assumptions about ourselves as well as others (Brooks, 2001a,b, 2004; Brooks & Goldstein, 2001, 2003). Lisa's teacher perceived Lisa's problems with learning in a judgmental way, describing her as lazy and unmotivated. In contrast, Bret's teacher interpreted his learning problems not as a lack of motivation but rather as his lacking certain skills—skills that she felt could be reinforced.

Our assumptions, which we may not even think about or be aware of, play a significant role in determining our expectations and behavior. Even seemingly hidden assumptions have a way of being expressed to others. Not surprisingly, people begin to behave in accord with the expectations we have of them and when they do, we are apt to interpret this as a sign that our expectations are accurate. What we fail to appreciate is the extent to which our expectations subtly or not-so-subtly shape the behavior of others.

If we examine the school environment, it should not be surprising to discover that educators possess many different assumptions about the process of education and about students with learning disabilities. Given these differences, a question can be posed, namely, "What is the mindset of an effective educator?" or worded somewhat differently, "What are the assumptions and behaviors of an educator who is most likely to enrich the hearts and minds of students with learning disabilities and reinforce their motivation and hope?"

In attempting to answer this question in this chapter, I will draw upon the many interactions I have had with educators as well as my experiences as a principal of a school in a locked-door unit of a psychiatric hospital, as a consultant to both public and independent schools, and as a therapist for numerous children and adolescents with learning disabilities. My journeys have introduced me to teachers, school administrators, and other school staff who are skilled in nurturing the "whole" student, who appreciate the need to focus not only on developing the intellectual lives of youngsters but also their emotional lives, and who, through their words and actions, demonstrate a profound commitment to creating school climates in which all students will thrive.

These talented educators possess a mindset that guides their teaching style and their interaction with students, a mindset that fortifies a love of learning, even in those children and adolescents struggling with learning problems. The more aware educators are of the tenets of this mindset, the more they can rely on constructive guideposts in their interactions with students.

THE ASSUMPTIONS AND MINDSET OF EFFECTIVE EDUCATORS

The following are several of the key characteristics of the mindset of effective educators. I believe that educators who embrace and incorporate this mindset in their teaching activities will lessen the feelings of low self-esteem and limited confidence experienced by many students with learning disabilities while helping them to lead more productive, hopeful, fulfilling lives.

All Students Desperately Want to Learn and to Succeed

I use the word "desperately" on purpose to emphasize each child's dream to be successful. Can you imagine a four-year-old saying, "I hope when I begin school I have difficulty learning. I hope I fail many tests and have trouble completing my homework so that my parents and teachers will constantly nag me to try harder and do better"? I believe that every child desires to learn and achieve in school. Effective educators subscribe to this belief and understand that when a student appears to give up, it is a sign that the student is feeling overwhelmed, vulnerable, and defeated.

All-too-often struggling students are anointed with accusatory labels such as "lazy" or "unmotivated." Once students are viewed as possessing these pejorative qualities, adults are likely to fall into the trap of becoming increasingly punitive and controlling rather than encouraging and supportive. These students frequently hear, "You could do it if you wanted to" or "You just don't try hard enough." As Dr. Mel Levine (2003) has eloquently espoused in his book *The Myth of Laziness*:

> When we call someone lazy, we condemn a human being. I am convinced that laziness is nothing more than a myth—hence the title of this book. Everybody yearns to be productive. Every kid would prefer to do his homework and be praised for its quality. Every grown-up would like to generate output that merits a raise or promotion. It's all part of a natural search for both recognition and self-satisfaction. As I've said, it's a basic drive. Therefore, when someone's output is too low, we shouldn't accuse or blame that individual. Instead, we should wonder what could be thwarting that person's output, obstructing his or her natural inborn inclination to produce. (p. 9)

I am sensitive to the issue of blaming since at the beginning of my career when children or adolescents did not improve in therapy with me or in the school at which I was principal, I was quick to label them "resistant," "oppositional," "unmotivated," and "manipulative." My use of such negative words essentially served to blame the very youngsters I was supposed to be helping. One of the most noteworthy changes in my mindset or perspective occurred when I began to accept the notion that whether or not a child benefited from therapy or learned in school has as much, if not more, to do with the attitude, style, and behavior of the therapist or educator than what the child brings into the situation (Brooks, 1997).

I am not implying that teachers should blame themselves when their techniques are not effective with a challenging student. Rather, I am advocating that instead of blaming the student through the use of accusatory labels, we should attempt to define and understand the student's strengths and vulnerabilities and ask what is it that we can do differently so that the student may become increasingly cooperative and more comfortable engaging in the process of learning. In essence, we shift the emphasis from blame to empowerment.

As an example, I worked with Billy, an angry and depressed 10-year-old with learning disabilities. He dealt with his anxieties about school by hiding behind the bushes of the school instead of entering the building. In our first meeting, Billy informed me that he hid behind the bushes because he liked the bushes better than he liked school. Rather than engage in a debate about the merits of bushes versus schools, I shifted my focus to his perceived strengths and asked him what he liked to do and thought he did well.

While many youngsters respond to such a question with a shrug and "I don't know" (if that is their response, I simply say, "That's okay, many kids aren't sure what they're good at but it's something we can think about"—I never want to put children on the spot, especially those with learning and/or language problems, by insisting they answer quickly), Billy's face lit up as he said, "I love to take care of my pet dog." Billy proceeded to spend much of the session in an animated fashion describing how to treat pets.

With Billy's permission, I spoke with the school principal who offered Billy the "job" of "pet monitor" of the school, which entailed his ensuring that the pets were cared for, writing a short story with the assistance of his teacher about pet care (the book was bound and placed in the school library), and lecturing in each class of his elementary school about the care of pets. Billy's motivation to attend school, to write, and to learn increased noticeably. He was fortunate to have a teacher and principal who possessed the courage to change their approach or script rather than expecting him to make the first move. Once they provided opportunities for Billy to pursue his interests and to be recognized positively by his peers and teachers, his seeming "resistance" disappeared.

Educators who appreciate the desire of all students to achieve in school will be more inclined to "join" the child in figuring out the most effective strategies for learning. The educational process is enriched when we understand the ways in which each student learns and we free ourselves of accusatory or judgmental remarks and interactions.

Addressing the Social-Emotional Needs of a Student is Not an Extra Curriculum Activity

At one of my workshops, I was involved in a discussion of the significant influence that educators have on the social-emotional life of students. A high school science teacher challenged the emphasis I placed on social-emotional factors by contending, "I am a science teacher. I know my science and I know how to convey science facts to my students. Why should I have to spend time thinking about the student's emotional or social life? I don't have time to do so and it will distract me from teaching science."

I know that there are many teachers and school administrators who would take issue with the views expressed by this science teacher, who believe as I do that focusing on a student's social and emotional development may be as integral as teaching specific academic skills and content (Brooks, 1999a, 2004; Cohen, 1999). However, I am also aware that there are many others who would concur with this teacher's opinion, especially as state-mandated achievement tests dominate the world of education. I believe that it is unfortunate that a dichotomy has emerged prompting some educators to perceive that nurturing a student's emotional and social health is mutually exclusive from the task of teaching academic skills.

I am convinced based on my own experiences as well as the observations I have heard from many educators, that strengthening a student's sense of self-esteem is not an "extra" curriculum; if anything, a student's sense of belonging, security, and self-confidence in a classroom provides the scaffolding that supports the foundation for enhanced learning, motivation, self-discipline, responsibility, and the ability to deal more effectively with obstacles and mistakes (Brooks, 1991, 1999a).

This focus on social-emotional factors is of special importance when working with children with learning disabilities. These youngsters, given their history of learning difficulty and failure, are especially vulnerable to feelings of frustration, low self-worth, and helplessness (Brooks, 1999b, 2001a; Canino, 1981; Deci, Hodges, Pierson, & Tomassone, 1992; Licht, 1983), feelings vividly captured in interviews and therapy I conducted. The following are a representative sample of comments I received from students when describing their learning disabilities:

"I was born to quit and God made me that way."

"It (learning disability) makes me feel terrible. It makes me realize that there is a barrier that stops me from having a happy and successful future."

"I always get confused. I don't think I'll ever learn. I must have half a brain."

"I have no friends. Everyone teases me. I wish I was never born."

"Sometimes I feel unrespected, unconfident, lower than other people. I also feel I could never do half the stuff I want to do and that makes me feel frustrated."

Caitlin was seven years old when I first met her in therapy. She had reading and attentional problems and was referred by her parents and teacher because of her lack of confidence, her frustration and disappointment about not learning to read as quickly as her peers, and her reported headaches. In therapy I invited Caitlin to write a story about her difficulties. I told her, as I do all my patients, that I often read stories written by children at my workshops so that parents, teachers, and doctors can gain a better understanding of how children feel and can be more helpful to them.

Caitlin was motivated to write such a story with my assistance. She decided to use as a main character a dog named Hyper who had difficulty learning and concentrating, an obvious representation of herself. The theme of low self-esteem was evident at the beginning of the story when she wrote:

Hyper told herself that she would get over this problem some day, but she wondered if she really would. She was worried that when she grew up and her own puppies asked her something, she would not know the answer and they would wonder why their mother was not very smart. Thinking about this made Hyper feel very upset. She wasn't sure what to do about it.

Caitlin's words poignantly captured not only her low self-esteem, but also a fear expressed by many children and adolescents with learning disabilities, namely, that their condition in life will not improve. In essence, when this fear dominates a child's mindset, it indicates that a major feature of emotional and physical well-being is in danger of being lost. That feature is hope.

I met Matt when he was a young adolescent. He was diagnosed with both learning disabilities and ADHD, was depressed, and entertained little hope for the future. His description of school reminds us of the way in which many youngsters with special needs experience school and should prompt us to become even more committed to creating school environments that provide realistic accommodations for students with learning and attentional problems. Matt wrote:

School has been and still is something I dread profusely. Going to school has been like climbing up a tremendous, rocky mountain with steep cliffs and jagged, slippery rocks. This mountain is very grey and always covered in dark, murky, cold clouds. I step forth to take on this task of climbing this huge mountain. Each step is a battle against strong, howling, icy winds. The winds contain frigid rain that slams against my body, trying to push me down. I keep battling my way up. Sometimes I am knocked down and sometimes I have to stop to regain my strength. My body is numb. My hands shake like leaves in the wind as I claw myself up the mountainside. Not being able to open my eyes, I blindly claw myself up the steep cliff. I stop because I am in such great pain. I look up and see that my struggle has hardly begun. Sometimes I just do not want to go on any further.

In college, Matt, feeling more self-confident, expanded on his story of "The Mountain" and noted that the mountain could become "your grave or your greatest triumph."

As you reflect upon the words of Caitlin and Matt as well as other youngsters with learning disabilities, place yourself in their shoes as they sit in a classroom. If we do not address their social-emotional concerns, their negative feelings about learning, and their sense of helplessness and hopelessness, they will not benefit from our instruction. I am not advocating that teachers become therapists, but that they recognize that the psychological readiness and emotional state of a student to learn is an integral part of the educational process.

Empathy Is an Essential Skill of an Effective Educator

I believe that one of the most important skills for a teacher to possess is empathy. Empathic educators are able to place themselves inside the shoes of their students and perceive the world through a student's eyes. Goleman (1995) highlights empathy as a major component of emotional intelligence.

Being empathic invites us to ask, "Whenever I say or do things with students, am I saying or doing these things in ways that my students will be most responsive to my message? Would I want anyone to say or do to me what I am saying or doing with my students?" For example, a teacher may desire to motivate a student with learning disabilities by exhorting the student to "just try harder." While the teacher may be well-intentioned, such a remark is frequently experienced in a negative, accusatory way. When students feel accused, they are less disposed to be cooperative. Consequently, the teacher's comments are not likely to produce the desired results.

However, if this teacher had been empathic, he or she would have wondered, "If I were struggling in my role as a teacher, would I want another teacher or my principal to say to me, 'If you just tried harder you wouldn't have this problem?'" I believe that the teacher would answer "no" to this question.

To highlight the significance of empathy, I have asked educators at my workshops to think of a teacher they liked and one that they did not like when they were students. I next ask them to think of words they would use to describe each of these teachers. Finally, I comment, "Just as you have words to describe your teachers, your students have words to describe you. What words would you hope they used to describe you? Why do you hope they use these words? What words would they actually use?"

Teachers who appreciate the importance of empathy as a vital teaching skill regularly ask these questions of themselves. I have met teachers who have assumed a proactive stance by requesting anonymous feedback from students; they have had the courage to ask students to draw and describe them, to list what they like about the class, and what they would like to see changed. Such an exercise communicates the message to students, "I want to understand your perspective. I respect your opinion, I value your input, you are a vital participant in the learning process."

Empathic educators appreciate and understand the frustrations experienced by students with learning disabilities such as Caitlin and Matt; consequently, they connect more effectively and constructively with these students so that the process of learning is enhanced.

All Students Learn Differently and We Must Teach Them in Ways in which They Learn Best

There is a vast array of research in the fields of education, developmental psychology, and the neurosciences indicating that each child is different from birth, that children have different temperaments, learning styles, and kinds of intelligence (Brooks, 1998; Carey, 1997; Chess & Thomas, 1987; Gardner, 1983; Hallowell, 1996; Keogh, 2003; Kurcinka, 1991; Levine, 2002, 2003). Yet, even with this burgeoning amount of research, I still hear some educators say, "We must treat all students the same. If we make an accommodation for this student, what will the other students feel? We must be fair."

I would not want any student to feel that a teacher is being arbitrary and unfair. However, we must recognize that fairness does not imply treating each student the same or expecting the same amount of work from each student. It has been my experience that if at the beginning of the school year, teachers assume a proactive stance and explain to their students that we all learn differently and that these differences require the implementation of a variety of accommodations, students will be less likely to feel that the teacher is unfair. What is unfair, however, and a prescription for frustration, anger, and failure, is to require students to learn and perform in identical fashion although they possess different learning and temperamental styles.

Some educators have expressed concern that making accommodations is very time-consuming and impractical. If they have 30 students in their class, they envision the need to create 30 different educational plans. However, in my consultations and workshops, when I describe the most common types of accommodations I have recommended for students with learning disabilities, most educators have remarked that these are realistic and achievable and do not require significant modifications in the classroom. Some of these accommodations include, but are not limited to:

1. Allowing students to take un-timed tests.
2. Establishing a maximum time for homework each night so that the student does not burn out or experience a meltdown. Parents can verify that their child has worked for the maximum amount of time.
3. Providing assignments for the entire week on Monday (or at the end of the previous week) so that parents can help their children organize their time and work.
4. Allowing students with attentional and learning difficulties to have two sets of books, one at home and one at school, to lessen the pressure they experience about the possibility of losing books.
5. Permitting students with writing difficulties to use computers for all written work.

Effective teachers appreciate the "one size fits all" approach does not promote fairness but rather frustration and anger. The time and energy spent implementing accommodations will be far less than the time and energy spent attempting to teach and manage frustrated and angry students.

Educators Have a Lifelong Impact on Students and Their Resilience

As noted earlier, many students with learning disabilities are burdened with feelings of doubt and anxiety about their future. Effective educators understand that what they say and do each day in their classrooms can have a lifelong influence on their students (Brooks, 1991; Brooks & Goldstein, 2001). This understanding of their impact adds meaning and purpose to their work, empowering them and lessening feelings of burnout (Brooks & Goldstein, 2004).

In the past 15 to 20 years there has been an increased effort to define those factors that help at-risk youth to overcome adversity and become resilient (Brooks, 1994; Brooks & Goldstein, 2001, 2003; Katz, 1997; Werner & Smith, 1992). Schools especially have been spotlighted as environments in which self-esteem, hope, and resilience can be reinforced. For example, the late psychologist Julius Segal (1988), in discussing resilient youth, writes:

> From studies conducted around the world, researchers have distilled a number of factors that enable such children of misfortune to beat the heavy odds against them. One factor turns out to be the presence in their lives of a charismatic adult—a person with whom they can identify and from whom they gather strength. And in a surprising number of cases, that person turns out to be a teacher.

A basic belief that permeates the mindset of effective educators is that they are in a unique position to be a "charismatic" adult in a child or adolescent's life and they actively seek opportunities to do so. These educators recognize that all of their words and actions in the classroom can have a profound impact on students, an impact that goes far beyond today, next month, or next year. This influence, while relevant to all students, may have greater urgency for students with learning disabilities who are often weighed down by feelings of vulnerability and hopelessness.

How does one become a "charismatic" adult in a student's life? There are many ways, some surprisingly simple. For instance, in research I conducted in which I asked educators to recall their most positive memories of school when they were students, I discovered it is often the seemingly small gestures that have the most longlasting impact (Brooks, 1991). A smile, a warm greeting, a note of encouragement, a few minutes to meet alone with a student, and an appreciation and respect for different learning styles are but several of the characteristics that define a "charismatic" teacher. These gestures are powerful demonstrations of acceptance and caring.

When I emphasize the need for educators to be the "charismatic" adults in the lives of students I am not minimizing the importance of educators being very well-versed and knowledgeable about the subject matter they are teaching. "Charismatic" teachers possess expertise in their subject areas but they also appreciate that if students are to learn from them, they must touch their hearts as well as their minds.

The theme of teachers as "charismatic adults" was vividly captured in a poem written by 13-year-old Nickolas Walker, a poem about Ms. Alex Scott, one of his eighth grade teachers. His mother, Tammy Young, is also an educator. She told me about the impact that Ms. Scott had on Nickolas, a very articulate, likeable young adolescent who has struggled with learning and attentional problems. Nickolas titled the poem "The Black Sea" and he wrote a very moving dedication—"Dedicated to Alex Scott, the teacher who saved me."

The following is Nickolas' poem:

Before I met you,
I lay trapped beneath the Black Sea,
Where the ordinary was mandatory.
You pulled me up—unconscious,
And waited for me to awaken.
It took me some time,
But I did pull through.
You taught me so much,

Now I must move on.
Your job, however, is not complete,
For others lie stranded
Beneath the Black Sea.
Waiting for you,
To reach them—like me.

Ms. Scott was obviously a "charismatic" adult for Nickolas, a teacher from whom he gathered strength. I believe that every educator can serve in this capacity, working closely with parents to nurture self-worth, confidence, hope, and resilience in children.

Students Will Be Increasingly Motivated to Learn from Us if We First Meet Their Basic Needs

Effective educators recognize that if learning is to take place in their classrooms and if they are to assume the role of charismatic adult, their first task is to create a safe environment in which all students feel respected, secure, comfortable, and motivated to learn. This task assumes greater importance when interacting with students with learning disabilities. As noted earlier, such students often encounter more frustration and failure in school than their peers who do not have learning problems. Consequently, they feel more vulnerable when exposed to classroom assignments. As one teenager reported, "School is the place where my deficits rather than my strengths are highlighted."

Psychologist Edward Deci is one of the foremost researchers in the area of motivation (Deci & Flaste, 1995; Deci, Hodges, Pierson, & Tomassone, 1992). Deci suggests that students will be more motivated to confront and persevere at tasks when certain basic needs have been met. Deci has highlighted three such needs for fostering motivation in all students. They are: (a) to belong and feel connected to the school (I would also add the words "to feel welcome"), (b) to feel a sense of autonomy and self-determination, and (c) to feel competent.

Let's examine these needs and their application more closely. We must also remember that if educators are to meet these needs successfully in students, they must feel that these same needs are being met for them.

To Belong and Feel Connected: Effective educators ask, "How do I help each student feel welcome in my classroom? How do I reach out to all students? How do I make certain that no student feels unknown, teased, or alienated in school?" When I queried students of all ages what a teacher or school administrator could do each day to help them feel welcome in school, the two most frequent responses were being greeted warmly by name and having a teacher smile at them. Obviously, seemingly small gestures can go a long way to helping students feel welcome.

Also, if students are to feel welcome and connected, we must teach them in ways in which they can learn most effectively. As noted earlier, this requires that we provide appropriate accommodations.

The importance of feeling welcome and known by staff was reinforced in a report about safe schools issued by the U.S. Department of Education (Dwyer, Osher, & Wagner, 1998). They note:

> Research shows that a positive relationship with an adult who is available to provide support when needed is one of the most critical factors in preventing school violence. Students often look to adults in the school community for guidance, support, and direction. Some children need help overcoming feelings of isolation and support in developing connections to others. Effective schools make sure that opportunities exist for adults to spend quality, personal time with children. (pp. 3-4)

Relatedly, a Massachusetts Department of Education (1988) report about at-risk students also captures the significant role an educator can assume:

> Possibly the most critical element to success within school is a student developing a close and nurturing relationship with at least one caring adult. Students need to feel that there is someone within school they know, to whom they can turn, and who will act as an advocate for them. (p. 17)

At the very core of success in school is the relationship that teachers develop with their students. When there is a lack of connection between teacher and students, any learning strategies and techniques used by the teacher will be weakened.

To Feel Autonomous and Possess a Sense of Self-Determination: At the core of most theories of motivation and self-worth are the concepts of ownership and self-determination (Adelman & Taylor, 1983; Deci & Flaste, 1995; Dicintio & Gee, 1999; Kohn, 1993). Motivation is reinforced when students feel that their voice is heard and respected, and when they believe they have some control over what transpires in their lives. To practice self-determination requires solid problem-solving, decision-making, and organizational skills. Since these skills are often lagging in youngsters with learning disabilities, they are at a disadvantage in developing a sense of ownership. Exacerbating the situation is that adults are more likely to dictate commands to these youngsters with learning problems than they are to those without such problems.

Thus, while children with learning disabilities yearn to accomplish things on their own, their limited skills in key areas make it difficult for them to do so. They feel that they are constantly being told what to do (often, they are) and that their lives are being directed by others. Consequently, they are less likely to be cooperative or engage in activities that they feel are being imposed on them. If anything, their main motivation may be to avoid what others wish them to do and a power struggle is likely to ensue.

Educators working with students with learning disabilities appreciate that as an initial step they must de-mystify for students with learning disabilities the nature of the disability (Levine, 2002). Once this understanding is in place the next step is to teach students to set realistic short-term and long-term goals, to develop and implement strategies to achieve these goals, and to establish new goals or attempt different strategies when necessary. In addition, it is essential that educators provide these students with ongoing opportunities to use and nurture these problem-solving skills (Shure, 1994).

The following are a few examples:

A group of students with special needs was engaged in conducting research about existing charities. Based on their research findings, they determined which charity to support and the most effective ways of raising money. These activities enhanced their self-esteem and reinforced the academic skills that were involved in the project.

Teachers can give students a choice of which homework problems to do. For instance, if there are eight problems on a page, students can be permitted to choose for themselves which six of eight to complete. In feedback I have received from educators, they report receiving more homework on a regular basis when allowing their students some choice.

The question of ownership is also strongly implicated in effective discipline techniques. The mindset of effective educators understands that a major goal of discipline—in addition to establishing a safe and secure environment—is to develop self-discipline, which requires teaching and educating students, not humiliating or intimidating them (Curwin & Mendler, 1988, 1997; Glasser, 1969; Mendler, 1992). Self-discipline and self-control are known to be significant predictors of readiness for as well as success in school (Blair, 2002; Strayhorn, 2002a, b).

Yet, many children with learning and attentional problems, especially those with a diagnosis of ADHD, demonstrate major difficulties developing self-discipline. Adults describe such children as "acting before they think," and unfortunately these children, who are most in need of limits and structure, are quick to experience any limits as unfair and arbitrary impositions on their lives. Thus, if teachers are to help these students develop self-control, they must help them understand the purpose of rules and engage them within reason in creating rules, guidelines, and consequences that govern the classroom (Brooks, 1991; Marshall & Weisner, 2004).

One strategy that I often recommend for accomplishing this feat involves teachers at the beginning of the school year reviewing several nonnegotiable rules with the class (typically involving issues of safety and security). Next, teachers can ask students what additional rules they believe are necessary for both students and teachers in order that the class run smoothly, the best ways to remember and/or be reminded of the rules so that students don't feel they are being nagged, and what the consequences should be if someone forgets a rule. Students are more likely to remember and adhere to rules that they have helped to create. Skillfully involving students in this process does not result in anarchy, but rather in an increased appreciation of the necessity for rules and an increased motivation to follow the rules (Curwin & Mendler, 1997; Marshall & Weisner, 2004). The process reinforces a feeling of ownership, a vital feature of motivation.

Before leaving the topic of self-determination and autonomy, it is important to note that when individuals become proficient problem solvers, they develop an increased sense of control of their lives. This feeling of control is a dominant part of the mindset of adults with learning disabilities who are leading successful lives. As Gerber, Ginsberg, and Reiff (1992) discovered, "Control is the key to success for adults with learning disabilities. . . . Control meant taking charge of one's life and adapting and shaping oneself in order to move ahead. . . . Control was the fuel that fired their success" (p. 479).

To Feel Competent: The third basic need described by Deci is the need to feel competent. As was noted earlier, many children with learning disabilities have low self-esteem and do not feel competent. Feelings of incompetence prompt these students to retreat from challenges and engage in avoidant behaviors that serve to intensify an already difficult problem.

Effective educators recognize that if students are to feel competent, they must receive realistic encouragement and feedback. Students know when we do not believe in them and when we expect them to fail. Students with learning disabilities, confronted with many frustrations and failures, typically require this encouragement even more than their peers in order to bolster their fragile self-esteem. A focus on encouragement should never be mistaken for giving false praise or inflated grades; students are quite perceptive in knowing when they are receiving undeserved positive evaluations (Brooks, 1999b).

To assist at-risk students to feel competent, educators must identify and reinforce what I have termed each student's "islands of competence" (Brooks, 1991). These islands are areas that are (or have the potential to be) sources of pride and accomplishment. We witnessed that with Billy when he was enlisted to display his interests in dogs through the role of a "pet monitor."

Researchers and clinicians have emphasized the importance of recruiting selected areas of strength or "islands of competence" in building self-confidence.

For instance, Rutter (1985), in discussing resilient individuals observed, "Experience of success in one arena of life led to enhanced self-esteem and a feeling of self-efficacy, enabling them to cope more successfully with the subsequent life challenges and adaptations" (p.604). Katz (1994) stated, "Being able to showcase our talents, and to have them valued by important people in our lives, helps us to define our identities around that which we do best" (p. 10).

I believe that at the beginning of the school year teachers should spend a few minutes with each student asking such questions as, "What do you enjoy doing? What do you think you do that's pretty good?" The more we can define a student's interests and islands of competence, the more effectively we can design and implement educational interventions that build upon a child's strengths and reinforce motivation.

There are numerous ways of helping students with learning disabilities feel more competent. One of the most obvious is to teach them in ways in which they can learn best in order to master the material. Another strategy that I frequently use, which can be linked to academic tasks, is to provide these students with an opportunity to help others. Helping others promotes a sense of ownership and pride. For example, students experience a more positive attachment to school and are more motivated to learn if they are encouraged to contribute to the school milieu (Brooks, 1990, 1991; Rutter, 1980; Werner, 1993).

Billy serving as "pet monitor" and teaching others about the care of animals illustrates the power of what I call "contributory activities." Other examples include: students with learning disabilities reading to younger children; a hyperactive child being asked to assume the position of "attendance monitor," which involved his walking around the halls to take attendance of teachers while the latter took attendance of students; and the use of cooperative learning in which students of varying abilities work together as a team with each bringing their unique strengths to different projects (Brooks, 1991, 1999b).

One of the most powerful approaches for helping students feel competent is to lessen their fear of failure, a fear that is magnified in students with learning disabilities. Many of these students engage in self-defeating coping strategies to avoid the risk of failure and humiliation. I have worked with many students who would rather be a class clown or a class bully than appear stupid. In their desperate attempt to avoid failure, they go down a path that takes them farther away from possible success.

As I have emphasized, effective teachers start with the assumption that each student comes to school wishing to learn and be competent. If students appear unmotivated, it is often a sign that they have given up. I believe that the fear of failure and humiliation is one of the greatest obstacles to learning and is more acute when children struggle with learning disabilities. This fear permeates every classroom and can serve to compromise the joy and enthusiasm that should be part of the learning process.

An effective intervention for overcoming a fear is to address it directly. It is for this reason that I advocate that at the beginning of the school year teachers ask their class, "Who feels they are going to make a mistake or not understand something in class this year?" Before any of the students can respond, teachers can raise their own hands as a way of initiating a discussion of how the fear of making mistakes affects learning. Teachers can share some of their own experiences making mistakes when they were students. They can involve the class in problem solving by asking what they can do as teachers and what the students can do as a class to minimize the fear of failure and appearing foolish. Issues of being called on and not knowing the answer can be discussed.

Openly acknowledging the fear of failure renders it less potent and less destructive. We can teach students with learning and attentional problems that not comprehending certain material is to be expected and that the teacher's role is to help them to learn. One teacher reported that when she engaged her class in this kind of discussion at the beginning of the year, she had the "most discipline-free year she had ever had." Students are less likely to misbehave and more willing to take appropriate risks when they do not feel vulnerable.

Effective teachers recognize that if children with learning disabilities are to succeed and become more hopeful in school, their basic needs to belong and feel connected, to be active participants in their own education, and to experience the joys of competence and accomplishment must be met. Teachers with such a mindset realize that it is their responsibility to provide the climate in which these needs can be satisfied.

Parents Are Our Partners, Not Our Adversaries

Effective teachers strive to develop and maintain close working relationships with parents, appreciating the importance of this bond in the child's success. Nor surprisingly, this task is smoother when the children involved do not present major learning or behavior problems in the classroom. However, when children do display these problems, it is a more formidable challenge to nurture teacher-parent relationships that are free of blame and accusation. For the sake of the child, it is a challenge that must be confronted.

I have witnessed many situations in which teachers and parents have slipped into the role of adversaries and it is the child who suffers. I have also visited schools in which a strong effort was made by both parents and teachers to ensure a collaborative and respectful relationship. For instance, in one elementary school teachers called each parent the day before school began to express their desire to work closely together; they encouraged the parents to call should they have any questions or concerns and they conveyed the wish for a positive relationship throughout the year.

The teachers in this school told me that they initiated the practice of calling parents before the beginning of the year when they realized that typically the first time they contacted parents was when there was a problem; thus, their initial contact centered around a negative issue, more likely adding tension and mistrust to the relationship. They reported that communicating with parents in a more positive way enhanced their relationship with parents and, very importantly, had a beneficial effect on the learning and motivation of the students. While this trusting, respectful relationship is important for success of all students, it has special relevance for parents of children experiencing difficulty in school since as one parent told me, "I am always poised for criticism when a teacher calls or I go to a school meeting. It is a very painful time for me."

It is obvious that when parents and teachers make an effort to establish a respectful relationship, the children are the beneficiaries.

Closing Reflections: Special Needs or Needing to Feel Special

In ending this description of the mindset of effective educators, there is one other component that requires highlighting and in many ways is interwoven with several of the others. I realize that for a variety of reasons, not the least of which is to secure accommodations and funding, we must use the label "special needs." In my conversations with educators who touch the minds and hearts of their students, I am left with the impression that it would be more in concert with their philosophy and approach if we replaced the term "special needs" with the words "every child (and I might add, every adult) who enters school needs to feel special."

I believe that the mindset and accompanying expectations and behaviors of effective educators are dominated by a motivation to help all students feel special, appreciated, and successful. We can accomplish this by being empathic, by treating students in the same ways that we would like to be treated, by finding a few moments to smile and make them feel more comfortable, by educating them in ways in which they can learn best given their learning style, by taking painstaking care to avoid any words or actions that might be accusatory, by minimizing their fears of failure, and by identifying, reinforcing, and displaying their islands of competence.

When we can achieve these goals, we will truly become the "charismatic" adults of children with learning disabilities. We will have touched their hearts and minds and in the process they will learn from us and carry the gifts of knowledge, acceptance, and resilience into their adult lives. What a wonderful legacy the effective educator bestows upon the next generation.

As educators commit themselves to develop a positive, hopeful mindset with high and realistic expectations, it would be helpful to keep in mind the words of Goethe: "Treat people as if they were what they ought to be, and you help them become what they are capable of being."

REFERENCES

Adelman, H., & Taylor, L. (1983). Enhancing motivation for overcoming learning and behavior problems. *Journal of Learning Disabilities, 16,* 384–392.

Blair, C. (2002). School readiness: Integrating cognition and emotion in a neurobiological conceptualization of children's functioning at school entry. *American Psychologist, 57,* 111–127.

Brooks, R. B. (1990). Indelible memories of school: Of contributions and self-esteem. *The School Field, 1,* 121–129.

Brooks, R. B. (1991). *The self-esteem teacher.* Loveland, OH: Treehaus Communications.

Brooks, R. B. (1994). Children at risk: Fostering resilience and hope. *American Journal of Orthopsychiatry, 64,* 545–553.

Brooks, R. B. (1997). A personal journey: From pessimism and accusation to hope and resilience. *Journal of Child Neurology, 12,* 387–395.

Brooks, R. B. (1998). Parenting a child with learning disabilities: Strategies for fostering self-esteem, motivation, and resilience. In T. Citro (Ed.), *The experts speak: Parenting the child with learning disabilities* (pp. 25–45). Waltham, MA: Learning Disabilities Association of Massachusetts.

Brooks, R. B. (1999a). Creating a positive school climate: Strategies for fostering self-esteem, motivation, and resilience. In J. Cohen (Ed.), *Educating minds and hearts: Social emotional learning and the passage into adolescence* (pp. 61–73). New York: Columbia Teachers College Press.

Brooks, R. B. (1999b). Fostering resilience in exceptional children: The search for islands of competence. In V. Schwean & D. Saklofske (Eds.), *Handbook of psychosocial characteristics of exceptional children* (pp. 563–586). New York: Kluwer Academic/Plenum Press.

Brooks, R. B. (2001a). Fostering motivation, hope, and resilience in children with learning disorders. *Annals of Dyslexia, 51,* 9–20.

Brooks R. B. (2001b). To touch a student's heart and mind: the mindset of the effective educator. *Proceedings of the 1999 Plain Talk conference sponsored by the Center for Development and Learning,* New Orleans (pp. 167–177). Cambridge, MA: Educators Publishing Service.

Brooks, R. B. (2004). To touch the hearts and minds of students with learning disabilities: The power of mindsets and expectations. *Learning Disabilities: A Contemporary Journal, 2,* 9–18.

Brooks, R. B., & Goldstein, S. (2001). *Raising resilient children.* New York: Contemporary Books.

Brooks, R. B., & Goldstein, S. (2003). *Nurturing resilience in our children: Answers to the most important parenting questions.* New York: Contemporary Books.

Brooks, R. B. & Goldstein, S. (2004). *The power of resilience: Achieving balance, confidence, and personal strength in your life.* New York: Contemporary Books.

Canino, F. J. (1981). Learned helplessness theory: Implications for research in learning disabilities. *Journal of Special Education, 15,* 471–484.

Carey, W. B. (1997). Understanding your child's temperament. New York: Macmillan.

Chess, S., & Thomas. A. (1987). *Know your child.* New York: Basic Books.

Cohen, J. (Ed.). (1999). *Educating minds and hearts: Social emotional learning and the passage into adolescence.* New York: Columbia Teachers College Press.

Curwin, R. L., & Mendler, A. N. (1988). *Discipline with dignity.* Reston, VA: Association for Supervision and Curriculum Development.

Curwin, R. L., & Mendler, A. N. (1997). Beyond obedience: A discipline model for the long term. *Reaching Today's Youth, 1,* 21–23.

Deci, E. L., & Flaste, R. (1995). *Why we do what we do: Understanding self-motivation.* New York: Guilford.

Deci, E. L., Hodges, R., Pierson, L., & Tomassone, J. (1992). Autonomy and competence as motivational factors in students with learning disabilities and emotional handicaps. *Journal of Learning Disabilities, 25,* 457–471.

Dicintio, M. J., & Gee, S. (1999). Control is the key: Unlocking the motivation of at-risk students. *Psychology in the Schools, 36,* 231–237.

Dwyer, K., Osher, D., & Wagner, C. (1998). *Early warning, timely response: A guide to safe schools.* Washington, D.C.: U.S. Department of Education.

Gardner, H. (1983). *Frames of mind.* New York: Basic Books.

Gerber, P. J., Ginsberg, R., & Reiff,, H. B. (1992). Identifying alterable patterns in employment success for highly successful adults with learning disabilities. *Journal of Learning Disabilities, 25,* 475–487.

Glasser, W. (1969). *Schools without failure.* New York: Harper & Row.

Goleman, D. (1995). *Emotional intelligence.* New York: Bantam.

Hallowell, E. (1996). *When you worry about the child you love.* New York: Simon & Schuster.

Katz, M. (1994, May). From challenged childhood to achieving adulthood: Studies in Resilience. *Chadder,* pp. 8–11.

Katz, M. (1997). *On playing a poor hand well.* New York: Norton.

Keogh, B. K. (2003). *Temperament in the classroom: Understanding individual differences.* Baltimore, MD: Brookes Publishing.

Kohn, A. (1993). Choices for children: Why and how to let students decide. *Phi Delta Kappan, 75,* 8–20.

Kurcinka, M. S. (1991). *Raising your spirited child.* New York: Harper/Collins.

Levine, M. D. (2002). *A mind at a time.* New York: Simon & Schuster.

Levine, M. D. (2003). *The myth of laziness.* New York: Simon & Schuster.

Licht, B. G. (1983). Cognitive-motivational factors that contribute to the achievement of learning-disabled children. *Journal of Learning Disabilities, 16,* 483–490.

Marshall, M., & Weisner, K. (2004). Using a discipline system to promote learning. *Phi Delta Kappan, 85,* 498–507.

Massachusetts Department of Education, Office of Student Services (1988). *Systemic school change: A comprehensive approach to dropout prevention.* Boston.

Mendler, A. N. (1992). *What do I do when. . .? How to achieve discipline with dignity in the classroom.* Bloomington, IN: National Educational Service.

Rutter, M. (1980). School influences on children's behavior and development. *Pediatrics, 65,* 522–533.

Rutter, M. (1985). Resilience in the face of adversity: Protective factors and resistance to psychiatric disorder. *British Journal of Psychiatry, 147,* 598–611.

Segal, J. (1988). Teachers have enormous power in affecting a child's self-esteem. *The Brown University Child Behavior and Development Newsletter, 10,* 1–3.

Shure, M. (1994). *Raising a thinking child.* New York: Holt.

Strayhorn, J. M. (2002a). Self-control: Theory and research. *Journal of the American Academy of Child and Adolescent Psychiatry, 41,* 7–16.

Strayhorn, J. M. (2002b). Self-control: Toward systematic training programs. *Journal of the American Academy of Child and Adolescent Psychiatry, 41,* 17–21.

Werner, E. (1993). Risk, resilience, and recovery: Perspectives from the Kauai Longitudinal Study. *Development and Psychopathology, 5,* 503–515.

Werner, E., & Smith, R. (1992). *Overcoming the odds: High risk children from birth to adulthood.* Ithaca, NY: Cornell University Press.

Chapter Two

Preventing Reading Problems: The application of an assessment-driven, classroom-based intervention in Texas schools

Angeliki Mouzaki, Ph.D.

University of Crete

Barbara R. Foorman, Ph.D. and Kristi Santi, Ph.D.

University of Texas-Houston

The ability to read fluently with comprehension has been the focus of many systematic and comprehensive investigations from a variety of disciplines that have yielded significant and converging outcomes over the last twenty years. Consistently within the research, reading interventions for children with reading problems continue to appear promising for elimination or remediation of the obstacles that hinder children from proficient reading and schooling. The general consensus is that a successful reading intervention should lead to the development of accurate and fluent text-based word reading skills that will enable the student to read and comprehend textual information in accord with what is expected from students of the same age (on or above grade level).

There is growing emphasis on prevention and early intervention concerning instructional practices that start as early as kindergarten. The goal of these interventions is to provide children (especially those considered at-risk for reading failure) with effective classroom-based reading instruction right from the beginning and guard them against impending reading problems. This approach, which is often described as first-tier intervention (Denton, Vaughn, & Fletcher, 2003; Mathes & Denton, 2002), is strongly supported by a growing body of empirical evidence. Reading problems—once they surface—typically persist throughout a child's school life. Several longitudinal investigations have demonstrated that reading disabilities diagnosed late (i.e., in second and third grade) persevere during the later school years even after the child has received the "standard" course of remedial services within the school system (Francis, Shaywitz, Stuebing, Shaywitz, & Fletcher, 1996; Juel, 1988; Torgesen & Burgess, 1998). Maturation and regular, school-based interventions are typically not sufficient to improve reading skills. The average special education class is often organized and equipped inadequately to advance students with reading problems towards reading mastery (Vaughn, Watson Moody, & Shay Schumm, 1998; Watson Moody, Vaughn, Hughes Tejero, & Fischer, 2000).

Alternatively, early reading performance (in kindergarten and the beginning of first grade) is very indicative of reading achievement in fourth and fifth grades (Francis et al., 1996; Juel, 1988; Torgesen, Wagner, & Rashotte, 1997). Again, several longitudinal studies have established reliable predictors of reading ability that could greatly improve the predictive accuracy of early screening practices (e.g., Fletcher et al., 2002; O'Connor & Jenkins, 1999; Scarborough, 1998; Torgesen, 2002; Vellutino, Scanlon, & Lyon, 2000; Wood, Hill, & Meyer, 2001).

In general, phonological awareness and letter-sound knowledge measured in kindergarten and at the beginning of Grade 1 are predictive of first-grade outcomes. At the beginning of Grade 1, word recognition ability emerges as an additional predictor of end of first grade reading ability. In Grade 2, word reading continues to be a strong predictor of Grade 2 outcomes, with reading fluency and reading comprehension becoming increasingly important predictors of reading outcomes (Bishop, 2003; Foorman, Fletcher, & Francis, 2004).

Large scale investigations conducted by Torgesen et al. (1997), Vellutino et al. (1996), and Foorman, Francis, Fletcher, Schatschneider, & Mehta (1998) provided evidence for the effectiveness of *early* intervention on students at-risk for reading failure. Early instructional intervention has a strong impact on reading skill outcomes among first- and second-grade children at risk for reading failure (Snow, Burns, & Griffin, 1998). Early intervention can be successfully delivered within the regular classroom as shown by studies that demonstrated significant reduction in the size of at-risk population for reading difficulties without implementing special pull-out programs (Foorman et al., 1998; Juel & Minden-Cupp, 2000). In fact, on a population basis, quality classroom prevention and early intervention can reduce the numbers of first and second graders who would be identified as reading disabled from around 20% to 5% (Fletcher & Lyon, 1998). Based on this evidence, Torgesen (2002) describes a comprehensive multi-layered plan to maximize the effectiveness of prevention for at-risk students: first, effective classroom-based instruction should be in place for the entire class and second, early identification of at-risk students should lead to more focused and intense instruction for this particular student group. The reading instruction offered to the at-risk group should be even more explicit, intensive, and supportive than the instruction offered to the entire class.

Based on this premise, in the remainder of this chapter, we describe in some detail, classroom instruction that is empirically shown as the most effective for improving reading skills for both at-risk and not-at-risk students.

Not surprisingly, the elements of reading instruction that are consistently described in the literature as necessary for reading success also serve as the basic components of early intervention programs (National Reading Panel, 2000; Rayner, Foorman, Perfetti, Pesetsky, & Seidenberg, 2001; Snow et al., 1998). These include: phonemic awareness and phonemic decoding skills, fluency in word recognition and text processing, extraction of meaning, vocabulary, spelling, and writing (Foorman & Torgesen, 2001). According to Torgesen et al., (1997), mastery of word identification skills leading to adequate orthographic representations, requires an emphasis on the development of alphabetic reading skills. In addition to the acquisition of the alphabetic principle, instruction should focus on the development of phonological processing skills. The alphabetic principle is defined as the "usable knowledge of the fact that phonemes can be represented by letters, such that whenever a particular phoneme occurs in a word, and in whatever position, it can be represented by the same letter" (Byrne & Fielding-Barnsley, 1989, p. 314). The preliterate child needs to become aware that individual phonemes are represented by one or more letters and also that phonemes are constantly represented by the same letters regardless of their position in a word (Byrne & Fielding-Barnsley). Moreover, according to Share & Stanovich's (1995) *self-teaching model* of reading acquisition, systematic and successful use of sublexical processes (print to sound conversion) facilitates the registration of orthographic representations in memory. This suggests that, phonological processing may play a self-teaching role for the development of knowledge of orthographic conventions which, in turn leads to fast, accurate, and efficient word reading and spelling (Share & Stanovich; Stanovich, West, & Cunningham, 1991).

In addition to the content of instruction, teaching methodology is also of primary importance. Growth of word-reading skills depends heavily on the explicitness of the instructional method (Snow et al., 1998; Torgesen et al., 1999). Moreover, effective reading interventions are typically intense. In successful programs, knowledgeable teachers use explicit and direct instruction to deliver appropriate content, in a scaffolding and systematic manner that builds self-confidence. The instructional content is frequently adjusted, based on the results of continuous assessments documenting the student's increasing level of competence (see Table 1). Instruction further includes practice in phonemic processing and phonics skills, reading practice on appropriate connected text and, finally, writing and comprehension instruction (Coyne, Kame'enui, & Simmons, 2001; Fletcher & Foorman, 1994; Moats, 1999; Snow et al., 1998; Torgesen, 1999;).

ASSESSMENT-DRIVEN CLASSROOM-BASED INSTRUCTION AS A PREVENTION/EARLY INTERVENTION MODEL

We argue that critical to the effectiveness of prevention and early intervention is assessment-driven instruction that leads to differentiated teaching. Early reading assessment that incorporates screening for risk, evaluations of skill development, and progress monitoring will ensure early identification of students with reading challenges and direct the allocation of extra resources (both within and outside the classroom).

Nevertheless, diagnostic student assessment may not produce the expected results unless certain other instructional components are in place. For instance, all students should be receiving first-tier effective reading instruction within the classroom that is tailored and continually adjusted to individual reading ability level. This type of instruction can be offered only to small groups of students who share similar profiles of reading development. The effectiveness of small-group

Table I

Characteristics of Effective Reading Programs.

Characteristics	Description
Knowledgeable teacher	The teacher has received substantial training on the theory—and research-based practices of effective reading instruction and had extensive opportunities for practice and reflection with colleagues and reading trainers/coaches.
Explicit/direct instruction	The teacher does not rely on the student's pre-existing knowledge and does not assume that the student will make inferences based on his/her own abilities and the presented information.
Intensive	The teacher provides a daily instructional session that lasts at least 30 minutes.
Supportive	The teacher supports the student emotionally in an attempt to boost self-esteem and confidence about reading. Also, the teacher scaffolds new learning on previous knowledge using carefully constructed personalized teaching sequences that evolve within the student's increasing level of competence, a concept often referred to as zone of proximal development (Vygotsky, Rieber, & Hall, 1999).
Systematic	The teacher follows a carefully planned instructional sequence for both the teaching session and the overall intervention plan. For example, each teaching session has a pre-determined sequence of instructional activities, and all sessions follow a well-defined instructional sequence of curriculum objectives.
Assessment based	The teacher formulates an intervention plan for each student based on individual characteristics and skills profile. The latter is derived from a thorough evaluation of the student's reading and cognitive skills. The assessment is repeated at regular intervals to reevaluate growth, document instructional effectiveness, and initiate necessary adjustments in instructional practices.

instruction in reading is well documented, advocated equally by experts and field-practitioners, and is shown to be comparably effective with one-to-one intervention programs (Mouzaki, 2001; Torgesen, 2002; Wise, Ring, & Olson, 1999). According to recent studies, small group instruction holds considerable promise for providing highly individualized in-class support before the small difficulties become more persistent and create learning barriers that are resistant to treatment (Abrami, Lou, Chambers, Poulsen, & Spence, 2000; Elbaum, Vaughn, Hughes, & Watson Moody, 1999; Foorman & Torgesen, 2001).

The primary challenge of implementing large-scale school reforms, including diagnostic assessments, is to incorporate them into the daily business of schools. Aspiring reform efforts should help teachers reformulate their beliefs and teaching practices, rather than layer new practices on top of old beliefs (Elmore, 1995). The implementation, sustainability, and effectiveness of assessment-based instruction depend heavily on teachers' general knowledge as well as their proficiency in implementing the specific instructional approach. Specific challenges concern (a) administration of the assessment, (b) interpretation of the assessment information to form an instructional plan, and (c) the implementation of small group instruction.

Assessment administration

While recent research has expanded and strengthened our definition of what constitutes a reliable, valid early reading assessment, there is a dearth of quantitative studies on the supports needed for large-scale effective implementation in the classroom (Valencia & Wixson, 1999). There is some evidence that sustained, in-classroom professional development is the strongest component for building teacher expertise regarding the use and interpretation of research-based assessment techniques (Strickland, Snow, Griffin, Burns, & McNamara, 2002). Traditionally, diagnostic student assessment in elementary school was performed by a specialist (i.e., special education teacher and/or school psychologist) with limited contribution from the classroom teachers. Student assessments administered by classroom teachers can be classified as either norm-referenced tests (NRT) or criterion-referenced tests (CRT). NRTs are designed to rank the student's general academic achievement in relation to a representative population (the norm group) of students as well as to discriminate between high and low achievers. CRTs are designed to assess students on specific curriculum areas as determined by teachers and the local curriculum. They are shorter in duration and scored immediately by the teacher to determine student growth on the specific curriculum implemented.

Typically, classroom teachers administer at least one NRT (i.e., Iowa Test of Basic Skills-ITBS: Riverside, Metropolitan Achievement Test-MAT:

Psychological Corporation), every year along with CRTs. NRTs are group-administered and the student record sheets are sent to the publisher for scoring. Scores typically take a few weeks to be computed and have little direct relevance to the local curriculum. Usually CRTs are given at the end of a chapter or unit of instruction. If a teacher notices that a student's performance over time is not at the expected level, a referral process is initiated. During this phase, a school psychologist conducts additional testing to determine specific skill levels and then reports back to the classroom teacher.

This structure is rapidly changing with the reformulation of the Elementary and Secondary Education Act, which became known as No Child Left Behind Act (NCLB, 2001), that brought early reading assessment into focus. The Reading First component of this Act encourages assessments in K-3 classrooms for screening, diagnosis, progress monitoring, and outcome measurement. These guidelines are prompted by empirical evidence that assessment-driven intervention is effective in improving reading achievement.

Low performing schools are also coming under the guidance of the NCLB Act and the Reading First Program. NCLB is a direct result of the suggestions made by the National Reading Panel (NRP, 2000) and the growing scientific consensus regarding reading acquisition. Reading First makes specific provisions for each of the five domains identified by the NRP, the three-tier model (advocating three levels of instructional support), and a variety of assessments needed to guide instruction. Reading First requires assessment for screening students to identify needed support: diagnosis to guide instruction; progress monitoring to benchmark student progress throughout the academic year; and outcome measures to evaluate student outcomes.

With NCLB, teachers in the regular classroom setting are responsible for conducting the screening, diagnosis, and progress monitoring throughout the year for students in their classrooms. Teachers in their new roles are asked to adhere to *individual* test administration procedures. Individual diagnostic assessment guidelines for reliable administration are often strict and do not allow accommodations for detecting skills not instantly revealed. In other words, teachers are required to temporarily abandon their didactic roles and beliefs of children's potential achievement in order to capture a valid and accurate profile of skill development that will guide instructional planning. Despite the many challenges of their new roles, teachers are more likely to use assessments when they find the information valuable to their understanding of student instructional needs, and when instructional leadership exists to help them understand how the changes are part of larger school improvement (Hawkins, Kulp, Gilbert, Mesa, & Schwarz, 1999; Paris, Paris, & Carpenter, 2001).

Interpretation of the assessment information to form an instructional plan

Teachers' abilities to understand their students' skills and needs affect both what they teach and how they teach it (Cohen & Ball, 1999). Integration of screening and diagnostic information produced by individual assessments into instructional planning is one of the most challenging steps of assessment-based instruction, especially for the novice teacher. According to Gresham, MacMillan, & Bocian (1997), teachers are very competent in identifying learning-disabled students as indicated by their referrals to school specialists for testing and diagnosis. Their intuitive screening ability, however, is rarely acknowledged by other school professionals, and their judgments are often mentioned as "suspicions." Furthermore, the traditional model of "wait-and-see" until the student is old enough for referral to the specialist, has left teachers ill prepared for making informed decisions regarding the content and instructional method that meet individualized students' needs.

Despite extensive guidelines linking assessment to instruction, early reading assessments vary in their overall structure, organization, specific components, and scores. Teachers are often overwhelmed by pressure from school and district officials and are left unsupported in their new roles as diagnosticians and curriculum planners. Professional development offered to teachers does not always address this need which is compounded by the lack of formal training during their basic studies. Regrettably, classroom instruction, in the traditional sense, does not take into account individual differences and is usually intended toward an abstract concept of the "average student."

Lately some instructional approaches, such as guided reading, and a plethora of leveled books for reading practice, have reinforced the discussion on differentiated instruction, and have increased teacher awareness of ways to customize their instruction for addressing individual student needs. To further support this trend current teacher professional development should focus on the study of student profiles and provide assistance on the decision-making process involved in planning small-group reading instruction.

Implementation of small group instruction

Small-group reading instruction is not the prevailing practice in elementary schools today (Schumm Shay, Watson Moody, & Vaughn, 2000; Watson Moody, Vaughn, & Shay Schumm, 1997). Part of this is justified by the criticism that was raised during the 1970s and 1980s from a group of studies arguing that same-ability grouping may have negative impact on the self-esteem and motivation of the students with reading problems, limit their socialization, and very frequently account for larger discrepancies between the high and low performing students (Calfee & Brown, 1979; Hiebert, 1983; Rosenholtz & Wilson, 1980).

According to Elbaum et al. (1999), reading instruction remains largely undifferentiated in both special and general education classes. This is not surprising if we consider the enduring negative connotation of the concept of small-group instruction and the considerable amount of extra work required for both planning and teaching. Small-group instruction poses many practical challenges, chief among which is the constant need to adapt instructional methods and materials (Lou et al., 1996). Teachers do not typically receive training in classroom management for small-group instruction and are hesitant to introduce a teaching method for which they are not adequately prepared. Finally, the alteration between homogeneous and non-homogeneous grouping for different instructional units and parts of the school day requires a substantial amount of organization, proactive management skills, and planning work that are often missing due to lack of experience or resources.

In 1998, a group of the world's leading experts on reading participated in the Committee on the Prevention of Reading Difficulties in Young Children under the auspices of the National Academies of Science. After reviewing current reading research, the Committee composed an influential document entitled *Preventing Reading Difficulties in Young Children* (Snow et al., 1998), and more recently another important work that focuses on the instructional implications of the above report. This work titled *Preparing our Teachers* succinctly summarizes the issues raised in previous paragraphs:

It is difficult for a teacher to gear instruction to struggling readers if the classroom is always managed in a whole-group manner. If children do not get instruction tailored to their needs, it is highly unlikely they will improve on their own. The whole group will move further and further ahead, while slower readers are left behind, still struggling with what the others take for granted. All teachers should know how to manage their classrooms so that they can provide instruction to different configurations of students, depending on the activity. Children may be assigned to groups that have the same range of abilities (homogeneous groups) or to groups that have a mix of ability levels (heterogeneous groups). Sessions with the whole class call for preparation and moment-to-moment teacher actions that are quite specialized. A different strategy and tactics are needed to teach one small group while the other students are less directly supervised. A good teacher can accomplish lesson goals with a small group while coordinating a class with some students working in pairs or small peer groups and others working on their own (Strickland et al., 2002, p.155).

To better understand the practical implications of this statement, a different class configuration should be adopted for reading instruction. In a class where the students are accustomed to working independently in small groups or in pairs, and engaging in highly individualized work, the teacher engages in proactive thinking to build student learning through carefully planned activities. Practice examples can be drawn by incorporating several well-known practices used daily in US classrooms today: independent reading and writing, center time, work with leveled books, etc. The distinguishing feature, however, is the creation of a coherent, assessment-based plan for addressing specific areas of reading behavior that have been established as critical for further development. This type of plan can only be formed by the teacher who has first-hand experience with students developing reading skill as it is reflected on a diagnostic assessment. Accordingly, instructional decisions are made and modified as indicated by subsequent assessments. These decisions concern the choice of direct teaching content and activities, choice of the type and materials for independent work, and the level of intensity of student engagement. For example, one day, a small homogeneous group of students may work on graphophonemic correspondences under teacher guidance and learn to apply this knowledge on a new concept such as consonant blends. After completing this activity, which takes only a small portion of the reading time, the students, may then practice independently their newly acquired knowledge on the computer station using special software. Subsequently, and while the teacher is attending another group with different needs, children in the first group may work in pairs reviewing learned sight words and marking their progress on a tracking sheet. Finally, they can sort words according to pre-specified features (such as consonant blends) or write sentences using these words.

It is obvious, that the group described above, won't have the opportunities to work on an individualized teaching plan under whole class instruction that moves all students to the same content at the same time without accounting for differences in the learning pace.

THE CASE OF TEXAS

In Texas, early reading assessment has been the centerpiece of a statewide reading initiative that emphasizes prevention and early intervention. The legislature mandated the use of K-2 diagnostic reading instruments in 1997, leading to the extension and validation of the Texas Primary Reading Inventory (TPRI) by academic researchers, and the corresponding development of the Spanish Tejas LEE. The TPRI is a one-on-one instrument designed to be administered by the classroom teacher. Currently, the TPRI and Tejas LEE (owned jointly by the Texas Education Agency and the University of Texas System) are used in more than 96% of the 1,100 districts in Texas and are on approved lists in several other states.

The Texas Primary Reading Inventory (TPRI)

The TPRI consists of a separate screening section and an inventory section for each of the three primary grades (K-2). With a short series of student-friendly tasks, the teacher can quickly gather information regarding the level of knowledge and skills on key reading concepts. By identifying students who are likely to experience success in reading, time can be spent gathering more detailed information for other students who may be likely to need instructional intervention. The inventory is aligned with the state curriculum standards and engages the student with inviting tasks and entertaining stories, while giving the teacher an opportunity to gather more data to help match reading instruction with specific student needs. If desired, the entire inventory can be given to all students to obtain a more complete picture of their strengths and needs. The inventory consists of the following components:

1. book and print awareness (knowledge of the function of print and of the characteristics of books and other print materials);
2. phonemic awareness (the ability to detect and identify individual sounds within spoken words);
3. graphophonemic knowledge (the recognition of the letters of the alphabet and the understanding of sound-spelling relations);
4. reading accuracy and fluency (the ability to read grade appropriate text accurately and fluently); and
5. reading comprehension (the understanding of what has been read).

The TPRI screening items tap into the following skill domains: phonological awareness and letter-sound knowledge in kindergarten and at the beginning of Grade 1, and word reading at the beginning and end of Grade 1, and again at the beginning of Grade 2.

In kindergarten, the initial screening task consists of a list of 10 uppercase and lowercase letters that the student is asked to identify by name and sound. The second screening task is a phonemic awareness activity in which the student is asked to listen to phoneme sequences that make up words. The student is then asked to produce the word. For example, the teacher says "sh - o - p" and the student says "shop."

In Grade 1, the initial screening task is again a list of 10 uppercase and lowercase letters that the student is to identify by name and sound. The second task, a list of words, selected for frequency and scaled for difficulty, is provided to determine the student's word recognition skill. The student is asked to identify the words. The final screening task is a phonemic awareness activity in which the student is asked to listen to words divided into their individual sounds and then asked to pronounce the words. In Grade 2, screening consists of a word identification task.

The purpose of the screening is early, rapid identification of children who do *not* need the inventory so that the teacher can focus on the children who do. In fact, the TPRI screen takes three to five minutes, depending on the grade. Performance cut-off points for the screening items were purposely set low so that over-identification rather than under-identification would occur. Over-identification rates in kindergarten and Grade 1 range from about 38% in kindergarten and 36% in Grade 1 to less than 15% at the beginning of Grade 2. These rates could be reduced, but then rates for under-identification, which were intentionally kept below 10% on the TPRI, would increase. The priority given to minimizing under-identification is sensible when the end result of under-identification is poor educational attainment for the student. At the same time, the consequences of over-identification are less severe, consisting primarily of increased assessment time (the teacher administers the entire inventory to the child), and closer monitoring of student progress.

The screen consists of those measures most predictive of reading success in a longitudinal sample of 945 children in a metropolitan school district in Texas. In that study children were assessed four times a year for literacy-related growth and at the end of Grades 1 and 2 for reading and spelling achievement (TPRI Technical Report, 1998). The items on the screen were selected on the basis of Item Response Theory (IRT) analyses from a larger set of items that discriminate success and failure on reading outcomes at the end of Grades 1 and 2. The initial battery included measures of phonological awareness, phonological (working) memory, rapid naming of letters and objects, expressive and receptive syntax, vocabulary, knowledge of letter names and sounds, and perceptual skills. For predictions involving Grades 1 and 2, the Woodcock-Johnson Broad Reading cluster (Woodcock & Johnson, 1989), which consists of letter-word identification, cloze-based reading comprehension, and reading vocabulary, was used. The criteria for risk were set to identify students who were six months below grade level, which, depending on the grade, corresponds to the lower 20th percentile.

To conform with the requirements of Reading First, the 2004–2005 edition of the TPRI includes a Grade 3 screen and inventory and a separate packet of fluency probes for monitoring progress in oral reading fluency in Grades 1–3.

TPRI and Teacher Mentoring

The purpose of the TPRI from its inception was to assist teachers in identifying those students who are more likely to succeed in learning to read. This way the teacher could easily identify the students who may be at-risk of having considerable difficulties with the reading process. The problem, however for most of the teachers is *how* to utilize classroom-based assessment data in planning effective reading instruction to address diverse student needs.

Surveys conducted as part of a large-scale implementation study with 299 teachers and 4,500 K-2 children in 52 schools across Texas showed that teachers made few administration errors, felt confident in their ability to administer the TPRI, found the results useful for evaluating students' strengths and weaknesses, but infrequently applied results to instruction (TPRI Technical Report, 1999). Field experience during the TPRI Implementation Study (1999–2000) indicated that teachers felt powerless in their efforts to translate the TPRI scores into instruction.

This phenomenon can be partially explained by the fact that the use of diagnostic instruments that aim to inform instruction is relatively new, even in the state of Texas. Initially, the training for the administration of the TPRI focused primarily on administration issues and logistics, rather than on the interpretation of the findings. In order to address this need, initially we developed specific materials that were included in the TPRI kit (TPRI Intervention Activities Guide, 2004). Also, the teacher training sessions offered were enriched as follows:

1. Authentic information (real TPRI scores) was used for practice.
2. Systematic guidance was provided so that teachers were able to become proficient in classifying the information obtained, grouping the students for instruction, and planning teaching lessons *within their existing curriculum.*
3. A variety of instructional activities was developed for use with small student groups as either an extension of the reading program or as main instructional strategies.

It seems that step-by-step demonstration of the thinking process toward forming a student intervention plan is of critical importance. For this purpose, we developed specific materials to use in the Texas schools that follow the grade level sequence for the primary grades (see http://www.TPRI.org). The sequence and materials are adapted to the time of the year the test is administered. In addition, appropriate technology (handheld system, Internet) was utilized to enable teachers to generate class summary reports and progress indicators for student groups or individual students.

Since 2002 a randomized study funded by the Interagency Education Research Initiative enabled the detailed examination of the administration format and data processing (paper, paper+desktop, handheld+desktop) in conjunction with the intervention support received by the teacher in order to translate the results to classroom instruction. The handheld system for the TRPI uploads data to web-accessible databases. The databases are linked to an online professional development website where assessment results are related to appropriate intervention activities, differentiated instructional resources, and strategies for classroom grouping. Similar training is delivered by TPRI training mentors who work with teachers in their classrooms to provide an effective model of teacher mentoring and support. Teachers are guided in their efforts to accurately interpret TPRI scores and make diagnostic decisions regarding students' reading abilities and performances as they are reflected in the TPRI Screening and Inventory data. Then they make decisions regarding instructional content, sequence, and method for teaching individual students and implement both whole-group and small-group reading instruction planned according to student scores on the TPRI.

DIFFERENTIATED INSTRUCTION BASED ON THE TPRI

Students vary widely in their learning needs and behaviors. In order to provide them with the type of instructional support that best fits their needs, teachers are encouraged to form homogeneous groups to engage in specialized work for a small part of the school day. Group formation is not an easy task and poses many challenges especially for the novice teacher. Classroom management for small group instruction demands high levels of skill and energy both in preparation and implementation. It is the kind of instruction, however that yields the most rewarding results for both teachers and learners through authentic personalized interactions that emerge and unfold dynamically around specific students' skill development.

Small group instruction is often mastered by both teachers and learners by allocating gradually increasing time periods for this type of teaching. Mastery is easier if a small number of groups (one to two) are formed initially with more groups added as teachers and students become more efficient and comfortable with small group work.

Generally, the purpose of whole-class instruction is to introduce new instructional units and concepts, practice with those concepts that are not mastered by more than two-thirds of the class, and provide periodic review of concepts previously taught. After a skill has been reviewed with the whole class, an activity based on this skill is placed on a workstation for student practice. As shown in Figure 1, when the teacher plans, for example, to introduce phoneme elision (elimination of a first or last phoneme in a spoken word) s/he might review initial and final phoneme identification first (i.e., a skill that is already mastered) while incorporating new skills. This way, the curriculum spirals and provides many opportunities for practicing mastered knowledge before expanding to new knowledge. The review of initial and final phonemes may be completed with the entire group of students, then be followed by leveled practice exercises designed for each small group of students. The introduction of a new concept (phoneme elision) may also be taught to the entire group of students, and additional practice (at different levels of difficulty) be incorporated into the small group instruction. Finally, after all groups have worked on the development of this concept

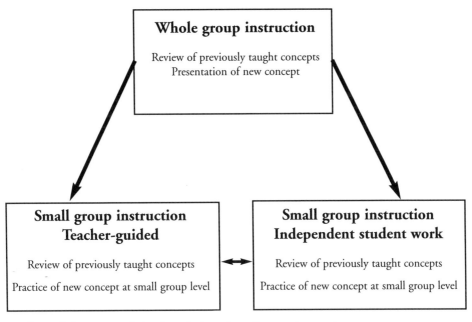

Figure 1. Instructional plan for whole and small group instruction

with the teacher during small group meetings, they practice the new learning again independently (in pairs or small group independent work).

It is important for small-group instruction, that the teacher develop a plan for what the rest of the class is doing while he is attending each of the small groups. A carefully planned management system should be in place outlining transition from one activity station to the next. This ensures uninterrupted teacher-guided and independent student group work. Work stations or center activities should always include familiar materials to ensure that students can operate without teacher assistance. Naturally, activities should also be instructionally valuable. While some teachers use activities from a variety of content areas not limited to reading, such as math, science, and writing, others focus exclusively on literacy activities. Still other teachers use a combination of the two. We generally recommend the formation of three to four small flexible groups in a classroom (averaging three to six students per group). Instructional needs of each student group may vary in terms of instructional intensity. For example, the *Most Independent* group might meet with the teacher for 20–25 minutes for three days a week. On the other two days, this group can work independently with minimal direction from the teacher. The *Least Independent* group has the most instructional needs and might meet with the teacher every day for 20–25 minutes. Sometimes students in the Least Independent group may need additional instructional time during the school day

Table 2

Sample Daily Lesson Planner

8:10-9:00	Whole Group Activities

— Morning routines

— Shared/Interactive Writing

Teacher and students take turns writing on a chart tablet. Teacher models and teaches phonemic analysis to spell words. She also uses "think aloud" strategy to create meaning out of the formed text. Each child writes a different part and then students chorally read the sentence.

— Review few high frequency words by random pointing and choral reading.

— Read Aloud of a new book after previewing new vocabulary words and concepts. Modeling a self-questioning strategy using "Think-Aloud." While reading students use meaning and structure cues to predict what comes next and are encouraged to self-monitor their understanding.

9:05-10:10			Small Group Instruction		
	Teacher Guided Differentiated small group instruction	**Writing Center** Independent journal writing	**Reading Corner** Partner reading leveled books to practice fluency	**Computer (2 students)** Log-in and choose between spelling or word games	**Listening Corner** Listening to stories on tape and filling out recording form
9:05-9:25	*P Group* (Kierra, Jose, Nicholas, Alexandra, Darrick) Word Ladders using known words and word patterns	Phillip, Annie Cari, Tyler, Carla, Kevin	Kendra, ConKelley, Morena, Brittany, Isabel	Noah, Larry	Jonathan, Maria, Joshua
9:25-9:45	*I Group* (Cari, Tyler, Annie, Brittany, Larry, Jonathan) Letter sound review. Say it and move it activity with blocks and letters.	Darrick, Isabel, Kendra, ConKelley, Joshua	Kierra, Jose, Carla, Kevin, Maria	Nicholas, Alexandra	Phillip, Morena, Noah
9:50-10:10	*MI Group* (Carla, Kevin, Isabel, Maria, Joshua) Practice reading and writing multi-syllabic words. Echo reading new book.	Nicholas, Alexandra, Morena, Brittany, Noah	Darrick, Larry, Jonathan, Phillip, Annie	Kierra, Jose	Kendra, ConKelley, Cari, Tyler

for reading instruction that some schools accommodate through pull-out programs. An example of classroom organization during small group instruction is presented in Table 2.

Forming Reading Groups

1. Identifying the Least Independent Group

    The Least Independent group consists of students who have the weakest reading-related skills. This group should be given the most immediate and intense reading intervention. The students in this group are "Still Developing" on the concept(s) assessed with the screening and have low scores on all or almost all of the tasks on the inventory, requiring instruction on all or almost all of the related skills. This group should meet with the teacher every day.

2. Identifying the Most Independent Group

    Students in the Most Independent group perform at a level higher than the class average or grade level expectations. Students who have developed the concept(s) assessed on the screening and have high scores on all or almost all the inventory tasks should be placed in that group. Children should be able to work independently with more challenging content and may serve as coaches to children in other student groups. Alternatively, they can be paired with students who require minimal assistance. This group usually works with the teacher three times a week.

3. Identifying Similar Profiles

    After the teacher forms the two groups as described in the first steps, one to two more groups remain to be organized. One option is to look at the remaining student scores in order to select the best criterion for grouping students who did not fit in either the Least Independent group or the Most Independent group. For example, identify groups that need support on phonemic awareness and graphophonemic knowledge. If student performances on the inventory tasks don't follow a predictable pattern, teachers should consider students' performances on the listening comprehension task. Generally teachers should look for similar performances and patterns of student strengths and weaknesses. The goal is to develop flexible groups based on the students' skill development and language proficiency. Most early assessments are organized in a way that the level of difficulty rises as the student progresses through the sequence of tasks. Initial tasks are less challenging than the later ones and teachers should take this into account when evaluating success patterns. Finally, it is important to keep in mind that not all students are expected to achieve perfect performance on all tasks at the beginning of the year. The kindergarten inventory tasks were constructed to address the whole range of skill development from beginning to the end of kindergarten in all areas described by the Texas Essential Knowledge and Skills document (TEA, 1998).

4. Merging Groups

A general rule of thumb is that the presence of more than four instructional groups might be difficult to manage. When the analysis of student profiles yields too many small groups, teachers should consider merging some of the groups in order to be able to manage and deliver effective instruction. The decision to consolidate groups of students for one or more target activities should be based on specific instructional goals. While the basic structure of three to four groups is maintained for most activities, the actual composition of the groups may change. Students may switch groups and groups may be merged at different times according to the instructional plan. Teachers save time and management effort, however, if they maintain a group composition for small-group instruction for a period of time (six to eight weeks).

A Classroom Example

Ms. Guerrero's class is a typical first-grade class consisting of 21 students from a small town in Texas. Ms. Guerrero administered the TPRI to each student at the end of September as follows: The TPRI screening was first administered to all students in the class; Ms. Guerrero then allocated time within the following week to administer the inventory to all students in the classroom regardless of their performance on the screening because she wanted to have information on all students in the class.

To effectively address individual needs with the classroom instruction, assessment information from each student should be inspected separately first. The student whose profile is presented in Table 3, was a very creative, sociable girl who was very popular among her peers. She was a hard worker and always tried to please her teacher. Annie was an only child and according to her teacher came from a stable and very literate family environment. Both her parents were actively involved in school activities. Annie's teacher reported that her overall language development was impressive for her age. She loved to listen to books read to her, she knew many authors of popular students' books and she was familiar with many book titles. At school, Annie was always involved in reading and writing activities and she was great at illustrating stories for her writing group. Annie came to first grade knowing all the letters of the alphabet and their associated sounds, and she recognized most of the print in the classroom along with a few common sight words. Her performance in reading, however, was erratic and she did not seem to respond to instruction consistently. One example was that her writing was still very immature, show-

Table 3

TPRI Screening and Inventory Performance Profile for Annie L.

Tasks	Scores	Performance description
Screening		
1 Letter Sound	10 of 10	Developed
2 Word Reading	0 of 8	Still Developing
3 Blending Phonemes	2 of 6	Still Developing
Inventory		
1 Phonemic Awareness (Blending word parts)	3 of 5	Still Developing
5 Graphophonemic Knowledge (Initial Consonants)	4 of 5	Developed
6 Graphophonemic Knowledge (Final Consonants)	3 of 5	Still Developing
10 Word List (Passage placement)	0 of 15	Passage Placement=1
11 Reading Connected Text	<90% accuracy	Frustrational Level
11 Listening Comprehension	5 of 5	Developed

ing that she had not yet mastered letter-to-sound correspondences.

According to the results of the TPRI screen, Annie required further evaluation before instructional objectives could be set. Her scores in the inventory section supported this notion by showing a rather typical pattern of a student with difficulties in phonological processing. She had difficulties in blending sounds both at the phoneme and the onset rime level (see Screening Task 3, Inventory, Phonemic Awareness Task 1). Her difficulty in distinguishing among the different sounds in words did not allow her to perform simple word building activities included in the "Graphophonemic Knowledge" section of the TPRI, despite her letter sound knowledge (see results of Screening 1). She was able to form seven simple words (mad, had, tad, dad, pan, pal, pap) by substituting initial and final consonants placed in front of her in the Graphophonemic Knowledge Tasks 1 and 2. Annie was not able to read any of the words given in the Word List accurately. Accordingly she was placed in the first TPRI passage for the assessment of reading accuracy and comprehension. Because she had many difficulties decoding the first sentence, her teacher read Story 1 to her. Her listening comprehension skills were excellent, and she answered without any problems both the explicit and implicit questions from the passage.

Based on this assessment and her overall classroom performance, Annie seemed to be an intelligent child with many book-related experiences from her home and school environment. Her difficulties with reading could not be accounted for by developmental delay. Rather, she showed specific deficits that could be addressed with appropriate instruction. Annie needed assistance in developing her phonemic awareness skills and applying these skills to word decoding. She could clearly benefit the most from individualized explicit instruction in phonemic awareness and letter-sound correspondences. Finally, instruction had to be offered in a systematic sequential manner, providing many opportunities for immediate feedback and modeling.

Grouping Phase for Forming Reading Groups

1. After all testing was complete, Ms. Guerrero filled out the *Class Summary Sheet* highlighting the names of students who were *Still Developing* on the Screening portion (Annie L., Cari C., Tyler B., Brittany M., and Larry T.). These students were placed in the *Intervention Group* (Group 1 as shown in Table 4) because they were the most likely to encounter problems in learning to read as indicated by their performance on the Screening portion of the TPRI. This group required the most frequent and intense instruction.

2. Then she prepared a classroom skills profile on the basis of the student scores across the different Inventory tasks. All students recognized the names of the letters of the alphabet and had mastered a significant number of letter-sound correspondences. Only a small group (five children) had difficulties answering explicit comprehension questions and only two had difficulty with the implicit questions. An important finding was that a significant number of students required more work on developing further phonemic awareness skills—specifically manipulating phonemes in words, such as deletion of individual phonemes in initial and final word positions.

3. Ms. Guerrero re-examined the students' performances in an effort to

Table 4

Classroom Small Instruction Groups

Group 1	Group 2	Group 3	Group 4
Intervention Group Work across all areas (I)	More work on phonemic awareness skills (PA)	More work on phonics skills/ word recognition (P)	Most Independent (MI)
Cari C.	Phillip C.	Kierra R.	Carla C.
Tyler B.	Morena C.	Jose R.	Kevin D.
Brittany M.	Kendra H.	Nicholas G.	Maria E.
Larry T. →	ConKelley P.	Alexandra C.	Joshua F.
Jonathan B. →	Noah B.	Darrick K.*[a]	Isabel N. *[b]
Annie L. →			

[a], [b] Asterisks indicate students who need extra work on comprehension skills.

group them into four small groups for providing differentiated instruction according to individual student needs. The *Least Independent* or Intervention Group (I) consisted initially of Annie, Cari, Tyler, Brittany, Larry (Still Developing on the Screening) and also Jonathan who had Developed on the Screening portion, but had very poor performance across several Inventory tasks. Annie, Larry, and Jonathan generally performed better than Cari, Tyler, and Brittany and the teacher made a note to move these three students to other groups according to the instructional focus in order for them to benefit from more challenging work.

4. It was relatively easy to identify the *Most Independent* group (MI). Carla, Kevin, and Isabel had a perfect score on almost all tasks with the exception of Isabel who had missed two of the five comprehension questions. Isabel had been noted for her erratic attention and Ms. Guerrero had decided to include her in the MI group and closely monitor her progress on listening comprehension. Two more children, Maria and Joshua, had shown some difficulty on the most challenging phonological awareness task, yet based on their overall level of skill development they were also placed in this group.

5. After forming the first two groups (totaling eleven), ten students remained unclassified. The teacher examined their individual profiles to find possible similarities. Four students showed difficulties with phonemic awareness skills assessed in the Inventory portion of the TPRI (Phillip, Morena, Kendra, ConKelley) and were grouped together. The teacher then decided to assign Noah to this group, although he lagged behind the other students. Noah could also participate in more basic work including letter-sound correspondence activities presented to the Intervention Group.

6. Finally, she reviewed scores for the remaining students (Kierra, Jose, Nicholas, Alexandra, and Darrick) and despite individual differences in their performances on certain tasks (especially comprehension), the four students had, in many respects, very similar instructional needs. It seemed that they could benefit from a direct approach to the development of a wide range of skills for recognizing words, without requiring the most intense intervention. Ms. Guerrero had placed an asterisk next to the names of Darrick and Isabel as a reminder that these two students would need extra work on comprehension skills.

Instructional Planning

After the completion of the initial student grouping, Ms. Guerrero planned to teach three small groups a day for approximately 20–25 minutes per group. This way she allocated about half of the morning reading instruction time to work with the small groups while the rest of the children were doing pre-planned center work at their level independently. Devoting approximately an hour of her reading instruction every day for teaching three small groups allowed her to meet with the Intervention (I) group every day, the Phonemic Awareness (PA) group four days per week, and the Most Independent (MI) and Phonics (P) groups three days per week. The rest of the teaching time was used for whole class reading instruction.

Regarding the content of her small group instruction, she wrote and posted on her desk a general sequence for each 20 minute lesson including the following components:

1. Brief review
2. Phonemic awareness
3. Letter sound correspondences
4. Word work (Word building, sight words)
5. Fluency practice with decodable text
6. Teacher Read-Aloud of advanced level text (Pre-teach vocabulary, Active Listening, Questioning and Comprehension strategies.)

This lesson plan was derived from the TPRI Intervention Activities Guide (TPRI, 2004) and was used with most groups as a complete sequential routine. She often focused, however, on elements from a particular lesson addressing specific, lingering weaknesses. These focused mini-lessons on specific skills contained a number of activities that shared the same objective in order to maximize the amount of practice provided. For example, while working with the P group one day she implemented the following activities instead of the usual daily sequence: (a) oral discrimination of a long sound from other sounds, (b) word building with consonant-vowel-consonant (CVC), consonant-vowel-consonant-silent e (CVCe) and derivatives (*cap-cape >caps, capes*), (c) practice reading word parts and whole word reading (*rab, bit, rabbit*), (d) sight word review (flash cards in pairs), (e) fluency practice with decodable text using sight words and previously taught sounds.

Especially for the Intervention group Ms. Guerrero planned lessons that focused on phonemic processing and word building activities every day for approximately 10 minutes of each session. Specifically, she worked on listening activities that aimed to help all students distinguish and manipulate different sounds in words (practicing oral blending and segmenting word parts and speech sounds to form and alter words). She also used handheld mirrors to help children locate parts of their mouths while they were producing different speech sounds. In the remaining time, she worked with the students on practicing letter-sound correspondences and the formation of single-syllable (CVC) words. At this point she introduced blending, a critical skill for word decoding.

Some of the activities she used frequently with this group as suggested in the TPRI Intervention Activities Guide (2004), were:

1. *Say the sound* In this activity different objects or picture cards were used along with small plastic chips. The students were asked first to name the items and then pronounce the words, one sound at a time while moving the chips as they were saying each sound. Ms. Guerrero had selected cards that represented words of increasing difficulty (from three phonemes to four, etc.).

2. *Detecting medial sounds with word building* In this activity each student was provided with a small set of plastic letters. The teacher initially demonstrated how to build a particular word (i.e. hit) and then how to convert it to other words with different middle vowels (i.e., hot, hut, hat).

3. *Closed word sorts and word sort according to sound* In this activity the students were given a set of word cards and were told which distinctive feature to use for sorting. Then the teacher would assign marks or headings for each word group. The students began by reading the word on their card and placing it under the appropriate heading. A variation of this activity, that was used to practice long vowel sounds, began by asking the students to brainstorm words that contain the long /a/ sound (i.e. make, rain, eight, day, etc.). The teacher wrote each word on an index card and placed the cards randomly on a stack adding several more similar words. Then students were asked to sort the words according to their spelling of the long /a/ sound (i.e., a, ai, eigh, ay). The teacher helped them blend and pronounce the words and the students at the end underlined the letters that make the long /a/ sound (TPRI, 2004).

As the students became more skilful at manipulating the sounds in words, more time was devoted to word building activities, by moving from oral blending and segmentation tasks, to forming the target word with letters and finally to word reading. They were also gradually advanced from simple CVC words to longer words and more complex letter patterns. The sequence followed for the word work was: words with digraphs and blends, long vowel patterns, other vowel patterns, consonant doubling, plural endings, compound words, simple inflectional endings, etc. Finally, all students in the I group also received individualized assistance whenever possible. Working with phonics rules and practicing reading with simple decodable text was especially beneficial for this group as documented by periodic assessments completed approximately every six weeks. Ms. Guerrero was especially watchful of the students' daily performance and she re-grouped the students as needed. After the mid-year Inventory

Table 5

Modified Instruction Groups After Mid-year Assessment.

Group 1	Group 2	Group 3	Group 4
Intervention Group Work across all areas (I)	More work on phonics skills/ word recognition (P)	More work on reading comprehension (C)	Most Independent (MI)
Cari	Annie	Jonathan	Carla
Tyler	Phillip	Kierra	Kevin
Brittany	Morena	Darrick	Maria
Larry	Kendra	Isabel	Joshua
Noah	ConKelley		Nicholas
	Jose		Alexandra

assessment the groups were re-formed as shown in Table 5 to accommodate changing learning needs.

Classroom management

A critical issue for effective implementation of small group instruction is classroom management. Ms. Guerrero had anticipated that children may take some time to adjust to independent work and for this reason she wanted to present children with clear roles and expectations and a support system to be activated each time they needed assistance. During the first month she used assistance from a teacher aid, employed by the school, in order to complete all individual assessments with the students. Later she introduced student independent work for gradually increasing time periods with the assistance of another adult (parent volunteer). She also created a rotation chart that clearly illustrated group assignments and rotations during the reading time and encouraged the children to use it without having to ask an adult for help in finding their group. Finally, she posted and reinforced the use of a sign that contained tips (along with signs and pictures) on what steps were appropriate when someone needed help while working independently (for example: Look at the station's work list, ask a classmate for help, use your brain, etc.). Ms. Guerrero had taken great efforts to positively reinforce all the students who followed these suggestions.

In terms of the physical environment she made sure that group stations (computer station, reading corner, writing center, and listening post) were arranged evenly, and placed physical barriers (cabinets, shelving, etc.) among the group stations allowing for some privacy and control of noise levels. She also had

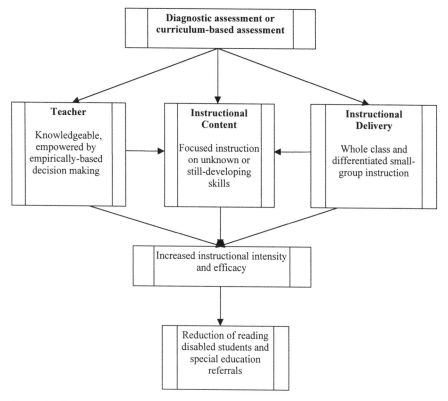

Figure 2. Outcomes of effective assessment-based intervention

placed adequate seating and had supplied each area with enough materials to sustain work in each group for at least a week. She had made sure that each group station encompassed a wide range of activities that were designed to require application of the skills learned during small and whole group instruction at different entry levels. Her goal was to replenish materials every week and renew the activities at each center at even longer time periods. Finally, in order to further ensure the effectiveness of her planning, she had organized a reward system to motivate students to work collaboratively without disruptions.

CONCLUSION

Quality classroom instruction and early identification of at-risk learners can significantly reduce the number of students with long-term reading disability. The Texas Primary Reading Inventory was developed through the Texas Reading initiative in an effort to improve classroom reading instruction in kindergarten through Grade 2 and achieve early identification of students at-risk for reading difficulties. The classroom case outlined exemplifies a model of training and instruction for early intervention using the TPRI with children who enter first grade with diverse needs and abilities (See Figure 2). Many teachers we have worked with during the past six years know how to individualize instruction based on children's progress on the assessment. The Intervention Activities Guides in the TPRI and Tejas LEE kits are valuable resources, but even more valuable is in-classroom coaching in how to translate TPRI and Tejas LEE results to differentiated instruction (Foorman & Moats, 2004). While in-classroom staff development is considered the most effective support method for scaling literacy initiatives (Snow et al., 1998), it is costly and requires a highly organized delivery infrastructure. An alternative approach, that has been very popular among teachers is to employ informal reading inventories as the main assessment tool in the context of literature-based approaches to instruction. Unfortunately, many informal reading inventories lack empirical evidence regarding reliability and validity. Even in districts and states where early reading assessment is widely used, the information from K-3 assessments is not regularly collected, nor does it inform instruction. The suggested application of this assessment-driven, classroom-based intervention in the Texas schools highlights the practical utility of K-3 assessments for identifying at-risk students, informing instruction, and monitoring student outcomes so that students emerge from Grade 3 as successful, independent readers.

REFERENCES

Abrami, P. C., Lou, Y., Chambers, B., Poulsen, C., & Spence, J. (2000). Why should we group students within-class for learning? *Educational Research and Evaluation, 6* (2),159–179.

Bishop, A. (2003). Prediction of first-grade reading achievement: A comparison of fall and winter kindergarten screenings. *Learning Disability Quarterly, 26* (3) 189–200.

Byrne, B., & Fielding-Barnsley, R. (1989). Phonemic awareness and letter knowledge in the child's acquisition of the alphabetic principle. *Journal of Educational Psychology, 81*(3), 313–321.

Calfee, R., & Brown, R. (1979). Grouping students for instruction. In D. L. Duke (Ed.), *Classroom management. Seventy-eighth yearbook of the national society for the study of education* (pp.144–182). Chicago: University of Chicago Press.

Cohen, D. K., & Ball, D. L. (1999). *Instruction, capacity and improvement.* CPRE Research Report Series RR-43. The Consortium for Policy Research in Education.

Coyne, M. D., Kame'enui, E. J., & Simmons, D. C. (2001). Prevention and intervention in beginning reading: Two complex systems. *Learning Disabilities Research & Practice, 16* (2), 62–73.

Denton, C. A., Vaughn, S., & Fletcher, J. M. (2003). Reading instruction for struggling students: Bringing research-based practice to scale. *Learning Disabilities Research and Practice, 18* (3), 201–211.

Elbaum, B., Vaughn, S., Hughes, M., & Watson Moody, S. (1999). Grouping practices and reading outcomes for students with disabilities. *Exceptional Children, 65* (3) 399–415.

Elmore, R. F. (1995). Structural reform and educational practice. *Educational Researcher, 24* (9), 23–26.

Fletcher, J. M., & Foorman, B. R. (1994). Redefining learning disabilities: Commentary on Berninger and Abbott. In G. R. Lyon (Ed.), *Better measurement of learning disabilities* (pp.185–200). Baltimore: Paul H. Brookes.

Fletcher, J. M., Foorman, B. R., Boudousquie, A., Barnes, M., Schatschneider, C., & Francis, D. J. (2002). Assessment of reading and learning disabilities: A research-based, treatment-oriented approach. *Journal of School Psychology, 40,* 27–63.

Fletcher, J. M., & Lyon, G. R. (1998). Reading: A research-based approach. In W. M. Evers (Ed.), *What's gone wrong in America's classrooms* (pp.49–90). Stanford, CA: Hoover Institution Press.

Foorman, B. R., Fletcher, J. M., & Francis, D. J. (2004). Early reading assessment. In W. Evert (Ed.), *Testing student learning, evaluating teacher effectiveness* (pp. 81–125). Stanford, CA: The Hoover Institution.

Foorman, B. R., Francis, D. J., Fletcher, J. M., Schatschneider, C., & Mehta, P. (1998). The role of instruction in learning to read: Preventing reading failure in at-risk children. *Journal of Educational Psychology, 90,* 37–55.

Foorman, B. R., & Moats, L. C. (2004). Conditions for sustaining research-based practices in early reading instruction. *Remedial and Special Education, 25* (1), 51–60.

Foorman, B. R., & Torgesen, J. K. (2001). Critical elements of classroom and small-group instruction promote reading success in all children. *Learning Disabilities Research and Practice, 16* (4), 202–211.

Francis, D. J., Shaywitz, S. E., Stuebing, K. K., Shaywitz, B. A., & Fletcher, J. M. (1996). Developmental lag versus deficit models of reading disability: A longitudinal, individual growth curves analysis. *Journal of Educational Psychology, 88,* 3–17.

Gresham, F. M., MacMillan, D. L. & Bocian, K. M. (1997). Teachers as "Tests": Differential validity of teacher judgments in identifying students at-risk for learning difficulties. *The School Psychology Review, 26* (1), 47–60.

Hawkins, J., Kulp, K. M., Gilbert, J., Mesa, L., & Schwarz, J. (1999). *Final summary report: Technology integration in Chicago Public Elementary Schools, 1997–1998.* New York: EDC Center for Children and Technology.

Hiebert, E. H. (1983). An examination of ability grouping for reading instruction. *Reading Research Quarterly, 18,* 231–255.

Juel, C. (1988). Learning to read and write: A longitudinal study of fifty-four children from first through fourth grade. *Journal of Educational Psychology, 80,* 437–447.

Juel, C., & Minden-Cupp, C. (2000). Learning to read words: Linguistics units and instructional strategies. *Reading Research Quarterly, 35,* 458–92.

Lou, Y., Abrami, P. C., Spence, J. C., Poulsen, C., Chambers, B., & d'Apollonia, S. (1996). Within-class grouping: A meta-analysis. *Review of Educational Research, 66* (4), 423–458.

Mathes, P. G., & Denton, C. A. (2002). The prevention and identification of reading disability. *Seminars in Pediatric Neurology, 9,* 185–191.

Moats, L. C. (1999). *Teaching reading IS rocket science.* Washington, DC: American Federation of Teachers.

Mouzaki, A. (2001). *The Literacy Lab: A school-based intervention program for students with reading difficulties.* Unpublished doctoral dissertation. University of Houston.

National Reading Panel (2000). *Teaching children to read: An evidence-based assessment of the scientific research literature on reading and its implications for reading instruction.* Washington, DC: National Institute of Child Health and Human Development.

No Child Left Behind Act (2001), 20 U.S.C. §§ 6301 et seq.

O'Connor, R. E., & Jenkins, J. R. (1999). The prediction of reading disabilities in kindergarten and first grade. *Scientific Studies of Reading, 3,* 159–197.

Paris, S. G., Paris, A. H., & Carpenter, R. D. (2001). *Effective practices for assessing young readers.* CIERA Report No. 3–013. Michigan: Center for the Improvement of Early Reading Achievement.

Rayner, K., Foorman, B., Perfetti, C. A., Pesetsky, D., & Seidenberg, M. S. (2001). How psychological science informs the teaching of reading. *Psychological Science in the Public Interest, 2,* 31–74.

Rosenholtz, S. J., & Wilson, B. (1980). The effect of classroom structure on shared perceptions of ability. *American Education Research Journal, 17,* 75–82.

Scarborough, H. S. (1998). Early identification of children at risk for reading disabilities: Phonological awareness and some other promising predictors. In B. K. Shapiro, A.J. Capute, & B. Shapiro (Eds.), *Specific reading disability: A view of the spectrum* (pp.77–121). Hillsdale, NJ: Erlbaum.

Schumm Shay, J., Watson Moody, S., & Vaughn, S. (2000). Grouping for reading instruction: Does one size fit all? *Journal of Learning Disabilities, 33* (5), 477–489.

Share, D. L., & Stanovich, K. E. (1995). Cognitive processes in early reading development: Accommodating individual differences into a model of acquisition. *Issues in Education, 1*(1), 1–5.

Snow, C. E., Burns, M. S., & Griffin, P. (Eds.). (1998). *Preventing reading difficulties in young children.* Washington, DC: National Academy Press.

Stanovich, K. E., West, R. F., & Cunningham, A. E. (1991). Beyond phonological processes: Print exposure and orthographic processing. In S. A. Brady & D. P. Shankweiler (Eds.), *Phonological processes in literacy: A tribute to Isabelle Y. Liberman* (pp. 219–235). Hillsdale, NJ: Lawrence Erlbaum Associates.

Strickland, D., Snow, C., Griffin, P., Burns M. S., & McNamara, P. (2002). *Preparing our teachers: Opportunities for better reading instruction.* Washington D.C.: Joseph Henry Press.

Texas Essential Knowledge and Skills (1998). Austin, TX: Texas Education Agency. Retrieved from http://www.tea.state.tx.us/teks/ under teks.

Texas Primary Reading Inventory. (2004). Austin, TX: Texas Education Agency.

Texas Primary Reading Inventory. Intervention Activities Guide (2004). Austin, TX: Texas Education Agency.

Texas Primary Reading Inventory Technical Report (1998). Austin, TX: Texas Education Agency. Retrieved from http://www.tpri.org under researchers and psychometrics.

Texas Primary Reading Inventory Technical Report (1999). Austin, TX: Texas Education Agency. Retrieved from http://www.tpri.org under researchers and psychometrics.

Texas Primary Reading Inventory Technical Report (in preparation). Austin, TX: Texas Education Agency. Retrieved from http://www.tpri.org under researchers and psychometrics.

Torgesen, J., Wagner, R., & Rashotte, C. (1997). Prevention and remediation of severe reading disabilities: Keeping the end in mind. *Scientific Studies of Reading, 1*(3), 217–234.

Torgesen, J. K. (1999). Reading disabilities. In R. Gallimore, A. Bernheimer, G. MacMillan, D. Spence, & S. Vaughn (Eds.), *Developmental perspectives on children with high incidence disabilities: Papers in honor of Barbara K. Keogh* (pp. 157–182). Mahwah,

NJ: Lawrence Erlbaum Associates.

Torgesen, J. K. (2002). The prevention of reading difficulties. *Journal of School Psychology* *40* (1), 7–26.

Torgesen, J. K., & Burgess, S. R. (1998). Consistency of reading-related phonological processes throughout early childhood: Evidence from longitudinal-correlational and instructional studies. In J. Metsala & L. Ehri (Eds.), *Word recognition in beginning literacy* (pp. 161–188). Hillsdale, NJ: Erlbaum.

Torgesen, J. K., Wagner, R. K., Rashotte, C. A., Rose, E., Lindamood, P., Conway, T., et al. (1999). Preventing reading failure in young children with phonological processing disabilities: Group and individual responses to instruction. *Journal of Educational Psychology, 91,* 579–93.

Valencia, S. W., & Wixson, K. K. (1999). *Policy-oriented research on literacy standards and assessment.* CIERA Report No. 3–004. Michigan: Center for the Improvement of Early Reading Achievement.

Vaughn, S., Watson Moody, S., & Shay Schumm, J. (1998). Broken promises: Reading instruction in the resource room. *Exceptional Children, 64,* 211–25.

Vellutino, F. R., Scanlon, D. M., & Lyon, G. R. (2000). Differentiating between difficult-to-remediate and readily remediated poor readers: More evidence against the IQ-achievement discrepancy definition of reading disability. *Journal of Learning Disabilities, 33* (3), 223–238.

Vellutino, F. R., Scanlon, D. M., Sipay, E. R., Small, S. G., Chen, R., Pratt A., et al. (1996). Cognitive profiles of difficult to remediate and readily remediated poor readers: Early intervention as a vehicle for distinguishing between cognitive and experiential deficits as basic causes of specific reading disabilities. *Journal of Educational Psychology, 88,* 601–638.

Vygotsky, L. S., Rieber, R. W., & Hall, M. J. (1999). *The collected works of L. S. Vygotsky: Scientific legacy*: *Vol. 6. Cognition and language.* Kluwer Academic Publishers.

Watson Moody, S., Vaughn, S., Hughes Tejero, M., & Fischer, M. (2000). Reading instruction in the resource room; Set up for failure. *Exceptional Children, 66* (3), 305–16.

Watson Moody, S., Vaughn, S., & Shay Schumm, J. (1997). Instructional grouping for reading: Teachers' views. *Remedial and Special Education, 18* (6), 347–356.

Wise, B. W., Ring, J., & Olson, R. K. (1999). Training phonological awareness with and without explicit attention to articulation. *Journal of Experimental Child Psychology, 72,* 271–304.

Wood, F., Hill, D., & Meyer, M. (2001). *Predictive assessment of reading.* Winston-Salem, NC: Author.

Woodcock, R. W., & Johnson, M. B. (1989). *Woodcock-Johnson Psychoeducational Battery-Revised.* Allen, TX: DLM Teaching Resources.

Chapter Three

SELF-MONITORING TO IMPROVE ACADEMIC AND BEHAVIORAL PERFORMANCE

Melody Tankersley , Ph.D.

Kent State University

Richard J. Cowan, Ph.D.

Kent State University

Bryan G. Cook, Ph.D.

University of Hawaii

Learning disability is an extremely complex and frequently misunderstood construct (Kavale & Forness, 1995). The complexity of the disability is evidenced by the many differing behavioral and psychological characteristics students with learning disabilities (LD) typically present both across the population (i.e., interindividual variation) as well as within their own profiles of ability (i.e., intraindividual variation) (Hallahan & Kauffman, 2003). To remediate the various areas of deficit associated with LD, special educators have developed and refined specific instructional interventions (Vaughn & Linan-Thompson, 2003). For example, because difficulty in reading is a prominent trait of many students with LD, a number of techniques have been advanced to improve reading proficiency and comprehension for these learners (Lerner, 2000). Although the appropriate use of learning strategies is a concern for many students in specific curricular areas in which they may struggle, seminal research has shown that students with LD often have difficulty identifying and using strategies associated with learning in general—regardless of the content area (e.g., Hallahan & Reeve, 1980; Torgesen, 1977). In fact, authorities in the field often characterize students with LD as inefficient learners who lack systematic strategies for remembering, monitoring, and directing their own academic and social learning (see Hallahan & Kauffman, 2003). Self-monitoring represents an effective learning strategy that can address this pervasive difficulty for individuals with LD which, when used appropriately, improves the learning and behavioral outcomes of students with (and without) LD.

In addition to considering research regarding the effectiveness of self-monitoring, it is also important to take into account the ease with which teachers can implement the intervention as it is designed (i.e., with fidelity). Significantly, the procedures of self-monitoring incorporate many aspects that enhance the likelihood that teachers will find it acceptable to use in their classrooms (e.g., requires only a short amount of time to implement, is a positive approach for improving academic and behavioral performance, is implemented in the natural learning environment) (see Tankersley & Talbott, 1992). In contemporary discussions of the research-to-practice gap that plagues the field of education, it has been noted that although special educators have developed a vast array of instructional practices that have been validated by research, the outcomes of students with disabilities are frequently less than desirable because many teachers do not use these practices at all, and those that do use them often fail to do so properly (e.g., Cook &

Schirmer, 2003). As such, the literature base reviewed in this chapter indicating that self-monitoring can both positively impact student outcomes and is relatively easy for teachers to use in a variety of settings is particularly meaningful and encouraging. Before exploring what the research literature tells us about the effectiveness and "useability" (Carnine, 1997) of self-monitoring in greater depth, the theoretical foundations of the practice will be briefly discussed. The chapter will conclude with a description of how to set up and implement self-monitoring for students with LD.

SELF-MANAGEMENT: THE FOUNDATION OF SELF-MONITORING

Cognitive training is an instructional technique that provides students with explicit strategies for solving problems while involving them to the greatest extent possible in their own learning. With cognitive training, the student is taught to use specific self-directed instructions, cognitions, or problem-solving strategies that will lead to successful, self-managed behavior (Hallahan, Kauffman, & Lloyd, 1999). Self-management, then, is the goal of cognitive training and specific interventions can help promote students' independence and self-reliance as they change or maintain their own behavior (Fantuzzo & Polite, 1990).

With self-management interventions, students are taught to use strategies that will increase their appropriate academic or social skills (and/or decrease inappropriate academic or social skills). Indeed, self-management interventions promote independence and self-reliance by teaching students to engage in specific strategies in an effort to change a targeted behavior (Shapiro & Cole, 1994).

Self-management strategies may also promote personal responsibility for learning and behavior. Because students are taught specific strategies that they (instead of a teacher, for example) manage, students' beliefs that they are able to select and control their behavior are encouraged (e.g., Graham, Harris, & Reid, 1992). Encouraging personal attribution for behavior is an especially important aspect of intervention for students with LD, as they often attribute their successes and failures to others rather than to their own effort and behavior (Hallahan & Kauffman, 2003). Self-management strategies encourage personal attribution as well as independence and self-reliance.

Self-monitoring is one type of self-management intervention. With over 25 years of research that confirms its effectiveness in improving academic and social behavior of students in schools, self-monitoring is a well established and widely studied intervention (Cole & Bambara, 2000). The purpose of this chapter is to provide an overview of self-monitoring and its effectiveness for students with LD, as well as to discuss considerations for setting up a self-monitoring intervention in the classroom to enhance the self-management of students with LD.

SELF-MONITORING

In the late 1970s and early 1980s, researchers at the University of Virginia Learning Disabilities Research Institute (Hallahan et al., 1983) conducted a series of studies regarding the effectiveness of self-monitoring for students with LD. The results showed that self-monitoring was effective for improving students' academic, task-related, and social behaviors and that teachers could easily implement it with precision. Since that time, systematic study of the application and effects of the intervention have resulted in a better understanding of self-monitoring as well as a number of recommendations and considerations for its implementation with students. In the following sections, we define self-monitoring and describe how it has been implemented.

Defining Self-Monitoring

Self-monitoring is a two step process that includes self-assessment and self-recording (Nelson & Hayes, 1981). First, one must assess whether a target behavior has occurred (self-assessment). Then, a record of the assessment result is noted in some overt way (self-recording). For example, in one of the early studies of self-monitoring as an intervention for students with LD, a 7-year-old boy was taught to assess and record his on-task behavior when he heard a tape recorded tone cue him to do so (Hallahan, Lloyd, Kosiewicz, Kauffman, & Graves, 1979). When the boy heard the cue, he was to ask himself, "Was I paying attention?" and then check a box on his recording sheet indicating the answer of his assessment ("Yes" or "No"). Independent data showed use of the self-monitoring procedure increased the student's on-task behavior as well as his academic productivity in math and handwriting.

The effectiveness of self-monitoring has been noted consistently through research. Many studies have demonstrated that the process of observing one's own behavior in order to assess its occurrence and subsequently making a record of that observation has a positive effect on the frequency, rate, duration, and/or intensity of the behavior being observed. Although the exact reasons why self-monitoring is effective are not entirely clear, the resulting change in behavior from this two-step process is most often theoretically linked to reactivity—the very act of engaging in self-assessment and self-recording can lead to positive behavioral changes (Mace & Kratochwill, 1988). Some scholars (e.g., Maag, 2004) liken the principles of reactivity to those of negative reinforcement in that as persons seek to avoid an unpleasant behavior (e.g., making note that they had engaged in an undesirable behavior), they engage in the undesirable behavior less often or in an alternative positive behavior more often. For example, a student may avoid the "guilt" associated with reporting five interruptions by engaging in interruptive behavior less often. Therefore, the interruptive behavior decreases because of the student's increased awareness of the behavior, brought about by the act of self-assessing and then making a record of its occurrence.

Applications of Self-Monitoring

Self-monitoring has been demonstrated to be a robust intervention in that it has been implemented with students of diverse characteristics, for a variety of behaviors, and in different settings. In the following sections, we discuss each of these areas of application of self-monitoring, focusing in particular on its application with students with LD.

Students. Self-monitoring has been implemented with students of varying ages and with students who present a variety of differences in ability in academic and social performance. For example, self-monitoring interventions have been implemented with students in preschool, (e.g., Connell, Carta, Lutz, Randall, & Wilson, 1993; Strain, Kohler, Storey, & Danko, 1994), kindergarten (e.g., Storey, Lawry, Ashworth, Danko, & Strain, 1994), elementary school (e.g., Maag, Rutherford, & DiGangi, 1992), middle school (e.g., Carr & Puntzo, 1993), and high school (e.g., Flores, Schloss, & Alper, 1995). Moreover, students with developmental disabilities (e.g., Boyle & Hughes, 1994; Hughes, Korinek, & Gorman, 1991), attention deficit disorders (e.g., Mathes & Bender, 1997), emotional and behavioral disorders (e.g., McDougall & Brady, 1995), autism (e.g., Newman et al., 1995), and LD (e.g., Shimabukuro, Prater, Jenkins, & Edelen-Smith, 1999) have used self-monitoring interventions successfully.

Among the studies that have introduced self-monitoring interventions to students with LD, students also differed in relation to age and ability. For example, Lloyd, Bateman, Landrum, and Hallahan (1989) and Maag, Reid, and DiGangi (1993) taught elementary students with LD to self-monitor their attention to task and their academic productivity. Trammel, Schloss, and Apler (1994) taught eight high school students with LD to self-monitor their homework assignments and Blick and Test (1987) taught nine high school students with LD to monitor their on-task behavior. Moreover, some students with LD who used self-monitoring also had other behavioral or learning concerns. For example, Shimabukuro et al. (1999) investigated the effects of self-monitoring of academic productivity and accuracy on the academic performance and on-task behavior of three students with LD who also had been diagnosed with attention deficit disorder.

Behaviors. The self-monitoring literature suggests that there are a wide variety of behaviors for which a self-monitoring program may be developed and implemented. The behaviors targeted may be readily observable to others (such as inappropriate verbalizations) or observable only to the individual self-monitoring (such as negative thoughts). Specific examples in the research include [has worked for] evidence of support for the use of self-monitoring as related to increasing on-task behavior, increasing task completion, increasing productivity, increasing work accuracy, reducing calling-out behaviors, increasing the use of positive statements, increasing positive social behaviors, decreasing aggression, and decreasing negative statements (DiGangi & Maag, 1992; Webber, Sheuermann, McCall, & Coleman, 1993). With such a long and assorted list, Cole and Bambara (2000) appositely summarized their discussion by saying that "almost any relevant target behavior may be successfully self-monitored by children and adolescents in school settings" (p. 205).

Although self-monitoring can be used with a variety of behaviors, its application with students with LD has been primarily focused on increasing on-task behavior or academic performance. For example, numerous studies have shown that when students with LD self-monitor their on-task behavior, their rate, frequency, or duration of attention increases (e.g., Blick & Test, 1987; Hallahan, Lloyd, & Stoller, 1982; Maag et al., 1992; Marshall, Lloyd, & Hallahan, 1993; Prater, Joy, Chilman, Temple, & Miller, 1991; Rooney, Hallahan, & Lloyd, 1984; Rooney, Polloway, & Hallahan, 1985). Most applications of self-monitoring of on-task behavior follow the procedures established by Hallahan et al. (1979) in which students ask themselves whether they were paying attention each time a variable-interval tone occurs, and then record their judgments on recording sheets.

For example, in the Prater et al. (1991) study, five adolescents with learning disabilities were taught to self-monitor their on-task behavior in educational settings particular to each student (e.g., resource classroom, general education social studies, study hall). Each student was taught to self-monitor by assessing their on-task behavior when they heard a tone and then recording a "+" if they were on-task or a "−" if they were off-task. The results of independent observations showed that all students increased their on-task behavior in the educational settings in which self-monitoring procedures were implemented.

Similar to self-monitoring of on-task behavior, when students with LD self-monitor their academic performance—typically defined as academic productivity or academic accuracy—increases in those outcomes occur (e.g., Harris, 1986; Harris, Graham, Reid, McElroy, & Hamby, 1994; Lloyd et al., 1989; Maag et al., 1993). Self-monitoring academic productivity typically involves recording the extent to which or rate at which a task has been completed. For example, Maag et al. taught fourth-grade students to record the number of math problems completed at cued times. Similarly, Harris asked students with LD to count the number of spelling words they practiced at the end of each class period for a record of productivity. The results of these studies showed that when students self-monitored their productivity, they completed more academic work.

In addition to productivity, academic performance is also concerned with issues of accuracy. For example, Rooney et al. (1985) taught students with LD that whenever they completed a specially marked problem on their worksheets, they were to compare their answer to the answer sheet and record their accuracy. Similarly, Shimabukuro et al. (1999) taught students to self-correct their independent work and compute their accuracy score, record it, and then graph it. These self-monitoring procedures resulted in an increase in students' academic accuracy in both studies.

Settings. Research has shown that self-monitoring can be introduced in different educational settings and situations. Studies have investigated the extent to which self-monitoring is effective with students with LD in general education classrooms (e.g., Maag et al., 1992), resource rooms (e.g., Lloyd et al., 1989; Trammel et al., 1994), self-contained classrooms (e.g., Harris et al., 1994; Marshall et al., 1993), and special schools (e.g., Shimabukuro et al., 1999) and found that the procedures are appropriate for each of these settings and that academic and social behaviors were improved across all of these different environments. Moreover, self-monitoring procedures have been incorporated to address specific behaviors while students were engaged in differing academic tasks and situations. For example, studies have addressed on-task behavior, academic performance, and other target behaviors while students with LD were working in such curricular areas as math (e.g., Heins, Lloyd, & Hallahan, 1986; Maag et al., 1993) and spelling (e.g., Harris, 1986; Harris et al., 1994) as well as in differing instructional groupings such as group instruction (e.g., Shimabukuro et al., 1999) and independent work (e.g., Lloyd et al., 1989).

SUMMARY

The results of over 25 years of investigating the effects of self-monitoring on the academic and social behaviors of students with LD are impressive. Self-monitoring has been established as an effective intervention for students with LD across the school-age span, for addressing a variety of behaviors, and in different settings and situations. In the following sections, we discuss considerations for setting up a self-monitoring intervention in the classroom.

SETTING UP A SELF-MONITORING INTERVENTION

Although each student-behavior-setting combination requires individualized planning and consideration on the part of the educational team, there exists a common set of sequential factors to consider when designing and implementing a self-monitoring intervention. Specifically, it may be beneficial for the educational team to consider the following phases or elements of the intervention: (a) clearly specifying and defining the target behavior(s), (b) selecting a monitoring method, (c) determining a frequency schedule for self-monitoring, (d) selecting a monitoring device, (e) training the individual, and (f) monitoring the accuracy of the individual's self-report data (adapted from Shapiro, Durnan, Post, & Levinson, 2002). These factors appear in Table 1, and are discussed in greater detail in the following sections.

Table 1

Steps for Setting up a Self-monitoring Intervention

- Specify and determine the target behavior(s)
  - May be objective (e.g., physical aggression) or subjective (e.g., thoughts)
  - Student articulates his or her understanding by providing examples and non-examples of the target behavior
- Select a self-monitoring method
  - Options: frequency counting, interval counting, general (or holistic) monitoring
- Select the right schedule
  - Options: duration of subject or assignment, time sampling, momentary time sampling
- Select the recording device
  - Options: paper-and-pencil protocols, hand signals
- Train the student to self-monitor
  - Options: verbal instructions, direct instruction, modeling, practice with feedback, accuracy analysis
- Investigate the accuracy of self-monitoring
  - Goal: > 80% student-rater agreement

Specifying and Defining the Target Behavior(s)

The first step for the educational team is to specify and define the target behavior(s) to be monitored by the student. As indicated earlier, a variety of behaviors may be monitored. For example, the target behavior may be clearly observable by the student and others (e.g., raising one's hand to ask a question, hitting another student in the stomach, yelling out in class). It is not necessary, however, for the behavior to be observable by individuals other than the student; that is, the behavior of interest may be more subjective on behalf of the student who is self-monitoring (e.g., thoughts, feelings, internal physiological responses to situations). As previously stated, virtually any behavior of interest may be successfully monitored by children and adolescents in applied settings (Cole & Bambara, 2000; Shapiro et al., 2002). However, the most critical aspect of this first step is that the student clearly understands which specific behavior is being monitored. Once the student is informed of the behavior of interest (i.e., during the training phase of intervention implementation) it may be beneficial to ask the student to explain the differences between the desired and undesired behaviors, a process which may help determine understanding of the relationship and differences between the two. Understanding the behavior is critical if the team expects self-monitoring to be accurate. Indeed, accuracy is necessary for self-governance, which is the ultimate goal of self-monitoring.

Selecting a Self-Monitoring Method

The second step for the educational team is to select a self-monitoring method that makes the most sense for the student-behavior-setting combination under consideration. There are two primary methods of self-monitoring: frequency monitoring and general monitoring. Within the category of frequency monitoring, the team may choose between frequency counting and interval counting (Cole & Bambara, 2000; Shapiro et al., 2002; Webber et al., 1993).

Frequency counting involves having the student keep track of each occurrence of a predetermined, specific behavior for the duration of either a designated time period (e.g., during math) or a particular assignment (e.g., a worksheet). Frequency counting may be accomplished by having the student indicate with a checkmark or hash line each occurrence of a behavior. For example, a student might be taught to place a checkmark on a data collection form each time he or she makes a positive social comment. An alternative to a pencil-and-paper approach involves having the student either place a token in a designated container or move an object (e.g., a raw kidney bean or paperclip) from one pocket to another for each occurrence of the target behavior. Another frequency counting approach involves having the student either write down or circle a number representing the frequency of occurrences. For example, after completing each worksheet, a student might be taught to check his or her own work and determine the number of problems completed correctly. Older students and/or a teacher could divide this number by the total number of problems attempted (resulting in a percentage correct score) to monitor progress over time. Frequency counting is likely most useful when the behavior (a) is of low frequency, (b) is of short duration, and/or (c) has a discrete beginning and end (Alberto & Troutman, 2003). The frequency count approach to data collection may require some monitoring and prompts from the teacher, especially during the beginning phase of intervention.

Whereas the frequency counting approach is concerned with monitoring behavior occurring within the duration of a time period or work product (e.g., a worksheet), *interval counting* involves the student recording his or her own behavior following a specific, predetermined amount of time (i.e., it is not continuous). Units of time are often designated by the presence of a signal as a prompt to record information (e.g., Hallahan et al., 1979). The signal or cue to monitor behavior can come from a special audiotape that beeps at a pre-determined, programmable rate (i.e., a "beep tape"). As an alternative to the audio-tape method just described, there exists computer application software that may be programmed to beep regularly at user-determined time intervals. For individuals who are hearing impaired, or as a less intrusive means of signaling, a visual cue or a hand signal or nonverbal message (e.g., a gentle tap on the shoulder) from a teacher or paraprofessional may serve as the cue for the student. Once the signal is received by the student, he or she records the occurrence or nonoccurrence of the specific, predetermined behavior. In this case, the student may use a checkmark to indicate behavior occurrence, answer a yes or no question regarding incidence of behavior, or rate his or her behavior on a continuum (e.g., 0 = no occurrences, 1 = one time, 2 = several times).

Whereas the frequency and interval counting procedures are concerned with tallying the frequency of behavior, *general monitoring* is concerned with having the student reflect on his or her overall performance over a designated time period, using a more holistic lens. For example, the student might be asked a series of questions related to his or her own performance during a specific time or on a specific task: Did you listen while the teacher was talking? Did you raise your hand to speak? Did you listen while others were asking questions? Did you participate without disturbing others? Did you put your name on your assignment? Did you complete the assignment? Did you hand in the assignment? This procedure may be used in cases where the student's overall performance is of greater interest than the number of times he or she engaged in a particular behavior. A variation of this approach might involve a task analysis worksheet whereby the student marks off each component of an assignment. The latter approach may be of particular interest and benefit for students who lack organizational skills. The team may decide to use either frequency monitoring or general monitoring, or some combination thereof.

Determining the Right Schedule

Regardless of whether the educational team decides to use a frequency and/or general monitoring approach, the team will need to decide on a meaningful recording schedule. For the frequency counting approach, this involves determining how often the student should engage in self-monitoring. For example, the team may decide to start with only one time period (e.g., the duration of independent seatwork immediately following direct instruction in math). This means the student would self-monitor continuously throughout the duration of the specified time period. Once the student demonstrates intervention fidelity (i.e., accurately records frequency of engaging in target behavior) during this time period, the team may decide to expand the self-monitoring to include additional independent seatwork periods. For each student-behavior-setting combination there is likely to exist a unique schedule for implementing frequency counting.

For some students in some situations, an interval counting approach is likely to yield more meaningful results. When this is the case, there are many schedules that may be used for self-monitoring procedures. One approach is the time sampling method wherein the student monitors his or her behavior at the end of each specified time interval. For example, every 15 minutes, the student may be cued to take a moment to reflect on his or her behavior over the last 15-minute period. Teams working with students for whom they designate the general monitoring approach will likely have the student engage in self-monitoring following either a designated time period, or following an assignment or portion of an assignment. The frequency with which the student uses general monitoring will depend on the goals and objectives of the student's educational team.

An alternative to this approach is momentary time sampling (sometimes referred to as "spot checking;" Cole & Bambara, 2000). With this procedure, the student monitors his or her behavior for that designated moment only (i.e., indicating whether or not he or she was engaged in the target behavior at that exact moment of time only). For example, Lloyd et al. (1989) used tape recorded tones that occurred at irregular intervals (mean inter-tone interval of 45 seconds) to prompt students to monitor their on-task behavior. Such a momentary time sampling method is often incorporated into self-monitoring on-task interventions as it provides multiple opportunities for the student to monitor and also serves as a reminder to re-engage in the task. Again, the use of this approach and the way the moment of self-monitoring is defined will depend on the goals and objectives of the student's educational team.

Selecting a Recording Device

There are a variety of recording devices available for students engaged in self-monitoring. For example, mechanical counters similar to golf counters may be easily worn and used by students (Cole & Bambara, 2000; Shapiro et al., 2002). Alternatively, hand signals may be used for younger children or with children for whom verbal communication is limited. For example, the student may give either a head nod or "thumbs up" indicating "yes" or "affirmative."

In addition to or in lieu of these devices, educational teams may select from a variety of paper-and-pencil procedures. Paper-and-pencil procedures vary, based on the needs of the student in the setting of interest. For example, the student may place a checkmark or hash line on a piece of paper or existing recording form for each occurrence of a specific behavior (i.e., frequency counting and recording; see Figure 1). Other paper-and-pencil strategies include having the student answer yes or no questions at the conclusion of a task, having the student rate his or her own behavior on a Likert scale (e.g., 1 = not at all, 2 = a couple of times, 3 = several times, 4 = most of the time; see Figure 2), and/or filling in boxes in a grid related to specific behaviors or tasks (Coleman & Webber, 2002). See Figure 2 for an example of a recording device that uses both yes/no and rating responses. As discussed previously, many self-monitoring programs also use interval counting, and incorporate signals to indicate times during an instructional period when students are to monitor their behavior. Simple checklists, such as the one illustrated in Figure 3, can be used as recording sheets for students to indicate "Yes" (the behavior was occurring at the end of the interval, the moment when the cue occurred) or "No" (the behavior was not occurring at the end of the interval, the moment when the cue occurred) responses. Although there are a variety of recording devices available for use by students for self-monitoring, paper-and-pencil procedures are among the most common means of recording during self-monitoring (Cole & Bambara, 2000; Coleman & Webber, 2002; Shapiro et al., 2002).

Name: Date:

Activity:

Directions: Place a hash mark (/) in the boxes below each time you

        (a) raise your hand, or (b) listen quietly while others speak.

Raise your hand to speak.
Listen quietly while others speak.

Figure 1. Sample recording form: Using paper-and-pencil approach to tallying behavior

---

Name: Date:

Activity:

Directions: Once you have finished your worksheet, answer the following
          questions by circling either "Yes" or "No."

1. Did you put your name on the paper?	Yes	or	No
2. Did you read the directions before starting?	Yes	or	No
3. Did you do all of the problems on the worksheet?	Yes	or	No
4. Did you check your work?	Yes	or	No
5. Did you hand in the assignment?	Yes	or	No

Directions: Once you have finished your worksheet, answer the following

questions by circling   **1** = never, **2** = sometimes, and **3** = most of the time.

	never	some times	most of time
1. Were you quiet while working?	1	2	3
2. Were you sitting in your seat?	1	2	3
3. Did you raise your hand to ask for help?	1	2	3

Figure 2. Sample recording form: Using Yes-No questions and Likert ratings to
          monitor behavior

Members of the educational team are encouraged to choose the device that
makes the most sense for the behavior of interest in the child, taking the specific setting(s) in which the student will be self-monitoring into consideration.
Shapiro et al. (2002) offers the following guidelines in selecting the self-monitoring device: it should (a) be readily available during times the behavior is likely to occur, (b) be portable so it may be used in more than one setting, (c) be
simple to access, (d) not be distracting (or embarrassing) to use, and (e) be relatively inexpensive. A review of the literature does not suggest that one device
is better than any of the others; rather, one can glean from the literature that
the process of self-monitoring as an intervention is what makes a difference in
behavior change.

Training the Student to Self-Monitor

The level of training and specific strategies used for training depend on
multiple factors, including student characteristics (e.g., age, skill-related

---

Name: Date:

Activity:

Directions: When you hear the beep, check the box "Yes" if you were on-task or check the box "No" if you were not on-task. After checking the box, go back to work until you hear the next beep.

Am I On-Task?

	Yes	No
1		
2		
3		
4		
5		
6		
7		
8		
9		
10		
11		
12		
13		
14		
15		
16		
17		
18		
19		
20		

Figure 3. Sample recording form: Indicating Yes-No responses at cued intervals to monitor behavior

strengths and limitations) and the complexity of the monitoring system. Based on the student-behavior-setting scenario under consideration, the intervention team may select from a variety of potential procedures, ranging from verbal instructions alone to multi-component training consisting of direct skill instruction, modeling of monitoring procedures, allowing the student to practice the skill, and providing specific feedback regarding appropriate and inappropriate use of the monitoring procedures (Firth & Armstrong, 1985; Shapiro et al., 2002). For younger children, it may be beneficial to use a story with drawings depicting the self-monitoring procedure to facilitate training (Cole & Bambara, 2000). To maximize the acquisition of self-monitoring skills, Frith and Armstrong recommend that training programs include: (a) an explicit target behavior definition, (b) simplified behavior counting and monitoring procedures, (c) specific and relatively short self-monitoring time periods, (d) educator reliability checks with specific feedback, and (e) sufficient practice to ensure fluency prior to implementing the complete procedure. Lloyd, Landrum, & Hallahan (1991) provides a script for introducing a self-monitoring program that incorporates each of those recommendations. In Table 2, we provide a training scenario adapted from the Lloyd et al. script and connect it to the recommendations of Frith and Armstrong.

In addition to selecting a means of training, the team will need to determine where to train. Training may occur in a designated training area, in the target setting, or both. For example, the team may opt to first train the target student in an isolated area (e.g., a resource room; to ensure success and minimize distraction), and then move into the criterion setting (e.g., an inclusive classroom; with initial support to facilitate the generalization of the newly acquired monitoring skill). The self-management intervention literature and general behavioral principles purport that training should occur in the target setting under real conditions to the greatest extent possible. The team should also keep in mind that periodic booster (i.e., retraining) sessions may be warranted, depending on the student, setting, and the nature of the behavior being monitored. Finally, as a means of motivating students to alter their behavior, the team might consider reinforcing the students as they learn and use self-monitoring. Because reinforcement to participate in the process may motivate the student to engage in self-monitoring, it may lead to greater treatment fidelity on the part of the student, who is a critical player in this self-governing approach to behavior modification. Reinforcement may be particularly relevant for younger students or students with more severe disabilities, but most applications of self-monitoring are successful without including reinforcement programs (Shapiro & Cole, 1994).

Investigating the Accuracy of Self-Monitoring

The utility of self-monitoring depends greatly on the student's ability to accurately monitor his or her own behavior. There are two issues to consider in relation to accuracy: (a) does the student accurately identify (assess) the occurrence or nonoccurrence of the target behavior? and (b) does the student accurately record the result of assessing the target behavior? In most self-monitoring studies and interventions, both issues of accuracy are determined by comparing the student's ratings to those of an independent observer (e.g., teacher, aide, peer), with an 80% student-observer agreement level being the "gold standard" (Kazdin, 1982; Shapiro et al., 2002). The logic behind this relationship is that students are able to adjust their level of performance to the extent necessary only when they have an accurate barometer of their present behavior level. This is a critical link in changing thought patterns, which is one of the three components of cognitive training techniques.

Table 2
Steps for Setting up a Self-monitoring Intervention

Training components	Examples of techniques to teach the components
Explicit target behavior	• Tell exactly what the behavior is to be recorded using clear, precise, and observable words • Model the defined behavior • Model exemplars and nonexamplars of the behavior and have the student distinguish between them • Ask the student to demonstrate the defined behavior
Simple behavior counting and monitoring procedures	• Have all materials needed readily available (e.g., cues, recording sheets, markers) • Model the use of the monitoring procedures (first without and then with the cue, if a cue is used) • Have student practice the monitoring procedures (first without and with the cue, if a cue is used) • Use videotapes to allow students to practice observing and recording the behavior (first without and with the cue, if a cue is used)
Specific and relatively short self-monitoring time periods	• Provide student the self-monitoring materials and have him or her engage in the entire self-monitoring procedure for 3–5 minutes • Provide feedback regarding use of the monitoring materials • Have student engage in entire self-monitoring procedure again for 3–5 minutes • Provide feedback regarding use of the monitoring materials
Educator reliability checks with specific feedback	• Assess student behavior at the same time student practices monitoring • Compare assessment with student recording of behavior at end of each practice session • Provide feedback regarding the accuracy of student self-monitoring • Retrain if agreement between educator assessment and student self-monitoring is not 100%
Sufficient practice to ensure fluency prior to implementing the complete procedure	• Have student engage in entire self-monitoring procedure again for 10–15 minutes • Provide feedback regarding use of the self-monitoring procedure • Move self-monitoring into the educational setting for longer periods of time

The educational team should pay particular attention to accuracy with which students demonstrate both their accurate assessment of the target behavior and their recording during training to ensure that the student is a good evaluator from the beginning of the behavior change process. Proper attention to accuracy during training, however, does not negate the necessity of continuing to monitor accuracy throughout the course of intervention. Continued accuracy is important if treatment effects are to be observed during intervention. Indeed, research suggests that students' awareness of their own accuracy of self-monitoring influences overall accuracy (e.g., Lloyd & Hilliard, 1989; Nelson, Lipinski, & Black, 1975). As previously discussed, it may be beneficial to reinforce students for accurately following the self-monitoring procedures (especially assessing the target behavior and recording at appropriate times), as a means of increasing their motivation to self-monitor, which bears considerable weight on both treatment fidelity and the potential effectiveness of the intervention.

CONCLUSION

The research-to-practice conundrum that is reported in all of education is of particular concern in special education. Criticism in both the scholarly (e.g., Brantlinger, 1997) and popular literature (e.g., Bolick, 2001) has charged that special education may not only be ineffective, but may actually incur damage to students (e.g., the proposed negative impact of labeling, lowered expectations) that outweighs any benefits such as improved academic performance that might be provided (Cook & Schirmer, 2003). Indeed, Fuchs and Fuchs (1995) proposed that critics' principal accusation is that special education simply doesn't work. Although Vaughn and Linan-Thompson (2003) recently indicated that special education has the promise to be truly special for students with LD due to the many effective practices developed (e.g., self-monitoring), it falls short of that goal because these instructional techniques are not pervasively implemented with fidelity in contemporary classrooms.

The purpose of this chapter was to provide an overview of self-monitoring and its effectiveness for students with LD, and to discuss considerations for setting up a self-monitoring intervention in the classroom to enhance the self-management of these students. By following the guidelines discussed in this chapter and summarized for use in the field on the checklist in Figure 4, educators can empower students to improve their own outcomes. Thus, self-monitoring has the potential to improve the education of students with LD meaningfully. But what makes self-monitoring such a powerful educational intervention are the features that enhance its useability: (a) it is effective with a variety of positive outcomes and in a variety of settings (this adaptability makes it an ideal strategy for

Directions: Once you have responded to each of the sub-category questions below by placing a checkmark on the designated line, place a checkmark on the line next to the category heading designated by a number (i.e., 1–6).

____ **1. Specify and determine the target behavior(s)**

     ____ Did the team specify a behavior of interest?

     ____ Did the team clearly define the behavior?

     ____ Did the team ask the student to provide specific examples and non-examples of the target behavior (during the training phase)?

____ **2. Select a self-monitoring method**

     ____ Did the team decide whether frequency monitoring is relevant?

     ____ If yes, did the team consider both frequency counting and interval counting?

     ____ Did the team decide whether interval counting was relevant?

____ **3. Select the right schedule**

     ____ Did the team determine when and how often it may be beneficial for the student to monitor his/her own behavior?

     ____ Did the team consider a continuous schedule?

     ____ Did the team consider a time sampling schedule?

     ____ Did the team consider a momentary time sampling schedule?

____ **4. Select the recording device**

     ____ Did the team consider a paper-and-pencil approach?

     ____ Did the team consider the use of alternatives (e.g., hand signals)?

____ **5. Train the student to self-monitor**

     ____ Did the team consider the student's cognitive ability when deciding on training procedures?

     ____ Did the team consider the complexity of the self-monitoring procedures when deciding on training procedures?

     ____ Did the team consider each of the following?
-direct instruction, modeling, practice with feedback, accuracy analysis, reinforcement for use of self-monitoring procedures?

____ **6. Investigate the accuracy of self-monitoring**

     ____ Did the team conduct a student-rater agreement analysis?

     ____ If yes, was level of agreement > 80% across at least three observations?

     ____ Did the team consider the use of rewards for accurate self-monitoring?

Additional Considerations:

Figure 4. Checklist for setting up a self-monitoring program

teachers of students with LD, a population with heterogeneous characteristics and needs served in a variety of settings) and (b) it is a relatively straightforward procedure that educators can implement (and maintain their use over time) as designed. By utilizing interventions such as self-monitoring (that have been shown to improve student outcomes and can be consistently implemented with fidelity in the classroom), educators can begin to bridge the research-to-practice gap and make special education truly special for students with LD.

REFERENCES

Alberto, P. A., & Troutman, A. C. (2003). *Applied behavior analysis for teachers* (6th ed.). Upper Saddle River, NJ: Merrill Prentice Hall.

Blick, D. W., & Test, D. W. (1987). Effects of self-recording on high-school students' on-task behavior. *Learning Disability Quarterly, 10,* 203–213.

Bolick, C. (2001, September 5). A bad IDEA is disabling public schools. *Education Week,* p. 56, 63.

Boyle, J. R., & Hughes, C. A. (1994). Effects of self-monitoring and subsequent fading of external prompts on the on-task behavior and task productivity of elementary students with moderate mental retardation. *Journal of Behavioral Education, 4,* 439–457.

Brantlinger, E. (1997). Using ideology: Cases of nonrecognition of the politics of research and practice in special education. *Review of Educational Research, 67,* 425–459.

Carnine, D. (1997). Bridging the research-to-practice gap. *Exceptional Children, 52,* 219–232.

Carr, S. C., & Puntzo, R. P. (1993). The effects of self-monitoring of academic accuracy and productivity on the performance of students with behavior disorders. *Behavioral Disorders, 18,* 241–250.

Cole, C. L., & Bambara, L. M. (2000). Self-monitoring: Theory and practice. In E. S. Shapiro & T. R. Kratochwill (Eds.), *Behavioral assessment in schools* (2nd ed.), (pp. 202–232). New York: Guildford Press.

Coleman, M. C., & Webber, J. (2002). *Emotional and behavioral disorders.* Boston, MA: Pearson Education Company.

Connell, M. C., Carta, J. J., Lutz, S., Randall, C., & Wilson, J. (1993). Building independence during in-class transitions: Teaching in-class transition skills to preschoolers with developmental delays through choral-response-based self-assessment and contingent praise. *Education and Treatment of Children, 16,* 160–174.

Cook, B. G., & Schirmer, B. R. (2003). What is special about special education? Overview and analysis. *Journal of Special Education, 37,* 200–204.

DiGangi, S. A., & Maag, J. W. (1992). A component analysis of self-management training with behaviorally disordered youth. *Behavioral Disorders, 14,* 281–290.

Fantuzzo, J. W., & Polite, K. (1990). School-based, behavioral self-management: A review and analysis. *School Psychology Quarterly, 5,* 180–198.

Firth, G. H., & Armstrong, S. W. (1985). Self-monitoring for behavior-disordered students. *Teaching Exceptional Children, 18,* 144–148.

Flores, D. M., Schloss, P. J., & Alper, S. (1995). The use of a daily calendar to increase responsibilities fulfilled by secondary students with special needs. *Remedial and Special Education, 16,* 38–43.

Fuchs, D., & Fuchs, L. S. (1995). What's "special" about special education? *Phi Delta Kappan, 76,* 522–530.

Graham, S., Harris, K., R., & Reid, R. (1992). Developing self-regulated learners. *Focus on Exceptional Children, 24*(6), 1–16.

Hallahan, D. P., Hall, R. J., Ianna, S. O., Kneedler, R. D., Lloyd, J. W., Loper, A. B., et al. (1983). Summary of research findings at the University of Virginia Learning Disabilities Research Institute. *Exceptional Education Quarterly, 4,* 95–114.

Hallahan, D. P., & Kauffman, J. M. (2003). *Exceptional learners: Introduction to special education* (9th ed.). Boston: Allyn & Bacon.

Hallahan, D. P., Kauffman, J. M., & Lloyd, J. W. (1999). *Introduction to learning disabilities* (2nd ed.). Boston: Allyn & Bacon.

Hallahan, D. P., Lloyd, J. W., Kosiewicz, M. M., Kauffman, J. M., & Graves, A. W. (1979). Self-monitoring of attention as a treatment for a learning disabled boy's off task behavior. *Learning Disabilities Quarterly, 2,* 24–32.

Hallahan, D. P., Lloyd, J. W., & Stoller, L. (1982). *Improving attention with self-monitoring: A manual for teachers.* Charlottesville, VA: University of Virginia.

Hallahan, D. P., & Reeve, R. E. (1980). Selective attention and distractibility. In B. K. Keogh (Ed.), *Advances in special education: Vol. 1: Basic constructs and theoretical orientations.* Greenwich, CT: JAI Press.

Harris, K. R. (1986). Self-monitoring of attentional behavior versus self-monitoring of productivity: Effects on on-task behavior and academic response rate among learning disabled children. *Journal of Applied Behavior Analysis, 19,* 417–423.

Harris, K. R., Graham, S., Reid, R., McElroy, K., & Hamby, R. S. (1994). Self-monitoring of attention versus self-monitoring of performance: Replication and cross-task comparison studies. *Learning Disability Quarterly, 17,* 121–139.

Heins, E. D., Lloyd, J. W., & Hallahan, D. P. (1986). Cued and noncued self-recording of attention to task. *Behavior Modification, 10,* 235–254.

Hughes, C. A., Korinek, L., & Gorman, J. (1991). Self-management for students with mental retardation in public school settings: A research review. *Education and Training in Mental Retardation, 26,* 271–291.

Kavale, K. A., & Forness, S. R. (1995). *The nature of learning disabilities: Critical elements of diagnosis and classification.* Mahwah, NJ: Lawrence Erlbaum.

Kazdin, A. E. (1982). *Single case research designs: Methods for clinical and applied settings.* New York: Oxford University Press.

Lerner, J. (2000). *Learning disabilities* (8th ed.). Boston: Houghton Mifflin.

Lloyd, J. W., Bateman, D. F., Landrum, T. J., & Hallahan, D. P. (1989). Self-recording of attention versus productivity. *Journal of Applied Behavior Analysis, 22,* 315–323.

Lloyd, J. W., Landrum, T. J., & Hallahan, D. P. (1991). Self-montoring applications for classroom intervention. In G. Stoner, M. R. Shinn, & H. M. Walker (Eds.), *Interventions for achievement and behavior problems* (pp.201–213). Washington, DC: National Association of School Psychologists.

Lloyd, M. E., & Hilliard, A. M. (1989). Accuracy of self-recording as a function of repeated experience with different self-control strategies. *Child and Family Behavior Therapy, 11,* 1–14.

Maag, J. W. (2004). *Behavior management: From theoretical implications to practical applications* (2nd ed.). Belmont, CA: Wadsworth/Thomson.

Maag, J. W., Reid, R., & DiGangi, S. A. (1993). Differential effects of self-monitoring attention, accuracy, and productivity. *Journal of Applied Behavior Analysis, 26,* 329–344.

Maag, J. W., Rutherford, A. B., & DiGangi, S. A. (1992). Effects of self-monitoring and contingent reinforcement on on-task behavior and academic productivity of learning-disabled students: A social validation study. *Psychology in the Schools, 29,* 157–192.

Mace, F. C., & Kratochwill, T. R. (1988). Self-monitoring. In J. C. Witt, S. N. Elliott, & F. M. Gresham (Eds.), *Handbook of behavior therapy in education* (pp. 489–522). New York: Plenum Press.

Marshall, K. J., Lloyd, J. W., & Hallahan, D. P. (1993). Effects of training to increase self-monitoring accuracy. *Journal of Behavioral Education, 3,* 445–459.

Mathes, M. Y., & Bender, W. N. (1997). The effects of self-monitoring on children with attention-deficit/hyperactivity disorder who are receiving pharmacological interventions. *Remedial and Special Education, 18,* 121–128.

McDougall, D., & Brady, M. P. (1995). Using audio-cued self-monitoring for students with severe behavior disorders. *Journal of Educational Research, 88,* 309–317.

Nelson, R. O. & Hayes, S. C. (1981). Theoretical explanations for reactivity in self-monitoring. *Behavior Modification, 5,* 3–14.

Nelson, R. O., Lipinski, D. P., & Black, J. L. (1975). The effects of expectancy on the reactivity of self-recording behavior. *Behavior Therapy, 6,* 337–349.

Newman, B., Buffington, D. M., O'Grady, M. A., McDonald, M. E., Poulson, C. L., & Hemmes, N. S. (1995). Self-management of schedule following in three teenagers with autism. *Behavioral Disorders, 20,* 190–196.

Prater, M. A., Joy, R., Chilman, B., Temple, J., & Miller, S. R. (1991). Self-monitoring of on-task behavior by adolescents with learning disabilities. *Learning Disabilities Quarterly, 14,* 164–177.

Rooney, K. J., Hallahan, D. P., & Lloyd, J. W. (1984). Self-recording of attention by learning disabled students in the regular classroom. *Journal of Learning Disabilities, 17,* 360–364.

Rooney, K. J., Polloway, E., & Hallahan, D. P. (1985). The use of self-monitoring procedures with low IQ learning disabled students. *Journal of Learning Disabilities, 18,* 384–389.

Shapiro, E. S., & Cole, C. L. (1994). *Behavior change in the classroom: Self-management interventions.* New York: Guilford Press.

Shapiro, E. S., Durnan, S. L., Post, E. E., & Levinson, T. S. (2002). Self-monitoring procedures for children and adolescents. In M. R. Shinn, H. M. Walker, & G. Stoner (Eds.), *Interventions for academic and behavioral problems II: Preventive and remedial approaches* (pp. 433–454). Bethesda, MD: National Association of School Psychologists.

Shimabukuro, S. M., Prater, M. A., Jenkins, A., & Edelen-Smith, P. (1999). The effects of self-monitoring of academic performance on students with learning disabilities. *Education and Treatment of Children, 22,* 397–414.

Storey, K., Lawry, J. R., Ashworth, R., Danko, C. D., & Strain, P. S. (1994). Functional analysis and intervention for disruptive behaviors of a kindergarten student. *Journal of Educational Research, 87,* 361–370.

Strain, P. S., Kohler, F. W., Storey, K., & Danko, C. D. (1994). Teaching pre-schoolers with autism to self-monitor their social interactions: An analysis of results in home and school settings. *Journal of Emotional and Behavioral Disorders, 2,* 78–88.

Tankersley, M., & Talbott, E. (1992). *Treatment acceptability: A review of student and teacher variables.* Unpublished manuscript, University of Virginia.

Torgesen, J. K. (1977). The role of nonspecific factors in the task performance of learning disabled children: A theoretical assessment. *Journal of Learning Disabilities, 10,* 27–34.

Trammel, D. L., Schloss, P. J., & Apler, S. (1994). Using self-recording, evaluation, and graphing to increase completion of homework assignments. *Journal of Learning Disabilities, 27,* 75–81.

Vaughn, S., & Linan-Thompson, S. (2003). What is special about special education for students with learning disabilities, *Journal of Special Education, 37,* 140–147.

Webber, J., Sheuermann, B., McCall, C, & Coleman, M. (1993). Research on self-monitoring as a behavioral intervention in special education classrooms: A Descriptive review. *Remedial and Special Education, 14,* 38–56.

Chapter Four

NATURALISTIC LANGUAGE TEACHING PROCEDURES FOR CHILDREN AT RISK FOR LANGUAGE DELAYS

Pete Peterson, Ph.D.

Johnson County Community College

Delays in language acquisition are one of the most prevalent disabilities in early childhood. It has been documented that 70% of 3-to-5-year old children with developmental disabilities have language delays (Wetherby & Prizant, 1992). Delays in language acquisition can have serious deleterious effects on the educational and social development of children (Goldstein & Kaczmarek, 1992; Ramey & Campbell, 1992; Warren & Kaiser, 1986). Children with developmental disabilities are known to be especially vulnerable to environmental conditions that may inhibit language acquisition (Tannock & Girolametto, 1992). Thus, the caregiver is viewed as having a "critical influence on the child and the child's language learning environment" (Hemmeter & Kaiser, 1990, p. 335). Some key interaction variables include the caregiver's responsiveness to child vocalizations, reciprocity in verbal interaction between caregiver and child, frequency of verbal interaction, and the availability of stimulating materials (Bradley & Caldwell, 1976; Hart & Risley, 1992; Huttonlocher, Haight, Bryk, Seltzer, & Lyons, 1991). For example, Hart and Risley (1995) found that the quantity and quality of talk directed toward children as well as parental responsiveness, feedback tone, and guidance style during the first three years of life were positively correlated with beneficial child language outcomes.

To address this need for language intervention in the child's natural settings, including the classroom and home, a number of related language teaching procedures have been developed. These include incidental teaching (e.g., Hart & Risley, 1975), mand-modeling (e.g., Rogers-Warren & Warren, 1980; Warren, McQuarter, & Rogers-Warren, 1984), and time-delay (e.g., Halle, Marshall, & Spradlin, 1979). Taken together, these procedures might be termed naturalistic teaching. Naturalistic language teaching approaches have been increasingly viewed as the treatment of choice for children at-risk or children with developmental disabilities (Noonan & McCormick, 1993; Tannock & Girolametto, 1992).

NATURALISTIC LANGUAGE TEACHING PROCEDURES

Incidental Teaching

Incidental teaching (Hart & Risley, 1968, 1974) involves the use of naturally occurring situations and the child's interests to facilitate language learning. Hart and Risley (1975) characterized incidental teaching as "the interaction between an adult and a single child, which arises naturally in an unstructured situation such as free-play and which is used by an adult to transmit information or give the child practice in developing a skill" (p.411). In this approach, the teacher or caregiver takes advantage of naturally occurring teaching situations to provide language-learning opportunities for the child. The situation or activity is "child selected" (Hart & Risley, 1975, p. 412), with the teacher or caregiver following the child's lead or interest.

Once a teacher identifies naturally occurring situations in which a child expresses interest, she or he then uses a series of graduated prompts to encourage the child's responses (Hart & Risley, 1974, 1975). Hart and Risley (1974) identified four levels of prompts associated with incidental teaching. The level of response is dependent on the child's response. A Level 1 prompt involved instituting a 30-second delay when the child displayed an interest in a specific object or material. At Level 2, the teacher prompted the child to ask for the desired object. At Level 3, prompts involved a more elaborate request by the teacher (e.g., the teacher showed the child the toy and asked "what is this?"). Finally, at Level 4, the correct response was modeled by the teacher and the child prompted to imitate the response. Teachers were taught to use the lowest level of prompt that would encourage the correct response by the child.

In one of the first studies of incidental teaching procedures, Hart and Risley (1968) successfully increased preschool children's use of adjective-noun combinations (e.g., red truck). Children were taught these combinations in a structured group setting. Although children increased their use of adjective-noun combinations in the structured settings, the behavior did not generalize to free play settings. To increase the "spontaneous" use of adjective-noun combinations in free play settings access to desired classroom materials (e.g., paints) was made contingent on the appropriate use of these combinations. Teachers used graduated levels of prompts similar to those described above to shape the children's verbal behavior.

Incidental teaching procedures have also been used to shape children's use of compound sentences (Hart & Risley, 1974, 1975). In these studies children were progressively required to increase the complexity of their statements. At first, children were required not only to name the object but also to describe how they would use that object (a compound sentence). Children participating in the studies increased their use of nouns, adjective-noun combinations, and compound sentences.

Mand-Model

The mand-model procedure (e.g., Rogers-Warren & Warren, 1980; Warren et al., 1984) is an extension of the incidental teaching model (essentially prompt levels 2, 3, and 4 of Hart and Risley, 1974). The mand-model procedure involves the teacher manding and/or modeling a response from the child. A mand is a request for a verbal response from the child (e.g., "Tell me what you want" or "Use your words"). If the child responds correctly, the teacher or caregiver praises the child and provides the object of interest. In modeling, sometimes known as child-cued modeling (Alpert & Kaiser, 1992; Kaiser, 1993), the teacher observes the focus of the child's interest (e.g., a toy fire truck) and models the correct verbalization (e.g., "That's a fire truck"). If the child makes the correct verbal response (e.g., "Fire truck"), the teacher then praises the child and provides the object of interest.

The mand-model procedure combines the mand and modeling procedures. In this procedure, the teacher observes the focus of the child's interest (e.g., the toy fire truck) and mands a response from the child (e.g., "Tell me what you want"). If the child makes an incorrect response (e.g., "Choo choo train"), the teacher then models the correct response (e.g, "Say fire truck").

Rogers-Warren and Warren (1980) successfully trained teachers to use the mand-model procedure along with contingent praise. The children participating in the study increased their rates of verbalization in general, as well as their rates of novel words and novel word combinations. Similarly, Warren et al. (1984) demonstrated the effectiveness of the mand-model procedure in promoting generalization across settings and maintenance over time by gradually fading the use of this procedure.

One difference between incidental teaching (e.g., Hart & Risley, 1975) and the mand-model procedure is that incidental teaching is more dependent upon the child's initiations. With the mand-model procedure, the teacher more directly controls the number of opportunities for the child to engage in the language interaction (Rogers-Warren & Warren, 1980). The procedure may be useful, then, for children with very low rates of initiation (Rogers-Warren & Warren; Warren et al., 1984).

Time-Delay

Another extension of incidental teaching is the time-delay or delayed prompt procedure (e.g., Halle, Baer, & Spradling, 1981). Time-delay has been defined as "nonvocal cues for vocal language" (Halle et al., p. 390). In the time-delay procedure, the teacher identifies a situation in which the child wants an object or assistance and then waits for the child to make a response. If this is unsuccessful, the teacher will then use the mand-model procedure. The time-delay procedure is especially useful for teaching children to initiate verbal interaction (Noonan & McCormick, 1993).

Halle, Marshall, and Spradlin (1979) used a time-delay procedure to increase children's "opportunity to respond" for two groups of institutionalized children. Initially, meal trays were withheld for 15 seconds. Of the first set of three children participating in the study, only one appropriately requested the meal tray. Next, modeling of the correct response was added to the delay resulting in an increase in appropriate responding. A second group of three children, who had observed the contingencies implemented for the first three, then participated in the delay condition. These children acquired the requesting behavior and generalized across meal settings and servers.

Charlop, Schriebman, and Thibodeau (1985) used a time-delay procedure to increase spontaneous speech in seven young boys with autism. Pretests were given to determine if each child could label certain preferred items and training was provided if the child did not have these skills in his repertoire. Next, training was provided in which the teacher modeled the correct response (e.g., "I want cookie"). The child would receive the item if he correctly imitated the response. Then a brief time-delay was introduced with delays beginning at two seconds. These were then systematically increased to 10 seconds. All children participating in the study, except one, acquired the target behavior.

Milieu Language Teaching

Incidental teaching, the mand-model procedure, and the time-delay teachnique have been combined with other strategies to encourage child language in natural environments (Alpert & Kaiser, 1992; Hart & Rogers-Warren, 1978). Hart and Rogers-Warren termed this approach "milieu language teaching." Kaiser (1993) defined milieu language teaching as "a naturalistic, conversation-based teaching procedure in which the child's interest in the environment is used as a basis for eliciting elaborated child communicative responses" (p. 77). Hemmeter and Kaiser (1994) later proposed "enhanced milieu teaching" as a more comprehensive approach to naturalistic language intervention. There are three components to this intervention model: (a) environmental arrangement, (b) responsive interaction techniques, and (c) milieu teaching procedures.

Environmental arrangement involves the arrangement of the child's environment to facilitate language teaching. The goal is to increase the child's engagement with the environment (Kaiser, 1993), while setting up situations in which the child is more likely to use language. For example, having toys or other objects of interest available will make it more likely that the teacher can use the situation to have the child verbalize a request for that toy or object (see Ostrosky & Kaiser, 1991). Another important part of environmental arrangement is to provide an "optimal affective environment for the child" (Kaiser, 1993, p. 76); that is, to keep the interaction nurturing and reinforcing for the child.

Responsive interaction techniques are designed to increase conversational interaction between teacher and child. These techniques include following the child's lead in terms of focus of interest, turn-taking, providing descriptive statements, imitating the child's verbalizations, and expanding on verbalizations made by the child (Kaiser, 1993). Milieu teaching procedures include modeling, mand-modeling, and time-delay. Each of these procedures builds upon the previous one, with later procedures incorporating components of earlier ones (Alpert & Kaiser, 1992), much like Hart and Risely's (1974) incidental teaching.

Effectiveness of Naturalistic Teaching

While little research has been conducted on the effectiveness of naturalistic teaching for children designated as having learning disabilities per se, it has been found to be effective for children from low-income families (e.g., Hart & Risley, 1975, 1980), children with mental retardation (e.g., Gobbi, Cipani, Hudson, & Lapenta-Neudeck, 1986; Warren, 1992), children with developmental delays (e.g., Angelo & Goldstein, 1990, Oswald, Lignugaris/Kraft, & West, 1990), children with language delays (e.g., Rogers-Warren & Warren, 1980; Warren et al., 1984), children prenatally exposed to drugs and in multiple risk families (Peterson, Carta, & Greenwood, 2005), and children with autism (e.g., Charlop et al., 1985; Hancock & Kaiser, 2002; Laski, Charlop, & Schriebman, 1988). Given the range of children for whom this approach is effective it would seem that it would also be useful in teaching children with learning disabilities.

Studies have demonstrated that children were able to acquire and generalize across a range of language targets, including single words (e.g., Charlop et al., 1985; Warren & Gazdag, 1990), combinations (e.g., Cavallaro & Bambara, 1982; Warren & Bambara, 1989), complexity of sentences (e.g., Hart & Risley, 1980), initiations and requests (e.g., Angelo & Goldestein, 1990; Warren et al., 1984; Warren, Yoder, Gazdag, Kim, & Jones, 1993), signing (e.g., Carr & Kologinsky, 1983; Kaczmarek, Hepting, & Dzubak, 1996), reading (e.g, Fabry, Mayhew, & Hanson, 1984), and receptive language (e.g., McGee, Krantz, Mason, & McClannahan, 1983; McGee, Krantz, & McClannahan, 1986).

NATURALISTIC TEACHING VS. TRADITIONAL LANGUAGE INTERVENTION

Naturalistic language teaching has been compared to more traditional, therapist-directed approaches to language intervention, such as discrete trial training (Fey, 1986; Spradlin & Siegel, 1982; Sundberg & Partington, 1998). Discrete trial training is conducted under highly structured conditions in which the therapist selects the stimulus items to be used during the teaching sessions, divides the language target skills into a series of independent tasks, presents these tasks in a series of massed trials until criterion is met, and provides the child an often arbitrary reinforcer combined with praise (Sundberg & Partington, pp. 224–256). In contrast, naturalistic teaching is considered "looser" (Sundberg & Partington), with less emphasis, at least initially, on the correctness of the child's response. This approach follows the child's lead in terms of the stimulus of interest and provides a "natural reinforcer" (usually the object of interest to the child). The reinforcers delivered in naturalistic teaching are considered to be be more functional in relation to the child's response than in the discrete trial training approach.

In the traditional therapist-directed approach (i.e., discrete trial training), language intervention is typically conducted in a speech therapy room and is highly structured by the therapist (Fey, 1986; Sundberg & Partington, 1998). Naturalistic teaching approaches typically work with the child in his or her natural setting (i.e., classroom or home) and usually follow the child's lead or interest, not in terms of the language skill being taught, but in relation to toys and other objects of interest to the child. This requires the teacher to respond more flexibly to naturally occurring language teaching opportunities as they occur throughout the day. The teacher must also be able to identify potential reinforcing contingencies that will be functional for the child in other settings (D. Baer, personal communication, May 30, 1996).

Naturalistic teaching procedures are advantageous in that the teacher or parent has far more opportunities throughout the day to engage in naturalistic teaching than would a speech therapist in a traditional pull-out program (Fey, 1986). Ideally, the use of naturalistic teaching procedures would become "automatic" to the teacher or parent and be used naturally throughout the day. Perhaps the most difficult part of this approach is teaching parents and teachers how to identify naturally occurring opportunities for language interaction.

A number of studies have compared naturalistic teaching with discrete trial training. Miranda-Linne and Melin (1992) found that although children acquired color adjectives faster through discrete trial training, they were more likely to generalize the new language skills following naturalistic teaching. Similarly, McGee, Krantz, and McClannahan (1985) reported that naturalistic teaching promoted greater generalization of new language skills across people and settings than did a more traditional trainer-directed approach. Seifert and Schwarz (1991) compared incidental teaching and direct instruction techniques and found that incidental teaching promoted great generalization across concepts to untrained concepts. Carr and Kologinsky (1983) initially used discrete trial training to teach signing to three children with autism. They then faded to incidental teaching. The results indicated that discrete trial training was best for training the correct form of the signs and incidental teaching was more likely to promote generalization and maintenance. Finally, Charlop-Christy and Carpenter (2000) compared discrete trial training, incidental teaching, and their modified incidental teaching (a combination of discrete trial training and incidental teaching). They found that their modified incidental teaching procedure was superior to either discrete trial training or incidental teaching alone.

It seems that discrete trial or other more structured, therapist-directed approaches may be necessary for establishing language skills initially but that naturalistic teaching strategies will promote better generalization of those skills.

NATURALISTIC TEACHING AND GENERALIZATION OF LANGUAGE SKILLS

Researchers and therapists have been concerned for some time about the poor generalization of children's language skills following traditional speech and language intervention (Fey, 1986, 1988; Guess, Keogh, & Sailor, 1978; Warren, 1988). Fey (1986) has called this a "black mark" on the history of language intervention. Problems in achieving generalization can occur, for example, if the generalization environment is too dissimilar to the training situation (e.g., Hemmeter, Ault, Collins, & Meyer, 1996; McGee, Almeida, Sulzer-Azaroff, & Feldman, 1992) or if the child's newly learned language skills are not reinforced in the generalization environment (e.g., Carr & Kologinsky, 1983; Warren & Bambara, 1989).

Generalization occurs when new skills learned in the teaching environment transfer to other situations without further training in those new environments or situations (Stokes & Baer, 1977). Stokes and Baer identifies a number of methods that have been utilized to promote generalization. Some of these methods include: (a) introduce behaviors that will contact naturally occurring contingencies of reinforcement in the generalization settings, (b) provide a range of examples of the target behavior, (c) vary the training routine enough to provide the child exposure to a wider range of stimuli, or "train loosely," and (d) make it difficult for the child to discriminate the contingencies, possibly through the use of an intermittent schedule of reinforcement.

Naturalistic teaching procedures have a number of common characteristics that make them very effective tools for promoting generalization of the child's newly learned language skills. As listed in Kaiser, Yoder, and Keetz (1992, p. 9) these include: (a) language teaching that follows the child's lead or interest, (b) the use of multiple, naturally occurring examples, (c) explicit prompts for the child's use of language, (d) the use of natural consequences to reinforce the child's verbal behavior, and (e) naturalistic teaching strategies that are embedded in the ongoing interaction between teacher and child.

These common characteristics are compatible with the strategies proposed by Stokes and Baer (1977) for promoting generalization of functional language skills in children (Warren & Kaiser, 1986). Following the child's lead or interest and the use of natural consequences increase the probability that the child's behavior will contact naturally occurring contingencies of reinforcement. The loose structure of this approach makes it more likely that the child will be exposed to multiple exemplars (Laski et al., 1988), including variations in location, position of trainer, time of day and so on (see Baer, 1981). This may prevent the behavior from coming under too narrow a range of stimulus control (Kirby & Bickel, 1988). Similarly, the embedded nature of the ongoing teaching interaction may make some of the contingencies less discriminable, perhaps creating "multiple stimulus control" (Halle et al., 1981). In addition, the fact that training is conducted in natural contexts makes it more likely that stimuli common to a wide range of potential language environments will be present. This would be a case of "programming common stimuli" (Stokes & Baer, 1977). Finally, it may also be that the language skills taught in the naturalistic language teaching approach, as compared to more traditional speech and language therapy, are more functional for the child and more likely to generalize to other settings and persons (Fey, 1986; Guess et al., 1978; Sundberg & Partington, 1998). In a review of the naturalistic teaching literature, Peterson (2005) found that 94% of the studies measuring for generalization effects demonstrated generalization.

Teaching Teachers and Parents To Use Naturalistic Language Teaching Skills

A number of studies have successfully trained teachers (e.g., Halle et al., 1981; Kaiser, Ostrosky, & Alpert, 1993; Warren et al., 1984) and parents (e.g., Alpert & Kaiser, 1992; Hemmeter & Kasier, 1994; Laski et al., 1988; Peterson et al., 2005) to implement naturalistic language teaching strategies. The most common strategies for teaching parents and teachers how to implement naturalistic teaching strategies include didactic presentation, modeling, roleplaying, feedback both during interaction with the child and via videotape (e.g., Alpert & Kaiser; Hester, Kaiser, Alpert, & Whiteman, 1995; Kaiser & Hancock, 2003; Kaiser, Hancock, & Hester, 1998; Kaiser et al., 1993; Peterson et al., 2005). Kaiser and Hancock also had parents keep detailed notes of their naturalistic teaching interaction with their children. Kaiser et al. (1998) trained parents as "co-interventionists" in which the therapist models and coaches the parent while they are both involved in a naturalistic teaching interaction with the child. In addition to direct modeling and coaching, the therapist can provide "functional support" to the parent by facilitating certain tasks (e.g., arranging the environment).

IMPLEMENTING NATURALISTIC TEACHING IN THE CLASSROOM AND HOME

There are three essential ingredients for the successful implementation of naturalistic teaching procedures in the classroom and home. These are (a) sensitivity to the child's interests, (b) strategic arrangement of the teaching environment, and (c) appropriate use of naturalistic teaching techniques (i.e., mand-model, time-delay).

Sensitivity to the Child's Interests

The best naturalistic teachers are those who are keenly aware of the child's interests both in general and at the moment. While more of an art than a science, a naturalistic teacher should be able to "read" the contingencies surrounding the child's behavior. The teacher must be able to track the child's changing interests and adjust accordingly. Naturalistic teachers can sense when to push for more and when to back off a little without "giving in" to the child. Knowing when to use specific naturalistic teaching strategies and when to change activities depends, in part, on this sensitivity. Sensitivity can be developed through coaching and experience. In addition, the teacher should keep her or his interaction with the child nurturing, positive, and reinforcing (Kaiser, 1993). The Naturalistic Observation Checklist (Figure 1) is an example of an instrument designed for training teachers and collecting data regarding fidelity of treatment. During a training or assessment opportunity an observer collects data on sensitivity to the child's interests, environmental arrangement, and the use of naturalistic teaching techniques. Data can be expressed as pure frequency count or as rate per minute. Furthermore, an observation system utilizing a

---

Environmental Arrangement

_____ Are interesting toys and materials available to the child?

_____ Does the teacher respond to teaching opportunities?

_____ Is the teacher aware of the child's immediate interest?

_____ Does the teacher follow the child's lead or interest?

_____ Is the affective environment positive and nurturing?

Use of Responsive Interaction and Milieu Teaching Procedures

Mark each time teacher uses a procedure	Naturalistic Teaching Procedure	Rate per Minute
	Descriptive Statements	
	Imitation	
	Expansions	
	Model	
	Mand	
	Mand-Model	
	Time-Delay	

Figure 1. Naturalistic teaching observation checklist

---

computer program with codes for both teacher behavior (e.g., descriptive statements, mand-model) as well as child verbal response (e.g., correct response) could be employed to determine the conditional probabilities of a child's verbal behavior following a specific naturalistic teaching behavior by the teacher (see Peterson et al., 2005). Conditional probability data can be a very useful feedback tool for training naturalistic teachers.

Environmental Arrangement

There are a number of strategies that can be used by the teacher to establish a more effective naturalistic teaching environment. Ostrosky and Kaiser (1991) offer a number of useful recommendations for arranging the teaching environment, including (a) making sure that toys, books, and other items of specific interest to the child are available, (b) putting toys and other interesting items out of reach, (c) not providing enough of something of interest so that the child will ask for more, (d) sabotaging, or "forgetting" an important item in a multi-step task so that the child will have to ask for it, (e) giving the child opportunities to make choices, and (f) arranging situations so that the child has to ask for assistance. Each of these strategies is designed to encourage functional language use by the child by arranging a situation in which the child must initiate a request.

The teaching area should include numerous materials (e.g., toys, books) that one is reasonably certain will be of interest to the child. For example, if the child is interested in jungle animals the teacher should make sure that there are toy jungle animals, books with pictures of jungle animals, and perhaps a jungle animal puzzle present in the teaching area. One should never assume that any particular toy, book, object, or activity will be of interest to an individual child (e.g., "Every child likes dinosaurs!"). Once again, the teacher needs to know the child's interests. These toys, books, and objects can be put out of reach so that the child has to request them. The teacher can then employ time-delay, model, mand, or mand-model procedures to prompt the correct verbal response from the child.

Teachers can also arrange a teaching opportunity by providing only some of what is needed to complete a task or activity (e.g., Ostrosky & Kaiser's, 1991, inadequate portions). Some examples might include providing only a small amount of paint needed for a painting project or only a small portion of a snack, so that the child will have to ask for more. This has the added benefit of "priming the pump" in terms of an introduction of a potential reinforcer in incomplete form. A closely related strategy is "sabotage" (e.g, Ostrosky & Kaiser). Sabotage is often accomplished through teaching the child a sequence of behaviors leading to a common outcome and then withholding materials necessary for completion of one of the behaviors. For example, a child might be taught to make chocolate milk using a glass, spoon, chocolate mix, and milk. Assuming that chocolate milk is a reinforcer for the child, after she has mastered the skill of making chocolate milk, the sequence can be "sabotaged" in that materials for one of the steps is withheld (e.g., the glass). Now the child has to verbally request the glass (or milk, or chocolate mix, etc.) in order to make her chocolate milk. This is also a case of arranging the situation so that the child has to ask for assistance.

Giving children an opportunity to choose is another strategy for establishing opportunities to use naturalistic teaching techniques. Depending upon the the child's abilities, one may have to teach the child to make choices, perhaps by at first giving the child a choice between a highly desired item and a non-desired item, employing time-delay, model, mand, and mand-model as needed. Later, the teacher can work toward giving the child choices of more equal value.

Naturalistic Language Teaching Techniques

At the core of naturalistic teaching are the teaching techniques themselves. Table 1 summarizes naturalistic language teaching techniques including descriptive statements, imitating, expansion, modeling, manding, mand-modeling, and time-delay. These techniques can be skillfully and flexibly combined to encourage children's verbal behavior and should be tailored to each child's language learning needs. For example, if a child has the verbal repertoire to request preferred objects but does not do so, time-delay may be a useful strategy to increase that child's verbal initiations. Another child, however, may not have the verbal repertoire to make requests. Then the mand-model procedure would be more appropriate.

Hart and Risley's (1974) levels of incidental teaching provide a fairly well structured example of how these might be combined for naturalistic teaching. As discussed earlier in this chapter, Hart and Risley recommended that the teacher begin with the lowest level of prompt necessary to encourage the child's verbal response beginning with, perhaps, the Level 1 time-delay. If the child does not respond, the teacher would then prompt the child to ask for the desired object. If the child still does not emit the desired response the teacher would then use a more elaborate response by pointing to the object and asking, "What's this?" If this still does not work, the teacher would then model the correct response and the child would be prompted to imitate the teacher.

For example, a teacher with Michael knows that he very much likes fire trucks and fire fighters. The teacher would already have made sure that there were toy fire trucks, books about fire trucks, and perhaps a fire fighter costume available in the room. The teacher observes that Michael is interested in the toy

Table I
Naturalistic Language Teaching Techniques

Technique	Description
Descriptive Statements	Caregiver makes a statement that describes the child's ongoing activities (e.g., "You're picking up the train"), or some other event in the immediate environment (e.g., the phone rings and teacher says, "The telephone is ringing").
Imitating	Caregiver directly imitates a verbal statement made by the child. For example, child says, "fire truck," mom says, "You're right. That's a fire truck."
Expansion	Caregiver expands on the child's statement. The caregiver responds to the child's utterance by repeating it, but adds syntactic or semantic information to what the child said. For example, child says, "fire truck," mom expands by saying, "That's a big red fire truck."
Model	Caregiver produces a word, phrase or sentence with the intention that the child will imitate the verbal behavior. For example, the caregiver, following the child's lead, observes the child's possible interest and models, "I want the red fire truck." Please note that model is different than descriptive statements in that the caregiver intends for the child to imitate the response.
Mand	Caregiver requests an appropriate response from the child. For example, the child is gesturing toward the toy fire truck and mom says, "Tell me what you want."
Mand-Model	Caregiver combines a mand and model at the same time. For example, the child is still interested in the toy fire truck and mom says, "Michael, say I want the red fire truck."
Time-Delay	Caregiver recognizes a situation in which the child wants an object or assistance and then waits to see if the child emits the correct response. The caregiver may use some form of visual prompt (e.g., holding the toy up) or assume a questioning look (e.g., raised eyebrows) or both. For example, mom notices that the child is interested in the toy fire truck, picks up the truck so that the child can see her holding it and then she simply waits for a response from the child.

Adapted from the Combined Milieu, Responsive-Interactive and Hybrid Language Teacher Code (Alpert, Keefer, & Fischer, 1992)

fire truck that has been placed out of reach. The teacher can tell that Michael is interested because he has been standing in front of the shelf that the toy fire truck is on and looking at the toy for some time. First, the teacher moves near the shelf and looks at Michael with an expectant look (communicating non-verbally, "Tell me what you want"). If Michael says "fire truck," the teacher will provide the toy and might also use an expansion like "the big red fire truck" or "You want the red fire truck." If Michael does not emit the correct response to the time-delay within 30 seconds, the teacher would then prompt him by saying "Tell me what you want." If Michael does not state what he wants verbally the teacher might then prompt him further by manding "What is this?" If Michael says "fire truck," she can then give Michael the toy (and probably use one of the expansions described above). If Michael does not say "fire truck" the teacher will then move to the next level of prompt and first model the correct response, "I want the fire truck," and then prompt Michael by saying, "Say I want the fire truck." If Michael successfully emits the response he can then play with the fire truck. If not, then he does not get to play with the toy. It should be noted, however, that shaping may be required here. If a child is only capable of getting out part of a word, for example "truh" (for fire truck), the teacher will need to start with that and shape close approximations as time goes on (later "truck," then "fff truck," then "fire truck").

In conclusion, naturalistic teaching has been demonstrated to be an effective approach to children's language intervention and may be particularly useful in facilitating the generalization and maintenance of children's language skills following intervention. The skillful combining of sensitivity to the child's interests, thoughtful arrangement of the teaching environment, and flexible use of naturalistic teaching techniques can lead to a positive and productive language interaction between teacher and child.

ACKNOWLEDGMENTS

I would like to thank Don Baer, Judith Carta, Joe Delquadri and Charles Greenwood for their helpful comments on earlier versions of this manuscript.

Correspondence concerning this chapter should be addressed to Pete Peterson, Ph.D., Associate Professor of Psychology, Liberal Arts Division, Box 36, Johnson County Community College, 12345 College Blvd., Overland Park, KS 66210. Email: ppetersn@cccc.net

REFERENCES

Alpert, C. L., & Kaiser, A. P. (1992). Training parents as milieu language teachers. *Journal of Early Intervention, 16,* 31–52.

Angelo, D. H., & Goldstein, H. (1990). Effects of a pragmatic teaching strategy for requesting information by communication board users. *Journal of Speech and Hearing Disorders, 55,* 231–243.

Baer, D. M. (1981). *How to plan for generalization.* Austin, TX: PRO-ED.

Bradley, R., & Caldwell, B. (1976). Early home environment and changes in mental test performance 6 to 36 months. *Developmental Psychology, 12,* 93–97.

Carr, E. G., & Kologinsky, E. (1983). Acquisition of sign language by autistic children II: Spontaneity and generalization effects. *Journal of Applied Behavior Analysis, 16,* 297–314.

Cavallaro, C. C., & Bambara, L. M. (1982). Two strategies for teaching language during free play. *Journal of the Association for Persons with Severe Handicaps, 7,* 80–92.

Charlop, M. E., Schreibman, L., Thibodeau, M. G. (1985). Increasing spontaneous verbal responding in autistic children using the time-delay procedure. *Journal of Applied Behavior Analysis, 18,* 155–166.

Charlop-Christy, M. H., & Carpenter, M. H. (2000). Modified incidental teaching sessions: A procedure for parents to increase spontaneous speech in their children with autism. *Journal of Positive Behavior Interventions, 2,* 98–112.

Fabry, B. D., Mayhew, G. L., & Hanson, A. (1984). Incidental teaching of mentally retarded students within a token system. *American Journal of Mental Deficiency, 89,* 29–36.

Fey, M. E. (1986). *Language intervention with young children.* Austin, TX: PRO-ED.

Fey, M. E. (1988). Generalization issues facing language interventionists: An introduction. *Language, Speech, and Hearing Services in Schools, 19,* 272–281.

Gobbi, L., Cipani, E., Hudson, C., & Lapenta-Neudeck, R. (1986). Developing spontaneous requesting among children with severe mental retardation. *Mental Retardation, 24,* 357–363.

Goldstein, H., & Kaczmarek, L. (1992). Promoting communicative interaction among children in integrated intervention settings. In S. F. Warren & J. Reichle (Eds.), *Causes and effects in communication and language intervention* (pp. 81–111). Baltimore, MD: Paul H. Brookes.

Guess, D., Keogh, W., & Sailor, W. (1978). Generalization of speech and language behavior. In R. Schiefelbusch (Ed.), *Bases of language intervention.* Baltimore, MD: University Park Press.

Halle, J., Baer, D., & Spradlin, J. (1981). Teachers' generalized use of delay as a stimulus control procedure to increase language use in handicapped children. *Journal of Applied Behavior Analysis, 14,* 389–409.

Halle, J. W., Marshall, A. M., & Spradlin, J. E. (1979). Time delay: A technique to increase language use and generalization in retarded children. *Journal of Applied Behavior Analysis, 12,* 431–439.

Hancock, T. B., & Kaiser, A. P. (2002). The effects of trainer-implemented enhanced milieu teaching on the social communication of children with autism. *Topics in Early Childhood Special Education, 22,* 39–54.

Hart, B. & Risley, T. R. (1980). In vivo language intervention: Unanticipated general effects. *Journal of Applied Behavior Analysis, 13,* 407–432.

Hart, B. & Rogers-Warren, A. (1978). A mileau approach to teaching language. In R. Schiefelbusch (Ed.), *Language Intervention Strategies* (pp. *193*–235). Baltimore, MD: University Park Press.

Hart, B. M., & Risley, T. R. (1968). Establishing the use of descriptive adjectives in the spontaneous speech of disadvantaged children. *Journal of Applied Behavior Analysis, 1,* 109–120.

Hart, B. M., & Risley, T. R. (1974). Using preschool materials to modify the language of disadvantaged children. *Journal of Applied Behavior Analysis, 7,* 243–256.

Hart, B. M., & Risley, T. R. (1975). Incidental teaching of language in the preschool. *Journal of Applied Behavior Analysis, 8,* 411–420.

Hart, B. M., & Risley, T. R. (1992). American parenting of language-learning children: Persisting differences in family-child interactions observed in natural home environments. *Developmental Psychology, 28,* 1096–1105.

Hart, B. M., & Risley, T. R. (1995). *Meaningful differences in the everyday experiences of young American children.* Baltimore, MD: Paul H. Brookes.

Hemmeter, M. L., Ault, M. J., Collins, B. C., & Meyer, S. (1996). The effects of teacher-implemented language instruction within free time activities. *Education and Treatment of Children, 13,* 331–346.

Hemmeter, M. L., & Kaiser, A. P. (1990). Environmental influences on children's language: A model and case study. *Education and Treatment of Children, 13,* 331–346.

Hemmeter, M. L., & Kaiser, A. P. (1994). Enhanced milieu teaching: Effects of parent-implemented language intervention. *Journal of Early Intervention, 18,* 269–289.

Hester, P. P., Kaiser, A. P., Alpert, C. L., & Whiteman, B. (1995). The generalized effects of training trainers to teach parents to implement milieu teaching. *Journal of Early Intervention, 20,* 30–51.

Huttonlocher, J., Haight, W., Bryk, A., Seltzer, M., & Lyons, T. (1991). Early vocabulary growth: Relation to language input and gender. *Developmental Psychology, 27,* 236–248.

Kaczmarek, L. A., Hepting, N. H., & Dzubak, M. (1996). Examining the generalization of milieu language objectives in situations requiring listener preparatory behaviors. *Topics in Early Childhood Special Education, 16,* 139–167.

Kaiser, A. P. (1993). Parent-implemented language intervention: An environmental perspective. In A. P. Kaiser & D. B. Gray (Eds.), *Enhancing children's communication: Research foundations for intervention* (pp. 63–84). Baltimore, MD: Paul H. Brookes.

Kaiser, A. P., & Hancock, T. B. (2003). Teaching parents new skills to support their young children's development. *Infants & Young Children, 16,* 9–21.

Kaiser, A. P., Hancock, T. B., & Hester, P. P. (1998). Parents as cointerventionists: Research on applications of naturalistic language teaching procedures. *Infants & Young Children, 10,* 45–55.

Kaiser, A. P., Ostrosky, M. M., & Alpert, C. L. (1993). Training teachers to use environmental arrangement and milieu teaching with non vocal school children. *Journal of the Association for Persons with Severere Handicaps, 18,* 188–199.

Kaiser, A. P., Yoder, P. J., & Keetz, A. (1992). Evaluating milieu teaching. In S. F. Warren & J. Reichle (Eds.), *Causes and effects in communication and language intervention* (pp.9–47). Baltimore, MD: Paul H. Brookes.

Kirby, K. C., & Bickel, W. K. (1988). Toward an explicit analysis of generalization: A stimulus control interpretation. *The Behavior Analyst, 11,* 115–129.

Laski, K. E., Charlop, M. H., & Schreibman, L. (1988). Training parents to use the natural language paradigm to increase their autistic children's speech. *Journal of Applied Behavior Analysis, 21,* 391–400.

McGee, G. G., Almeida, M. C., Sulzer-Azaroff, B., & Feldman, R. S. (1992). Promoting reciprocal interactions via peer incidental teaching. *Journal of Applied Behavior Analysis, 25,* 117–126.

McGee, G. G., Krantz, P. J., Mason, D., & McClannahan, L. E. (1983). A modified incidental-teaching procedure for autistic youth: Acquisition and generalization of receptive object labels. *Journal of Applied Behavior Analysis, 16,* 329–338.

McGee, G. G., Krantz, P. J., & McClannahan, L. E. (1985). The facilitative effects of incidental teaching on preposition use by autistic children. *Journal of Applied Behavior Analysis, 18,* 17–31.

McGee, G. G., Krantz, P. J., & McClannahan, L. E. (1986). An extension of incidental teaching procedures to reading instruction for autistic children. *Journal of Applied Behavior Analysis, 19,* 147–157.

Miranda-Linne, F., & Melin, L. (1992). Acquisition, generalization, and spontaneous use of color adjectives: A comparison of incidental teaching and traditional discrete-trial procedures for children with autism. *Research in Developmental Disabilities, 13,* 191–210.

Noonan, M. J., & McCormick, L. (1993). *Early intervention in natural environments: Methods and procedures.* Pacific Grove, CA: Brooks/Cole.

Ostrosky, M. M., & Kaiser, A. P. (1991). Preschool classroom environments that promote communication. *Teaching Exceptional Children, 23*(4) 6–10.

Oswald, L. K., Lignugaris/Kraft, B., & West, R. (1990). The effects of incidental teaching on the generalized use of social amenities at school by a mildly handicapped adolescent. *Education and Treatment of Children, 13,* 142–152.

Peterson, P., (2005). *Naturalistic language teaching: Effective procedures for promoting generalization.* Manuscript in preparation.

Peterson, P., Carta, J. J., & Greenwood, C. R. (2005). Teaching enhanced milieu language teaching skills to parents of multiple risk families. *Journal of Early Intervention. 27(2), 94–109*

Ramey, C. T., & Campbell, F. A. (1992). Poverty, early childhood education, and academic competence: The Abecedarian experiment. In A. Huston (Ed.), *Children in poverty (pp. 190–221).* New York: Cambridge University Press.

Rogers-Warren, A., & Warren, S. F. (1980). Mands for verbalization. *Behavior Modification, 4,* 361–382.

Seifert, H., & Schwarz, I. (1991). Treatment effectiveness of large group basic concept instruction with Head Start students. *Language, Speech, and Hearing Services in the Schools, 22,* 60–64.

Spradlin, J. E., & Siegel, G. (1982). Language training in natural and clinical environments. *Journal of Speech and Hearing Disorders, 47,* 2–6.

Stokes, T. F., & Baer, D. M. (1977). An implicit technology of generalization. *Journal of Applied Behavior Analysis, 10,* 349–367.

Sundberg, M. L., & Partington, J. W. (1998). *Teaching language to children with autism or other disabilities.* Pleasant Hill, CA: Behavior Analysts, Inc.

Tannock, R., & Girolametto, L. (1992). Reassessing parent-focused language intervention programs. In S. F. Warren & J. Reichle (Eds.), *Causes and effects in communication and language intervention* (pp. 49–76). Baltimore, MD: Paul H. Brookes.

Warren, S. F. (1988). A behavioral approach to language generalization. *Language, Speech, and Hearing in the Schools, 19,* 292–303.

Warren, S. F. (1992). Facilitating basic vocabulary acquisition with milieu teaching procedures. *Journal of Early Intervention, 16,* 235–251.

Warren, S. F., & Bambara, L. M. (1989). An experimental analysis of milieu language intervention: Teaching the action-object form. *Journal of Speech and Hearing Disorders, 54,* 448–461.

Warren, S. F., & Gazdag, G. (1990). Facilitating early language development with milieu intervention procedures. *Journal of Early Intervention, 14,* 62–86.

Warren, S. F., & Kaiser, A. P. (1986). Incidental language teaching: A critical review. *Journal of Speech and Hearing Disorders, 51,* 291–299.

Warren, S. F., McQuarter, R. J., & Rogers-Warren, A. P. (1984). The effects of mands and models on the speech of unresponsive language-delayed preschool children. *Journal of Speech and Hearing Disorders, 49,* 43–52.

Warren, S. F., Yoder, P. J., Gazdag, G. E., Kim, K., & Jones, H. A. (1993). Facilitating prelinguistic communication skills in young children with developmental delay. *Journal of Speech and Hearing Research, 36,* 83–97.

Wetherby, A. M., & Prizant, B. M. (1992). Profiling young children's communicative competence. In S. F. Warren & J. Reichle (Eds.), *Causes and effects in communication and language intervention* (pp. 217–253). Baltimore, MD: Paul H. Brookes.

Chapter Five

Promoting Self-Efficacy and Academic Competency: Instructional Implications for Struggling Secondary Learners

Craig A. Michaels, Ph.D.
Queens College, City University of New York

Gloria Lodato Wilson, Ph.D.
Hofstra University

Howard Margolis, Ed.D.
Queens College, City University of New York

By secondary school, struggling learners[1] have experienced "considerable failure and negative competence feedback at school" (Grolnick & Ryan, 1990, p. 177). Consequently, many develop weak self-efficacy and motivation for academics. Frequent frustration and failure have taught them to believe that they cannot succeed, that they lack the ability, and that even enormous effort produces failure. Not surprisingly, many resist academics, carelessly rushing through school-related tasks, investing as little effort and thought as possible to protect themselves from frustration and failure. Ironically, this lack of cognitive engagement often produces even more frustration and failure.

IMPORTANCE OF MOTIVATION ☆ same as online class)

Most teachers will agree that it is far easier to teach motivated than unmotivated students. Motivated students are far more likely to cooperate and to cognitively engage in learning, increasing the likelihood of academic success (Guthrie & Davis, 2003). Consequently, motivation and engagement are critical factors in learning, especially for struggling learners.

> Struggling readers [for example] are often disengaged from the literacy of school . . . They are disaffected with school reading. They are at best passive and may actively avoid reading. Consequently, a primary challenge is to re-engage students. Students' reading motivation must be redeveloped to make possible the long process of acquiring cognitive skills for reading comprehension. (Guthrie & Davis, p. 70)

When assessing reading and language arts achievement, DiPerna, Volpe, and Elliott (2001) found that both prior achievement and motivation influenced current achievement. Analogously, Lan and Lanthier (2003) found that the combination of academic difficulties and poor motivation dramatically increased the likelihood that struggling learners would drop out of school. Kortering and Braziel (1999) reported that students with more positive levels of motivation had a greater likelihood of interacting with teachers and of completing school. Clearly, to reverse this trend, teachers must motivate struggling learners so that they in turn work to succeed in school.

---

1. "*Struggling learners*" is a general term that refers to students who find learning difficult, frustrating, or incomprehensible. The term encompasses (a) students with documented learning disabilities who receive special education services and supports; and (b) students, who for a variety of reasons (e.g., poverty, English language learning difficulties, cultural differences), struggle with learning and perform poorly. This second, and larger group, may not be eligible for special education; some however, may eventually be identified as students with learning disabilities.

IMPORTANCE OF SELF-EFFICACY

According to self-efficacy theory, self-efficacy can strengthen or weaken motivation (Wigfield, 2004). The two are positively correlated. Self-efficacy mediates and influences task choice, persistence, effort, and academic achievement (Bandura, 1997; Pajares, 1996, 2002, 2003; Zimmerman, 2000). Earlier, Torgesen (1997a) described this relation by suggesting that poor readers, reacting to past frustration and failure, often lacked the intention to learn. As a result, "the proper task attitude may never develop because of chronic failure due to specific cognitive difficulties [which in turn] . . . can lead to a withdrawal of effort, a loss of confidence, or a change in attitude" (Torgesen, 1977b, p. 32). At about this time, Brown (1978) suggested that early failures caused many adolescents to become passive and dependent, further eroding self-concept. To a large extent, Torgesen and Brown described the phenomenon that is now called *self-efficacy*—the personal and often private belief that one can or cannot succeed on specific tasks.

The relation between self-efficacy and motivation continues to be well documented (e.g., Wigfield, 2004; Wigfield, Guthrie, Tonks, & Perencevich, 2004; Zimmerman, 2000). Many educational researchers and practitioners believe that learners with a strong sense of academic self-efficacy will likely work harder and persevere longer when they encounter difficulties than will their peers with lower self-efficacy levels (Pajares, 1996; Pintrich & Schunk, 2002; Zimmerman, 2000). In contrast, struggling learners often resist or quickly quit activities they perceive as difficult or impossible for them (Wong, 1991; Wong & Wong, 1986). These struggling learners attribute success to easy tasks or luck instead of personal effort and attribute failure to low ability rather than insufficient effort (Alderman, 2004; Ormrod, 2003; Pearl, Bryan, & Donahue, 1980; Pintrich & Schunk, 2002).

Simply put, "no one works if they know that they will fail anyway" (Allington & Cunningham, 2002, p. 269). Unfortunately, many struggling learners even believe they will fail on activities that they could likely master. This only further exacerbates learning difficulties and impedes progress. In other words, "people's accomplishments are generally better predicted by their self-efficacy beliefs than by their previous attainments, knowledge, or skills... Self-efficacy beliefs are themselves critical determinants of how well knowledge and skill are acquired" (Pajares, 2002, p. 3).

Fortunately, research suggests that declining "motivation can be reversed with instructional practices designed to foster children's motivation" (Wigfield et al., 2004, p. 308). More specifically, teachers' manners and practices can play a pivotal role in improving academic achievements and strengthening self-efficacy (Allington & Johnston, 2001; Deshler, Schumaker, & Woodruff, 2004;

Linnenbrink & Pintrich, 2002, 2003; Pintrich & Schunk, 2002; Schunk & Zimmerman, 1997a). To achieve this with learners who doubt their competence, teachers must work to systematically strengthen struggling learners' self-efficacy by creating emotionally and psychologically safe classes in which sound pedagogy is practiced.

Although helping struggling learners strengthen their academic self-efficacy can be a difficult, lengthy process, teachers have two reasons for optimism. First, self-efficacy is not an immutable, global trait. Rather, it is a modifiable, task-specific set of beliefs derived largely from past experiences (frequent failures) and maladaptive attributions (e.g., "I failed because I'm dumb"). By structuring academics for frequent success, and helping learners attribute their successes to controllable factors, teachers can influence learners' academic self-efficacy, their belief that they have the ability to succeed. Second, teachers are in an excellent position to strengthen struggling learners' academic self-efficacy. Teachers can do this by establishing emotionally and psychologically safe classes, making informed curriculum decisions, and implementing instructional guidelines that promote success (discussed in detail later in this chapter).

RELATIONSHIP BETWEEN SELF-EFFICACY AND ACADEMIC COMPETENCY

Competency refers to the belief in one's ability to positively change one's life. The term is similar to *control*, as used by Reiff, Gerber, and Ginsberg (1997) to describe the central attribute or quality of highly successful adults with learning disabilities. Competency is also similar to *self-efficacy*, the "personal beliefs about one's capabilities to learn or perform behaviors at designated levels" (Schunk & Zimmerman, 1997b, p. 195). While personal competency is related to self-efficacy, academic competency is seen as actual attainment of a skill level. Thus, learners are considered academically competent if others, such as teachers and parents, judge them successful.

Research on highly successful adults with learning disabilities (Gerber, Ginsberg, & Reiff, 1992; Reiff et al., 1997; Reiff, Ginsberg, & Gerber, 1995) offers retrospective clues about competency, self-efficacy, and developing secondary supports for struggling learners. Extensive interviews identified three critical factors—control, internal decisions, and external manifestations—that differentiated highly successful adults with learning disabilities from the majority of their less successful peers:

- *Control* "refers to the drive to manage one's life [and involves] a set of internal decisions (conscious decisions to take charge of one's life) and external manifestations (adapting and shaping oneself to move ahead)" (Reiff et al., 1997, p. 101).
- *Internal decisions* subsumes three sub-themes: desire, goal orientation, and reframing. Specifically, "adults with learning disabilities must want

to succeed, must set achievable goals, and must confront the learning disability so that appropriate measures can be undertaken to heighten the likelihood for success" (Reiff et al., 1997, p. 103).

- *External manifestations* subsumes the four sub-themes of adaptability that tend to be present in highly successful adults with learning disabilities—"persistence, goodness of fit with one's work environment, coping behavior we call learned creativity, and the support of individuals in the development of success we refer to as social ecologies" (Reiff et al., 1997, p. 110).

We suggest that self-efficacy (i.e., the belief that "I can succeed if I try") influences these factors. After all, why try if you believe your limitations make failure inevitable? This research, although retrospective, strongly suggests that teachers who work with struggling learners should systematically foster these attributes. Because learners spend so much of their lives in school and because instructional activities and classroom routines dominate time in school, these attributes must be fostered in school; not doing so may inadvertently foster maladaptive, self-defeating beliefs and behaviors.

Figure 1. Conceptual map of the competency or self-efficacy inhibiting attributes professionals, families, and learners typically associated with the term, "Students with Learning Disabilities."

RECONCILING COMPETENCY AND LEARNING DIFFICULTIES

Educators often envision limited futures for struggling learners and communicate these beliefs to learners either directly through their words and actions or indirectly through their attitudes and decisions. Therefore, we suggest that secondary educators examine their beliefs about learning difficulties as part of the process of building self-efficacy and academic competency in struggling learners. According to Wilson and Michaels (2000), every learner's interaction in school with every professional or peer is a mirroring process that shapes a learner's self-efficacy and competency. Within this mirroring, self-efficacy and competency are either enhanced or diminished. This may be particularly true during adolescence, when various persona and identities are tested and the personal self emerges (Michaels, 1997).

When working with professionals, families, and struggling learners, the first author frequently asks them to brainstorm whatever comes to mind when they think about *competency* and *learning disabilities*. Figure 1 presents the typical concept map for learning disabilities that emerges and Figure 2 presents the typical map for competency. Part of what these two concept maps illustrate is that we, as

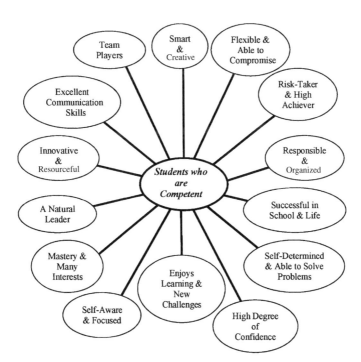

Figure 2. Conceptual map of the competency or self-efficacy promoting attributes professionals, families, and students typically associated with the term, "Students who are Competent."

teachers, tend to believe that we are dedicated to helping struggling learners achieve the self-efficacy and competency illustrated in Figure 2; yet the messages about self-efficacy and competency that learners internalize are often closer to Figure 1. While we do not suggest that teachers are solely responsible for this, we believe that all who work with struggling learners should explore the possibility that they are promoting and sustaining these beliefs.

CHANGING STRUGGLING LEARNERS' BELIEFS

To strengthen struggling learners' beliefs about their academic self-efficacy and competency, teachers need to provide emotionally and psychologically safe classes, use curriculum in an informed, systematic manner, and implement instructional guidelines that engage learners, produce frequent success, and teach them to make adaptive attributions.

Emotionally and Psychologically Safe Classes

Because many struggling learners are emotionally fragile and find schools tough, difficult, threatening places, attempts to improve self-efficacy and academic competence need to occur in classes they perceive as safe and supportive. Establishing emotionally and psychologically safe classes makes it more likely that struggling learners will attempt new activities about which they feel somewhat insecure. If the activities match their independent and instructional levels, the likelihood of success is high, setting the stage for strengthened self-efficacy and greater motivation. Table 1 presents several hallmark features of such classes.

When secondary teachers successfully create secure, welcoming, and motivating learning environments—environments that stress moderate challenge and frequent success—struggling learners' self-efficacy for academics will likely improve. Because they frequently achieve success, they will likely demonstrate the attributes of success (Raskind, Goldberg, Higgins, & Herman, 2002), as they begin to

- Engage in goal setting—establish and monitor goals.
- Acknowledge and use available support systems—ask for and accept help as needed.
- Develop greater emotional stability—cope with stresses and emerging issues.
- Demonstrate self-awareness—know who they are and begin to de-compartmentalize parts of their lives.
- Develop proactivity—actively participate in making decisions and engage in self-advocacy.
- Demonstrate perseverance—show a never quit attitude and a willingness to learn from their mistakes.

Table I

Hallmark Features of Safe Secondary Classrooms that Emphasize Motivational Principles

To promote motivation and self-efficacy, teachers should

- Run well-organized classes
- Encourage learners to actively solve problems and locate information
- Treat learners with respect
- Show interest in learners
- Give learners choices
- Relate curriculum to learners' lives and interests, in and out of school
- Be enthusiastic about their lessons and subject area
- Stimulate and maintain curiosity
- Engage learners in collaborative learning activities (e.g., cooperative learning, peer tutoring) rather than competitive ones (e.g., the best paper wins)
- Encourage sharing of both products and process in the classroom
- Match teaching approaches to lesson objectives
- Be clear and realistic about objectives and expectations
- Provide help, whenever needed, in socially appropriate ways that prevent embarrassment
- Compare learners' achievements to their past achievements, rather than to other learners'
- Provide frequent, immediate, task-specific feedback that includes corrective comments and justified praise
- Ensure that learners have the prerequisite knowledge and skill to master new topics and assignments
- Emphasize what is right about learners' work
- Challenge rather than frustrate learners

Note. From "Self-efficacy: A key to improving the motivation of struggling learners," by H. Margolis and P. P. McCabe, 2003, *Preventing School Failure, 47,* pp. 162–169. Copyright 2003 by Heldref Publications. Adapted with permission of the authors.

Informed Curriculum Decisions

Because the instructional hours in a day are few, the scheduled time for graduation usually less than five years away, and the drop-out rate high for struggling learners (e.g., 38% nationally for students with learning disabilities, according to Wagner, Blackorby, and Hebbeler, 1993), secondary level teachers must make informed curriculum decisions that can strengthen struggling learners' self-efficacy and academic competence.

Obviously, to strengthen self-efficacy, secondary learners who struggle with academics must become more academically competent. Although this is not a chicken and egg conundrum, it is almost impossible to increase academic self-

Table 2

Six Essential Curriculum Framework Strategy Elements for Struggling Learners

Framework Element/Strategy	Criteria or Features
1. *Big Ideas*—Concepts, principles, or heuristics that facilitate the most efficient and broad acquisition of knowledge	• Focus on essential learning outcomes • Capture rich relationships • Enable learners to apply what they learn in varied situations • Involve ideas, concepts, principles, and rules central to higher-order learning • Form the basis for generalization & expansion
2. *Conspicuous Strategies*—Useful steps for accomplishing goals or tasks	• Planned • Purposeful • Explicit • Of medium-level application • Most important in initial teaching
3. *Mediated Scaffolding*—Instructional guidance provided by teachers, peers, materials, or tasks	• Varied according to learner & experiences • Based on task (not more than learner needs) • Provided in the form of tasks, content & materials • Weaned or removed according to learner proficiency
4. *Strategic Integration*—Integrating knowledge as a means of promoting higher-level cognition	• Combines cognitive components • Results in a new & more complex knowledge structure • Aligns naturally with information (i.e., not forced) • Involves meaningful relationships • Links essential big ideas across lessons within a curriculum
5. *Primed Background Knowledge*—Preexisting information, background, or schema that affects new learning	• Aligns with learner knowledge & expertise • Considers strategic & proximal pre-skills • Readies learner for successful performance
6. *Judicious Review*—Structured opportunities to recall or apply information previously taught	• Sufficient • Varied • Distributed • Cumulative • Judicious

Note. From "A focus on curriculum design: When children fail," by D. C. Simmons & E. J. Kameenui, 1996, *Focus on Exceptional Children, 28*(7), pp. 1–16. Copyright 1996 by Love Publishing Company. Reproduced with permission of the publisher.

efficacy without directly addressing task performance or competency. Learners must begin by experiencing meaningful and substantial growth as poor self-efficacy tends to develop when learners' efforts repeatedly result in failure, failure impervious to change (Deci, Hodges, Pierson, & Tomassone, 2000). Thus, attempts to strengthen self-efficacy will likely produce questionable results if academic success and competence are not addressed effectively.

Consider, for example, Jensen, Lingren, Andersson, Ingvar, and Levander's (2000) study of unemployed adults with severe deficiencies in reading and writing. After an intensive ten week intervention program, participants' memory and reading and writing skills improved. Improved academic skill was accompanied by improved self-confidence and perspective taking. Clearly, curriculum and instruction that directly support skill development can improve learners' success, which, in turn, can strengthen self-efficacy, motivation, and academic competence. Effective instructional strategies and guidelines, however, will produce little of value unless careful consideration is given to curriculum design.

Curriculum design "refers to the way information in a particular domain (e.g., social studies, science, reading, mathematics) is selected, prioritized, sequenced, organized and scheduled for instruction within a highly orchestrated series of lessons and materials that make up a course of study" (Simmons & Kameenui, 1996, p. 5). By providing a logical structure and sequence, effective curriculum design should assist teachers to avoid or minimize learner frustration and failure, increasing the likelihood of strengthening learners' self-efficacy and academic competency. Teachers need to reflect on a series of critical questions to maximize the positive effects of curriculum design. We believe that addressing these questions will help teachers ensure that what is taught is valuable to learners and that instructional time is used effectively.

Does the curriculum offer a framework of strategies for helping all learners succeed? By focusing on core elements within a larger curriculum framework, teachers can develop curricula that support and guide struggling learners. Kameenui and his colleagues (Kameenui & Carnine, 1998; Simmons & Kameenui, 1996) describe six such core curriculum elements—big ideas, conspicuous strategies, strategic integration, mediated scaffolding, judicious review, and primed background knowledge. Table 2 highlights each core element's criteria or features. Focusing on these core elements can conceptually and practically support teachers as they think about and implement instructional strategies that will assist struggling learners.

- *Big ideas*—struggling learners often get bogged down in details. They miss the proverbial "forest for the trees." By focusing on Big Ideas—the fundamental concepts or "forest"—teachers can later connect the details or "trees." Figure 3 illustrates how the Big Ideas of history follows a problem-solution-effect model with categories that make the model applicable to major historical events.

- *Conspicuous strategies*—struggling learners frequently lack an adequate number of learning strategies (e.g., how to comprehend text and repair misunderstandings, how to write summaries); consequently, they rigidly apply one or two strategies to most situations, whether or not the strategies match the situation. Not surprisingly, applying a few strategies to many situations produces frustration and failure (Horner & Shwrey, 2002; Lenz, Deshler, & Kissam, 2004). Fortunately, when struggling learners are taught a task-specific strategy, they can apply it

Big Idea: In HISTORY, events can be understood through a Problem-Solution-Effect model. This model not only helps to understand a particular event, but can facilitate seeing how other events are connected and related

Problem	Solution	Effect
Many problems in history can be ascribed to economic and human rights issues	Most solutions to problems can be classified under moving; inventing; dominating; accommodating; tolerating	The effects of the solution can lead to the problem being solved; the problem continuing; or the creation of new problems

	Tolerating and Accommodating	
In the 1800's in the United States there were conflicts between the states concerning economics (the need differences between agriculture and industry) and human rights (slavery)	The states came up with a series of ways to address the human rights issue of slavery. The Missouri Compromise (1820) set up an agreement between pro-slavery factions in the US regarding which new states would become free states and which would become slave states.	**Problem Solved!** There was now a set plan for new states and the slavery issue.
		Problem Continues Slavery still exists and the basic human rights issue has not been solved.
		New Problems Marked the beginning of intensive sectional conflict over the human rights issue of slavery that eventually leads to the American Civil War.

Figure 3. Big Ideas in history [1]

[1]From "A focus on curriculum design: When children fail," by D. C. Simmons and E. J. Kameenui, 1996, *Focus on Exceptional Children, 28* (7), pp. 1–16. Copyright 1996 by Love Publishing Company. Adapted with permission of the publisher.

effectively (Ellis, 1986; Hughes, Ruhl, Schumaker, & Deshler, 2002), in the right situation. Once mastered, learners can be taught additional strategies. Curricula that incorporate specific and conspicuous strategies, strategies intentionally taught in a sequential, step-by-step fashion, offer learners opportunities for increased success. Following up on the Big Ideas illustrated in Figure 3, learners might be taught to use a problem-solution-effect graphic organizer to organize key historical information about reconstruction after the Civil War.

- *Strategic integration*—struggling learners often experience significant difficulties connecting new and previously learned information. Teaching them to connect what is taught to what they know, and then helping them do this, enables learners to better understand and remember new materials. This further reinforces Big Ideas. As part of the previous reconstruction example, teachers might help learners make personal connections by associating the historical events to learners' personal experiences (e.g., rebuilding a home after hurricane Ivan).

- *Mediated scaffolding*—struggling learners need teachers to intentionally provide whatever temporary supports are needed (e.g., academic, physical, social, emotional, motivational) to acquire a skill or concept. As successful learning occurs, teachers can then begin reducing or eliminating supports commensurate with learners' increased proficiency or knowledge. Through this process, teachers increase the likelihood of learner success and independence while sustaining motivation. Continuing with our reconstruction example, when learners write an essay, teachers might prompt them to review their graphic organizer to make sure they included all major points.

- *Judicious review*—practice does not ensure proficiency. To benefit struggling learners, practice must reinforce previously taught skills and concepts and must be easy enough not to practice or reinforce errors (Mastropieri & Scruggs, 2004). Additionally, it must be judicious: distributed (spaced over time), cumulative, integrated, and varied (Dixon, Carnine, & Kameenui, 1992, as cited in Simmons & Kameenui, 1996). In keeping with our example, teachers might briefly have a class play "Jeopardy," to review key concepts.

- *Primed background knowledge*—struggling learners also have difficulty activating and applying prior knowledge to current learning. Helping learners link what is taught to current knowledge facilitates learning. Sometimes, relevant background knowledge or associations must be directly taught to lay the foundation for the curriculum. This may be particularly true for English Language Learners. In our reconstruction

Table 3

Examples of Frequently Implemented Accommodations and Modifications/Adaptations for Struggling Secondary Learners

Accommodations	Modifications/Adaptations
• Does not change the content, conceptual difficulty • Changes the input and output methods	• Content is the SAME • Conceptual level changes slightly
Examples of Accommodations	Examples of Modifications/Adaptations
• Enlarge fonts/text • Present instructions verbally rather than in writing • Listen to a book on tape • Remove distractions from a worksheet or put fewer problems on each page • Allow a learner to use a word processor • Allow a learner to dictate answers to an essay exam	• Provide the learner with less material to learn • Simplify an assignment by reducing either performance expectations or the number of steps • Develop alternative assignments • Relate to the same content but be less complex • Have functional or direct applications • Reduce the performance standards • Adjust the pace of lesson

example, lessons can start with learners meeting in small groups to summarize what was discussed previously. This provides practice, activates background knowledge, and helps set the stage for new material.

Does the curriculum support a universally designed learning environment? Universal Design for Learning (UDL) emanates from architecture's Universal Design principles, which established guidelines for accessibility and maximum usage by the broadest potential audience (e.g., cabinets are accessible to those with and without disabilities, old and young, tall and short). Universal Design focuses on accessibility in the initial planning and design, rather than after completing a structure, minimizing the need for subsequent modifications and retrofitting.

Likewise, UDL centers on the curriculum design and planning stage, helping curriculum developers create curriculum with built-in strategies for differentiation and making adaptations to fit diverse learning needs (Bowe, 2000). As such, UDL incorporates strategies that emphasize mediated scaffolding, a variety of instructional and assistive technologies, and a variety of best-practice approaches to teaching and learning (Orkwis, 2003). Because of its potential flexibility, UDL can support learner self-efficacy and academic competence by minimizing initial failure and the subsequent need for accommodations and modifications.

To address struggling learners' needs, teachers might also have to make accommodations and modifications. Typically, *accommodation* refers to adjustments in timing, formatting, setting, scheduling, response, and/or presentation of materials without adjustments to performance expectations or learning objectives (i.e., learners are held to the same performance standards). In contrast, *modifications* or *adaptations* generally refer to changes in task demands (e.g., having to answer fewer test questions) or performance standards (e.g., having a lower passing grade). Table 3 lists examples of common accommodations and modifications that can enhance struggling learners' access to the general curriculum.

Is homework benefiting the learner? Homework is a pervasive component of academic life, especially in general education classes. Teachers assign it regularly and parents think it is important (Allington & Cunningham, 2002). Homework is often factored into grading practices, and teachers typically expect struggling learners to complete it independently and satisfactorily. While some do, many do not. Unfortunately, homework is often far more difficult and frustrating for struggling learners and their families than for typically achieving learners (Margolis & McCabe, 2004). Often, excessively difficult assignments, combined with learner characteristics (e.g., inattentiveness, disorganization), make completion nearly impossible (Bryan, Burstein, & Bryan, 2001; Hughes et al., 2002; Margolis & McCabe, 1997).

Along with diminished self-efficacy and damaged perceptions of competency, difficult homework assignments can lead to resistance or slipshod work that exacerbates learner frustration, parent disappointment, and teacher disapproval. In fact, homework can so adversely affect the self-efficacy of struggling learners with academic difficulties that homework may widen the achievement gap between learners with and without learning disabilities (Hughes et al., 2002). To overcome homework problems, Margolis and McCabe suggest that teachers

- Stress moderately challenging work that struggling learners can complete successfully without excessive, laborious effort.
- Limit the number of assignments.
- Make sure struggling learners know what homework is due and when it's due.
- Make sure struggling learners understand the assignment and have the needed materials at home.
- Keep organizational and written requirements doable by teaching needed self-regulatory skills and emphasizing practice assignments.
- Use shaping and behavioral contracts.

- Systematically use peer modeling.
- Teach learning strategies to the point of mastery.
- Frequently review homework, graph success, and teach self-monitoring strategies.
- Teach learners to attribute success to controllable behaviors (e.g., effort, persistence, correct use of strategies).
- Link homework to learners' short-term goals.
- Make homework interesting and worthwhile, tying it to discussions of learners' everyday lives.
- Let learners choose homework assignments and elicit their suggestions about homework.
- Use collaborative social structures to complete homework projects.

How does mandated high-stakes testing affect the curriculum? Manset and Wasburn (2000) contend that high-stakes testing (exams that affect promotion, placement, or graduation) not only produces "a narrowing of the curriculum to fit exams" (p. 164), but also negatively influences struggling secondary learners' self-efficacy, thereby increasing the risk of school drop out. They noted that struggling learners who fail competency tests doubt their ability to graduate (Catterall, 1989, as cited in Manset & Wasburn.)

In addition to the immediate damage that failing a high-stakes test inflicts on struggling learners, failure can further weaken self-efficacy by restricting learners' access to courses of personal interest. Some districts even prohibit learners from vocational programs unless they pass a certain number of high-stakes evaluations, thus blocking access to the very transition and vocational preparation programs that might enable them to demonstrate competence and enhance personal efficacy. While the importance of accountability, equity, and high standards should not be dismissed, the full impact of high-stakes testing on the self-efficacy of struggling learners may not yet be fully understood (Manset & Wasburn, 2000).

Although there are no easy solutions to the issues associated with high stakes assessment, teachers may be able to help struggling learners become more comfortable taking these types of tests. According to McCabe (2003), while the teaching of test taking strategies may not significantly influence test scores, they should increase confidence and allow learners to more accurately demonstrate their abilities. McCabe suggests that teachers

- Use materials that mimic the test so learners get more comfortable and confident with the format.
- First use passages at the learners' easy reading level, to build success and engender confidence.

- Model test taking strategies, and use peer models to do the same, to help struggling learners see and hear how competent test takers tackle questions and answers.
- Use charts and graphs to monitor learners' success and progress.

Does the curriculum promote student/family involvement and self-determination? Morningstar, Turnbull, and Turnbull (1995) reported that secondary learners with disabilities thought that educators gave little attention to getting their input for instructional planning and goal-setting and that they devoted little effort to transition planning. The researchers concluded that the majority of learners with disabilities had a vague sense of their future plans and that for help in developing post-school plans they generally turned to their families rather than educators. Heron and Harris (2001) speculated that perhaps learners and families were not fully involved in educational and post-school planning because (a) meetings were conducted without learners or families being present, (b) learners and families may have lacked basic information about services and supports necessary for full participation, and (c) professionals may not have encouraged learners and families to participate or express their needs and preferences.

Self-determination refers to the ability of learners to advocate, evaluate, and make choices in their lives (Grigal, Neubert, Moon, & Graham, 2003). More formally, it is "an educational outcome referring to acting as the primary causal agent in one's life and making choices and decisions regarding one's qualify of life free from undue external influence or interference" (Wehmeyer & Lawrence, 1995, p. 74). Logically, it resembles and emanates from self-efficacy: Without belief in one's ability to succeed on a particular task—self-efficacy—self-advocacy and planning (self-determination) are unlikely.

Frank discussion with struggling learners about their strengths and weaknesses often allows teachers to involve learners in planning how to enhance their competency and self-esteem. Many struggling learners may "already know a great deal about their disabilities, they just don't know what they know. Learners can identify when they get frustrated or in which activities they excel" (Zickel & Arnold, 2001, p. 72). Positively engaging learners in goal setting can also increase their willingness to advocate for curricula that allow them to develop their strengths and talents. Consistent with this, Zickel and Arnold developed the Self-Advocacy Circle, a four-component strategy that increased learner involvement and participation in IEP meetings. First, struggling learners are taught to engage in self-reflection; second, they are taught to set both short- and long-term goals; third, they create narratives to represent themselves at planning meetings; finally, they share their work with teachers and receive feedback on its clarity and comprehensiveness. Such goal setting and self-advocacy are related to self-determination.

Recent research on post-school transition planning and goal-setting linked learner and family participation and learner self-determination to increased graduation rates, employment, and other positive post-school outcomes (Benz, Lindstrom, & Yovanoff, 2000; Wehmeyer & Palmer, 2003). Wehmeyer and Palmer, for example, reported that among students with mental retardation and learning disabilities, those who had high self-determination at graduation were significantly more likely to live independently, have greater financial independence, and receive work-related benefits three years after graduation than those with low self-determination.

INSTRUCTIONAL GUIDELINES TO STRENGTHEN ACADEMIC SELF-EFFICACY AND COMPETENCY

As this chapter posits, learners with strong academic self-efficacy "participate more readily, work harder, persist longer, and have fewer adverse emotional reactions when they encounter difficulties than do those who doubt their capabilities" (Zimmerman, 2000, p. 86). Thus, it's critical that secondary teachers assist struggling learners in developing the belief that they can succeed if they make the effort to learn and apply what is taught. Without a self-efficacious attitude, learners may make only minimal efforts, making learning an objectionable chore.

Changing beliefs is hard, especially for adolescents who have struggled academically and failed for years. Fortunately, hard does not mean impossible; instead, it means that changing "can't do" beliefs about learning into "can do" ones requires teachers to systematically adhere to instructional guidelines likely to produce success, success that provides teachers with the opportunity to strengthen learners' self-efficacy: "Successes generally raise self-efficacy and failure lowers it" (Pintrich & Schunk, 1996, p. 180).

Fortunately, many promising suggestions are available that might help produce success and strengthen self-efficacy (e.g., Linnenbrink & Pintrich, 2002, 2003; Margolis & McCabe, 2004; Schunk & Zimmerman, 1997a). Effective teachers have many positive characteristics and simultaneously do many different things. According to Allington and Johnston's (2001) review, effective teachers are:

Caring
Persistent
Sensitive to individual needs
Have high expectations
Provide explicit instruction
Use behavioral routines
Schedule frequent library visits
Maximize opportunities to read

Focus on meaning

Provide opportunities to discuss what was read

Attend to students' academic and personal problems *Pay attention to everyone*

In other words, when trying to influence achievement, academic functioning, and beliefs (e.g., self-efficacy), teachers must consider many classroom factors simultaneously—including personal, environmental, instructional—as they act in concert and influence one another. Teachers must also remember that learning is complex (i.e., many other factors also influence student achievement and motivation). Teachers should carefully monitor all instructional activities and make adjustments based on struggling learners' successes. More specifically, teachers need to continually observe struggling learners' responses to instructional activities, listen to their concerns, and systematically evaluate progress. It is within this context that the teachers are encouraged to consider the suggestions below, while remembering that:

> Psychology and educational psychology are probabilistic sciences, not deterministic ones . . . Teachers [should] use psychological [and educational] research as a guide for their teaching rather than a prescriptive device for what will occur in every circumstance. That is, research suggests that following certain principles will most likely result in positive motivational outcomes, but there are always exceptions to these general principles. (Linnenbrink & Pintrich, 2003, p. 134)

Make sure assignments match struggling learners' independent, instructional, and comfort levels. In reviewing the difficulty of school work, Allington (2001) reported that "tasks completed with high rates of success were linked to greater learning and improved student attitudes toward the subject matter learned" (p. 44) and that "oral reading error rates of 5% or greater were linked to significant increases in off-task behavior" (p. 45). Similarly, Vaughn, Gersten, and Chard (2000) concluded that "teachers would enhance the effectiveness of their instruction by assuring that the task difficulty for students is a match with their abilities and emerging skills" (p. 111). Although a large body of experimental research has not identified absolute guidelines for independent, instructional, frustration, and comfort levels, the guidelines below typify what most authorities recommend.

If you expect struggling learners to successfully read and complete work without professional help (e.g., homework), assign material at their independent reading level, the level at which they independently, accurately, and quickly recognize at least 96% of the words in paragraphs and correctly answer 90% of the questions. If you are directly teaching learners, reading materials should be their instructional level, the level at which they correctly and quickly recognize more than 90% of the words in paragraphs and accurately answer 70% to

89% of questions (McCormick, 2003). For tasks with minimal reading (e.g., mathematics computation), consider Salvia and Ysseldyke's (2001) guidance: "Instruction is usually motivating [if] students can see that, with some effort, they will succeed. Depending on the student and the task, [appropriately] challenging material usually produces rates of correct student response of between 85 and 95 percent" (p. 25). The general principle is to avoid materials and tasks that learners struggle with or that create palpable anxiety. Instead, assign moderately challenging materials and tasks. If, however, the guidelines above create palpable anxiety, the materials and tasks are, for the moment, too difficult. Learners may resist the task, believing—perhaps erroneously—they lack the prerequisite skills and knowledge.

Think big, start small. It is important that teachers have realistically high expectations for struggling learners and that they focus on Big Ideas, "those concepts, principles, or heuristics that facilitate the most efficient and broadest acquisition of knowledge. . . . The keys that unlock a content area" (Kameenui & Carnine, 1998, p. 8). To create situations likely to engender the success needed to strengthen self-efficacy, teachers must be sure that they challenge rather than overwhelm struggling learners. Often, this means starting "small," with the simple rather than the complex, with the short rather than the long, with the concrete rather than the abstract, with the comprehensible rather than the incomprehensible. This dovetails with Swanson's (2000) finding that the success of students with learning disabilities was influenced by sequencing (e.g., breaking down activities, sequencing short activities), segmenting (e.g., dividing a target skill into parts and then synthesizing them), and controlling difficulty (e.g., sequencing tasks from easy to difficult).

To create expectations of success, expectations critical to strengthening self-efficacy, give struggling learners small, meaningful tasks that they can succeed on if they make a moderate effort. Select tasks that focus on Big Ideas; gradually increase the difficulty and complexity of tasks to match improved ability levels. If, however, learners make excessive errors or respond slowly and laboriously, the original independent and instructional levels may have overestimated their abilities. If so, lower the levels, analyze the task to identify and remove the obstacles to success, and quickly begin re-teaching the prerequisite skills and knowledge critical to success. This may require focused instruction in small interactive groups of three or fewer learners, greater time on tasks with high levels of success, and frequent practice and reinforcement throughout the day. Although this can be labor intensive, lowering difficulty levels and focusing on prerequisite skills and knowledge can produce high success rates, which can strengthen self-efficacy and increase motivation. As Linnenbrink and Pintrich (2003) concludes, "research has shown [that] students are motivated to engage in tasks and achieve when they believe they can accomplish the task" (p. 134).

Start with tasks similar to those on which struggling learners previously achieved success. Generally, success strengthens self-efficacy; failure weakens it (Bandura, 1997; Pintrich & Schunk, 2002; Wigfield, 2004). Moreover, "enactive experiences [student successes and failures] are the most influential source of efficacy belief because they are predicated on the outcomes of personal experiences" (Zimmerman, 2000, p. 88). "Students feel more confident that they can succeed at a task when they have succeeded at that task or at similar ones in the past" (Ormrod, 2003, p. 347).Together, these findings underscore the importance of ensuring that struggling learners' academic experiences are successful, as they influence self-efficacy beliefs.

To capitalize on struggling learners' past successes, and to help them anticipate success on present tasks, teachers might compare present to previous tasks on which learners succeeded or demonstrate to them how previously mastered strategies will likely produce success on the present task. In other words, incrementally introduce tasks that differ only slightly from those on which learners previously succeeded or give them tasks on which previously learned strategies will likely produce success.

Help struggling learners appreciate the value of tasks. Struggling learners are more likely to carry out difficult tasks they value than those they do not (Linnenbrink & Pintrich, 2002; Pintrich & De Groot, 1990; Pintrich & Schunk, 2002; Zimmerman, 2001). In other words, students will more likely engage in tasks they believe are "worth the effort" than those "not worth it" (Alderman, 2004; Good & Brophy, 2003; Horner & Shwery, 2002; Ormrod, 2003; Pintrich & Schunk, 2002; Schunk, 2001; Stipek, 1998; Zimmerman, 2001). Believing tasks are "worth the effort" relates to the importance and interest students assign to them and to the degree they believe the tasks relate to their goals (Horner & Shwery, 2002; Linnenbrink & Pintrich, 2002; Pintrich & De Groot, 1990; Stipek, 1998).

Thus, it's important to assign tasks that struggling learners immediately value—tasks they think are interesting or are important enough to help them achieve a personal goal—tasks like writing a letter to a brother in Iraq, reading an article on a topic of interest, earning the grade point average needed to play varsity basketball, reading instructions on downloading songs from the Internet. If, as is often true, a task's value is not immediately apparent, teachers should discuss how the task relates to students' daily lives and goals and how task success will benefit them.

Teach specific step-by-step strategies. Strategy instruction can be effective in assisting struggling learners to improve academic performance (De La Paz, 1999; Graham, Harris, & Troia, 2000; Lenz et al., 2004; Swanson, 2000; Vaughn et al.,

2000). In summarizing the literature on Self-Regulated Strategy Development (SRSD), a writing strategy, De La Paz, Owen, Harris, and Graham (2000) concluded, "SRSD has made significant and meaningful differences in children's development . . . [resulting in] improvements in four main aspects of students' performance: quality of writing, knowledge of writing, approach to writing, and self-efficacy" (p. 107).

When using strategy instruction, teachers should demonstrate how to use a highly structured, step-by-step learning strategy to achieve success on specific, important tasks at students' instructional level. Make each step explicit by modeling it while using verbal mediation. Teachers should give learners an acronym for the strategy and discuss and review the strategy frequently. Teachers can provide students with written instructions and illustrations for each step while also giving learners task-specific feedback as students review and practice the strategy. Students should explain to teachers when and why they used the strategy as well.

Systematically use other learners to model appropriate strategy usage. Students' self-efficacy can be strengthened by watching peer models, similar to themselves, learn and apply a new strategy. Struggling learners begin to believe they too can learn and use the strategy, which in turn, can strengthen their self-efficacy (Ormrod, 2003; Pintrich & Schunk, 2002; Schunk, 2001; Schunk & Zimmerman, 1997a). To increase the likelihood of success, peer models should, while successfully learning and carrying out the strategy, verbalize each step. Teachers and the peers should have the learners repeat or paraphrase the models' statements and discuss the strategy with them. Teachers and peer models then have to build in opportunities for struggling learners to practice the strategy while giving them task-specific feedback to increase the likelihood of success.

Often, peer models that also have had difficulty learning new skills and concepts are more effective in helping observing students learn than same-age models who quickly demonstrate mastery. Schunk, Hanson, and Cox (1987), for example, reports that students "who observed a single peer model coping with initial difficulties but gradually learning to work fraction problems demonstrated higher self-efficacy for learning, training performance, posttest self-efficacy and skill, and judged themselves more similar in competence to the model, compared with children who observed a single peer mastery model" (p. 60).

Give struggling learners frequent, immediate feedback when teaching something new. Properly phrased feedback can be highly motivating; it can help strengthen students' interest, persistence, and self-efficacy (Guthrie & Humenick, 2004; Schunk, 1999, 2003; Schunk & Zimmerman, 1997b). In analyzing much of the literature on motivating students to read, Guthrie and Humenick concluded that "combinations of specific goals and feedback can increase students' self-efficacy, which translates into higher effort and devotion to reading. . . . The concreteness of the goal, and information about progress toward the goal . . . foster students' motivational processes of self-efficacy and increase their confidence as readers" (pp. 337–338). In other words, teachers' use of properly phrased feedback enables struggling learners to continue to read extensively, which is a critical factor in developing reading abilities and positive attitudes toward reading (Allington & Cunningham, 2002). Thus, the structured feedback from teachers allows struggling learners to maintain their self-efficacy or confidence for reading, which in turn enables them to continue to engage in the process of reading.

When learning something new, struggling learners often make mistakes. In such situations, teacher feedback is critical, especially corrective feedback that permits them to improve their performance and clarifies what was done correctly. For feedback to be effective, it should be immediate, credible, and task-relevant: "Ryan, you used the TELLS strategy. You studied the story title, examined the page for clue words, and looked for important words. That's why you found six clue words and three important words. You made progress—you found twice as many clue words as you did yesterday. Great job." Such feedback is sensitive, positive, discrete, and informative—it reinforces the strategy by telling learners why they succeeded (Good & Brophy, 2003; Konold, Miller, & Konold, 2004; Pintrich & Schunk, 2002; Schunk, 1999, 2001; Schunk & Zimmerman, 1997a).

Provide multiple opportunities for guided and independent practice. Swanson (2000) found that effective remedial instruction required practice. Willingham (2004) underscored the importance of extensive practice: "For a new skill to become automatic or for new knowledge to become long-lasting, sustained practice, *beyond the point of mastery,* is necessary" (p. 31). Moreover, to avoid learning bad habits and skills, what is practiced must be correct. In other words, independent practice is most appropriate when students are at the accuracy level of learning and are moving on to the fluency phase. In supporting the development of accuracy, teachers should provide fairly immediate corrective feedback during guided practice—practice that takes place shortly after an initial concept or skill is taught (Mastropieri & Scruggs, 2004).

Teachers can have struggling learners frequently practice newly acquired skills and strategies with independent and instructional level materials they find interesting. Start with guided practice, to provide feedback and help learners understand how to correct mistakes. As learners' confidence, accuracy, and speed increase—when they achieve a high rate of success and can self-correct their mistakes—stress lightly supervised or independent practice and opportunities for learners to apply their new skills and knowledge in different situations (Mastropieri & Scruggs, 2004).

Help struggling learners set short-term goals of moderate challenge. Personally relevant goals—especially short-term, moderately challenging ones—energize and motivate students (Ormrod, 2003; Pintrich & Schunk, 2002; Schunk, 2003; Schunk & Zimmerman, 1997b). Goals are what students want to do, get, or achieve. As Rock (2004) noted, "goals must be reasonable, but not too easy, and students must perceive goals as 'under their control'" (p. 66). In analyzing the literature on reading motivation and achievement, Guthrie and Humenick (2004) found that content learning goals substantially increased both students' motivation and comprehension. In addition, when struggling learners are directly involved in setting goals for themselves, they are more invested and therefore more likely to achieve those goals, which in turn fuels self-efficacy (Deci & Chandler, 1986; Deci et al., 2000; Wehmeyer, 1996; Wehmeyer, Palmer, Agran, Mithaug, & Martin, 2000).

Struggling learners may fail to understand the importance of schoolwork and its relation to their goals, especially when schoolwork is perceived to be busy work or when teachers have not assisted learners to make these connections. Teachers can counter this tendency by meeting with struggling learners to set short-term goals they believe are important and achievable and to then assist them in gauging progress (Ames, 1990; Pintrich & Schunk, 2002; Rock, 2004). If they fall short of the mark, teachers will need to quickly intervene (i.e., show, describe, and reinforce the correct use of simple strategies likely to improve performance). Goals that learners believe are moderately challenging are far more motivating than goals they believe too easy or too difficult (Ames, 1990; Pintrich & Schunk, 2002; Stipek, 1998; Taylor, Harris, Pearson, & Garcia, 1995)—so teachers must assist students in choosing personally important, moderately challenging goals they can achieve with moderate effort.

Make struggling learners aware of their success. To increase students' self-efficacy and motivation, teachers can help students become more aware of their progress. Schunk (2003) suggests that "goal progress and accomplishment convey to students that they are capable of performing well, which enhances self-efficacy for continued learning" (pp. 160, 162). Fortunately, if materials and activities are at struggling learners' independent or instructional levels, this is relatively easy as learners will likely experience high rates of success.

To make progress obvious, teachers should consider meeting with learners frequently and privately to review and chart their progress (Pemberton, 2003). Teachers should also review what learners did that resulted in success and how they can better their performance. When possible, teachers can use visual displays to emphasize progress, as "displays that compare earlier successful attempts . . . with later ones can be powerful, tangible indicators to convince individuals of their capability" (McCabe, 2003, p. 17).

To promote independence, teach struggling learners how to monitor their progress for themselves. This need not be difficult, even for students with learning disabilities and attention problems. According to Shimabukuro, Prater, Jenkins, and Edelen-Smth (1999), "self-monitoring procedures were easy to learn and implement . . . and did not require . . . a lot of time closely monitoring the students" (p. 409). Additionally, these researchers found that teaching these students how to self-monitor and self-graph their progress improved their academic productivity and on-task behavior. Take the old adage, "Nothing succeeds like success," a little further: "Nothing succeeds like obvious, measured, ongoing, recognized success."

Use attribution feedback and teach learners to do the same. Attribution feedback and training are often successful in improving the attributions and academics of struggling learners (Robertson, 2000). Pintrich and Schunk (2002) found that "students can be taught to attribute outcomes to effort and that effort feedback produces beneficial effects on self-efficacy, motivation, and skills" (p. 320). Attributing success to the correct use of strategies also enhances self-efficacy and motivation as does combining strategy instruction with attribution training (Pintrich & Schunk, 2002). Borkowski, Weyhing, and Carr (1988), for example, found that students with learning disabilities who received a combination of summarization strategy instruction and attribution training about the efficiency of the strategy had greater improvements in reading comprehension than peers receiving only strategy instruction. Similarly, Chan (1996) found that combining reading strategy instruction with attribution training that attributed success to effective use of strategies and failure to ineffective use improved the reading comprehension and attributions of poor readers.

When learners succeed, tell them that they were responsible for their success: they made the effort, they persisted, and they correctly used the right strategy. Because they can control effort, persistence, and strategy use, they can repeat their success. When they do poorly on independent or instructional level tasks, stress the same controllable factors: they made a poor effort, they did not persist, or they used the wrong strategy or they used the right strategy incorrectly (Alderman, 2004; Ormrod, 2003; Pintrich & Schunk, 2002; Robertson, 2000). Of course, comments need to accurately reflect learners' effort, persistence, and strategy use. Afterwards, privately ask learners to explain why they succeeded or had difficulty and what they will do next time to ensure success.

Make encouraging comments and provide needed information. Verbal encouragement—a form of verbal persuasion—can improve self-efficacy, achievement, and commitment to attaining goals (Zimmerman, 2000). "Persuasive statements (e.g. 'I know that you can do this') can raise self-efficacy" (Schunk, 2001, p. 127), which in turn, can encourage struggling learners to temporarily involve themselves in schoolwork.

To persuade struggling learners to involve themselves in an activity, teachers must provide timely, focused, encouraging comments that promote effort, persistence, and correct strategy use with instructional or independent level materials and tasks (Pajares, 2002; Pintrich & Schunk, 2002; Schunk, 2001). If learners have difficulty, teachers must provide the explicit information students need to address the difficulty (Ames, 1990; Salend, 2001). Teachers' use of encouraging comments that provide important information about how to do better can transform pessimistic mind-sets into optimistic expectations. Teachers, however, must not use encouraging comments with frustration level materials and tasks; as repeatedly making encouraging comments in these situations erodes credibility.

Reward struggling learners for successfully completing tasks they think are boring or valueless. When struggling learners view tasks as boring or valueless, they are unlikely to become sufficiently engaged. Until they see their value or until they think about them and cognitively manipulate the critical concepts, they may need extrinsic rewards powerful enough to engage them cognitively. In such cases, teachers need to help students understand how task mastery can assist them while extrinsically rewarding them for reasonable efforts.

> Rewards are motivating because people expect that behaving in a given fashion will be rewarded. This belief, coupled with perceived importance or value of the reward, leads people to act in ways they believe will result in reward attainment . . . Rewards can also inform learners about their progress in skill acquisition and thereby sustain motivation. (Pintrich & Schunk, 2002, p. 322)

Over time and commensurate with success and positive perceptions of tasks, the frequency of extrinsic rewards can be reduced and eventually eliminated. While rewarding learners, teachers should give them a rich diet of materials and tasks likely to capture their interest. Eventually, interest, or intrinsic reinforcement, should prevail. In reading, for example, interesting, relevant texts have a powerful, positive influence on both motivation and comprehension (Guthrie & Humenick, 2004).

Surround struggling learners with peers who value learning. Often, peers exert far more influence on struggling learners' behavior and attitudes than do adults (Steinberg, Brown, & Dornbusch, 1996). Peers, for example,

> Offer new ideas and perspectives . . . They serve as role models and provide standards for acceptable behavior, showing what is possible, what is admirable, what is cool. They reinforce one another for acting in ways deemed appropriate for their age, gender, or ethnic group. (Ormrod, 2003, p. 73)

Grouping or tracking struggling learners with other poor achievers, many of whom routinely display unacceptable behavior or disdain for schoolwork, will likely erode struggling learners' motivation, confidence, and achievement

(Allington & Cunningham, 2002; Lipson & Wixson, 2003). To take advantage of potentially positive peer influences, teachers need to regularly involve struggling learners in lively, meaningful activities and discussions with average and high achievers who act in praiseworthy ways and whom the struggling learners respect and value.

One way to do this is to involve struggling learners in collaborative projects or cooperative learning activities or frequent peer sharing. Guthrie and Humenick (2004) suggest that "most students' intrinsic motivation for reading is increased when they can read together, share information, and present their knowledge to others" (p. 350). Of course, to be successful and strengthen self-efficacy, such activities must not exceed the struggling learners' abilities and must not require Herculean efforts (Margolis & McCabe, 2004). The literature on such learning is replete with practical ideas. Feldman and Denti (2001), for example, describe a variety of such activities, including the Think-Pair-Share strategy. In Think-Pair-Share, teachers

- Pose an open ended question (no single answer).
- Provide time for students to think of answers.
- Have students form pairs.
- Designate students in each pair as a "one" or a "two."
- Direct "ones" to share answers for a minute or two, then reverse the process.
- [Teachers then] randomly call on individuals to share with the class. (p. 275)

Capitalize on interests, every day. Teachers need to develop creative strategies for engaging students during the course of instruction. Wigfield et al. (2004), for example, hypothesized that hands-on science activities, as part of a larger program to influence motivation, would spark students' interest and that immediately connecting these activities to interesting texts would positively influence students' self-efficacy and motivation. They found that "children's intrinsic motivation to read (defined as reading curiosity and preference for challenge) increased during the course of the program, as did their self-efficacy for reading" (p. 306). Guthrie and Humenick (2004) also concluded that "interesting texts increase motivation for reading and comprehension of those texts . . . [suggesting that] children are more likely to comprehend texts that they find interesting than texts they do not" (p. 343).

By listening carefully to struggling learners, watching what they orient to, and administering interest inventories, teachers can learn about their interests. Teachers should then use this information every day to provide at least one moderately challenging academic activity students are likely to find interesting. Moderately challenging material increases the likelihood that struggling learners will become intellectually engaged. This, in turn, fosters a willingness to try new tasks, and this willingness is essential for strengthening self-efficacy.

CONCLUSIONS

It is critical that teachers systematically work to strengthen the self-efficacy and academic competence of struggling learners at the secondary level. Without adequate beliefs, borne of experience that they can succeed on moderately challenging tasks, struggling learners are likely to disengage or remain disengaged from mastering the curriculum. As indicated by the disappointing post-school outcomes of former special education students (e.g., Blackorby & Wagner, 1996; Johnson, Stodden, Emanuel, Luecking, & Mack, 2002) and the lack of productive employment and community participation of the vast majority of adults with disabilities (e.g., National Organization on Disability & Lou Harris & Associates, 2000), the effects of this disengagement are likely to be lifelong and debilitating.

While it is often difficult to change self-defeating beliefs about self-efficacy and competency, it can and must be done. Among other things, this requires that teachers and others involved with struggling learners (a) examine their own beliefs about disabilities and competency to assure that they support strengthening struggling learners' competency and self-efficacy; (b) stress success-oriented instructional practices within well-conceptualized curriculum frameworks and principles, such as those suggested by Kameenui and his colleagues (Kameenui & Carnine, 1998); and (c) create multiple opportunities for learners to experience academic success, without which attempts to strengthen self-efficacy will fail.

We know that the drop-out rate for struggling learners is much higher than that of general education students Wagner, Blackorby, and Hebbeler (1993), for example, reported a national drop-out rate for students with learning disabilities of 38%, while most states report dropout rates for students without disabilities at around 10% (Kortering & Braziel, 2002). We also know that the unemployment rate for adults with disabilities is astronomically high, approximately 80% (National Organization on Disability & Lou Harris & Associates, 2000). The time teachers have to change these potential and seemingly inevitable realities for their struggling secondary students is short and precious. If struggling learners are to succeed in high school, teachers must focus on both academic competency and self-efficacy—they go hand in hand. Moreover, the beliefs students hold about their abilities to succeed on specific tasks, their self-efficacy, influence every aspect of their lives. Teachers can and must work to strengthen the self-efficacy of all secondary learners, especially struggling learners.

The higher the sense of efficacy, the greater the effort, persistence, and resilience. Efficacy beliefs also influence individuals' thought patterns and emotional reactions. People with low self-efficacy may believe that things are tougher than they really are, a belief that fosters stress, depression, and a narrow vision of how best to solve a problem. High self-efficacy, on the other hand, helps to create feelings of serenity in approaching difficult tasks and activities. As a result of these influences, self-efficacy beliefs are strong determinants and predictors of the level of accomplishment that individuals finally attain. (Pajares, 1996, p. 544)

REFERENCES

Alderman, M. K. (2004). *Motivation for achievement: Possibilities for teaching and learning* (2nd ed.). Mahwah, NJ: Lawrence Erlbaum.

Allington, R. L. (2001). *What really matters for struggling readers: Designing research-based programs.* NY: Longman.

Allington, R. L., & Cunningham, P. M. (2002). *Schools that work: Where all children read and write* (2nd ed.). Boston: Allyn & Bacon.

Allington, R. L., & Johnston, P. H. (2001). What do we know about effective fourth-grade teachers and their classrooms. In C. M. Roller (Ed.), *Learning to teach reading: Setting the research agenda* (pp. 150–165). Newark, DE: International Reading Association.

Ames, C. A. (1990). Motivation: What teachers need to know. *Teachers College Record, 91,* 409–421.

Bandura, A. (1997). *Self-efficacy: The exercise of control.* New York: W. H. Freeman.

Benz, M., Lindstrom, L., & Yovanoff, P. (2000). Improving graduation and employment outcomes of students with disabilities: Predictive factors and student perspectives. *Exceptional Children, 66,* 509–529.

Blackorby, J., & Wagner, M. (1996). Longitudinal postschool outcomes for youth with disabilities: Findings from the National Longitudinal Transition Study. *Exceptional Children, 62,* 399–413.

Borkowski, J. G., Weyhing, R. S., & Carr, M. (1988). Effects of attributional retraining on strategy-based reading comprehension in learning-disabled students. *Journal of Educational Psychology, 80,* 46–53.

Bowe, F. (2000). *Universal design in education: Teaching nontraditional students.* Westport, CT: Greenwood Publishing Group.

Brown, A. L. (1978). The development of memory: Knowing when, where, and how to remember. A problem of metacognition. In R. Glaser (Ed.), *Advances in instructional psychology* (pp. 77–165). Hillsdale, NJ: Lawrence Erlbaum.

Bryan, T., Burstein, K., & Bryan, J. (2001). Students with learning disabilities: Homework problems and promising practices. *Educational Psychologist, 36,* 167–180.

Chan, L. K. S. (1996). Combined strategy and attributional training for seventh grade average and poor readers. *Journal of Research in Reading, 19,* 111–127.

Deci, E. L., & Chandler, C. L. (1986). The importance of motivation for the future of the LD field. *Journal of Learning Disabilities, 19,* 587–594.

Deci, E. L., Hodges, R., Pierson, L., & Tomassone, J. (2000). Autonomy and competence as motivational factors in students with learning disabilities and emotional handicaps. *Journal of Learning Disabilities, 25,* 457–471.

De La Paz, S. (1999). Self-regulated strategy instruction in regular education settings: Improving outcomes for students with and without learning disabilities. *Learning Disabilities Research & Practice, 14,* 92–106.

De La Paz, S., Owen, B., Harris, K. R., & Graham, S. (2000). Riding Elvis's motorcycle: Using self-regulated strategy development to plan and write for a state writing exam. *Learning Disabilities Research & Practice, 15,* 101–109.

Deshler, D. D., Schumaker, J. B., & Woodruff, S. K. (2004). Improving literacy skills of at-risk adolescents. In D. S. Strickland & D. E. Alvermann (Eds.), *Bridging the literacy achievement gap, grades 4–12* (pp. 86–105). NY: Teachers College Press.

DiPerna, J. C., Volpe, R. J., & Elliott, S. N. (2001). A model of academic enablers and elementary reading/language arts achievement. *School Psychology Review, 31,* 298–312.

Ellis, E. S. (1986). The role of motivation and pedagogy on the generalization of cognitive strategy training. *Journal of Learning Disabilities, 19,* 66–70.

Feldman, K., & Denti, L. (2001). High-access instruction: Practical strategies to increase active learning in diverse classrooms. In L. Denti & P. Tefft-Cousin (Eds.), *New ways of looking at learning disabilities: Connections to classroom practices* (pp. 267–285). Denver, CO: Love Publishing.

Gerber, P. J., Ginsberg, R., & Reiff, H. B. (1992). Identifying alterable patterns to employment success for highly successful adults with learning disabilities. *Journal of Learning Disabilities, 25,* 475–487.

Good, T. L., & Brophy, J. E. (2003). *Looking in classrooms* (9th ed.). Boston: Allyn & Bacon.

Graham, S., Harris, K. R., & Troia, G. A. (2000). Self-regulated strategy development revisited: Teaching writing strategies to struggling writers. *Topics in Language Disorders, 20(4),* 1–14.

Grigal, M., Neubert, D. A., Moon, M. S., & Graham, S. (2003). Self-determination for students with disabilities: Views of parents and teachers. *Exceptional Children, 70,* 97–112.

Grolnick, W. S., & Ryan, R. M. (1990). Self-perception, motivation, and adjustment in children with learning disabilities: A multiple group comparison study. *Journal of Learning Disabilities, 23,* 177–184.

Guthrie, J. T., & Davis, M. H. (2003). Motivating struggling readers in middle school through an engagement model of classroom practice. *Reading & Writing Quarterly: Overcoming Learning Difficulties, 19,* 59–86.

Guthrie, J. T., & Humenick, N. M. (2004). Motivating students to read: Evidence for classroom practices that increase reading motivation and achievement. In P. McCardle & V. Chhabra (Eds.), *The voice of evidence in reading research* (pp. 329–354). Baltimore: Paul H. Brookes.

Heron, T. E., & Harris, K. C. (2001). *The educational consultant: Helping professionals, parents, and students in inclusive classrooms* (4th ed.). Austin: Pro-Ed.

Horner, S. L., & Shwery, C. S. (2002). Becoming an engaged, self-regulated reader. *Theory into Practice, 41,* 102–109.

Hughes, C. A., Ruhl, K. L., Schumaker, J. B., & Deshler, D. D. (2002). Effects of instruction in an assignment completion strategy on the homework performance of students with learning disabilities in general education classes. *Learning Disability Research & Practice, 17,* 1–18.

Jensen, J., Lingren, M., Andersson, K., Ingvar, D.,& Levander, S. (2000). Cognitive intervention in unemployed individuals with reading and writing disabilities. *Applied Neuropsychology, 7,* 223–236.

Johnson, D. R., Stodden, R. A., Emanuel, E. J., Luecking, R., & Mack, M. (2002). Current challenges facing secondary education and transition services: What research tells us. *Exceptional Children, 68,* 519–531.

Kameenui, E. J., & Carnine, D. W. (1998). *Effective teaching strategies that accommodate diverse learners.* Columbus, OH: Merrill.

Kameenui, E. J., Carnine, D. W., & Dixon, R. C. (1998). Introduction. In E. J. Kameenui & D. W. Carnine (Eds.), *Effective teaching strategies that accommodate diverse learners* (pp. 1–17). Columbus, OH: Merrill.

Konold, K. E., Miller, S. P., & Konold, K. B. (2004). Using teacher feedback to enhance student learning. *Teaching Exceptional Children, 36,* (6), 64–69.

Kortering, J., & Braziel, P. (1999). School dropout from the perception of former students: Implications for secondary special education programs. *Remedial and Special Education, 20*(2), 78–83.

Kortering, J., & Braziel, P. (2002). A look at high school programs as perceived by youth with learning disabilities. *Learning Disability Quarterly, 25*(*Summer*), 177–188.

Lan, W., & Lanthier, R. (2003). Changes in students' academic performance and perceptions of school and self before dropping out of schools. *Journal of Education for Students Placed at Risk, 8,* 309–332.

Lenz, K. L., Deshler, D. D., & Kissam, B. R. (2004). *Teaching content to all: Evidence-based inclusive practices in middle and secondary schools.* Boston: Allyn & Bacon.

Linnenbrink, E. A., & Pintrich, P. R. (2002). Motivation as an enabler for academic success. *School Psychology Review, 31,* 313–327.

Linnenbrink, E. A., & Pintrich, P. R. (2003). The role of self-efficacy beliefs in student engagement and learning in the classroom. *Reading & Writing Quarterly: Overcoming Learning Difficulties, 19,* 119–137.

Lipson, M. Y., & Wixson, K. K. (2003). *Assessment and instruction of reading disability: An interactive approach* (3rd ed.). NY: Longman.

Manset, G., & Wasburn, S. (2000). Equity through accountability? Mandatory minimum competency exit examinations for secondary students with learning disabilities. *Learning Disability Research & Practice, 15,* 160–167.

Margolis, H., & McCabe, P. P. (1997). Homework challenges for students with reading and writing problems: Suggestions for effective practice. *Journal of Educational & Psychological Consultation, 8,* 41–74.

Margolis, H., & McCabe, P. P. (2003). Self-efficacy: A key to improving the motivation of struggling learners. *Preventing School Failure, 47,* 162–169.

Margolis, H., & McCabe, P. P. (2004). Resolving struggling readers' homework difficulties: A social cognitive perspective. *Reading Psychology, 25,* 225–260.

Mastropieri, M. A., & Scruggs, T. E. (2004). *The inclusive classroom: Strategies for effective instruction* (2nd ed.). Upper Saddle River, NJ: Pearson Merrill Prentice Hall.

McCabe, P. P. (2003). Enhancing self-efficacy for high-stakes reading tests. *The Reading Teacher, 57*(1), 12–20.

McCormick, S. (2003). *Instructing students who have literacy problems* (4th ed.). Upper Saddle River, New Jersey: Merrill/Prentice Hall.

Michaels, C. A. (1997). Preparation for employment: Counseling practices for promoting personal competency. In P. J. Gerber & D. S. Brown (Eds.), *Learning disabilities and employment* (pp. 187–214). Austin, TX: Pro-Ed.

Morningstar, M. E., Turnbull, A. P., & Turnbull, H. R. (1995). What do students with disabilities tell us about the importance of family involvement in the transition from school to adult life? *Exceptional Children, 62,* 249–260.

National Organization on Disability, Lou Harris and Associates (2000). *The NOD/Harris Survey Program on Participation and Attitudes: Survey of Americans with Disabilities.* Washington, DC: National Organization on Disability.

Orkwis, R. (2003). *Universally Designed Instruction.* (Report No. RIENOV2003). Arlington, VA: Clearinghouse on Disabilities and Gifted Education. (ERIC Document Reproduction Service No. ED475386)

Ormrod, J. E. (2003). *Educational psychology: Developing learners* (4th ed.). Upper Saddle River, NJ: Prentice Hall.

Pajares, F. (1996). Self-efficacy beliefs in academic settings. *Review of Educational Research, 66,* 543–578.

Pajares, F. (2002). *Overview of social cognitive theory and of self-efficacy.* Retrieved July 27, 2004, from http://www.emory.edu/education/mfp/eff.html

Pajares, F. (2003). Self-efficacy beliefs, motivation, and achievement in writing: A review of the literature. *Reading & Writing Quarterly: Overcoming Learning Difficulties, 19,* 139–158.

Pajares, F., & Schunk, D. H. (2001). Self-beliefs and school success: Self-efficacy, self-concept, and school achievement. In R. Riding & S. Rayner (Eds.), *Self-perception* (pp. 239–266). London: Ablex.

Pearl, R., Bryan, R., & Donahue, M. (1980). Learning disabled children's attributions for success and failure. *Learning Disabilities Quarterly, 3,* 3–9.

Pemberton, J. B. (2003). Communicating academic progress as a integral part of assessment. *Teaching Exceptional Children, 35*(4), 16–20.

Pintrich, P. R., & De Groot, E. V. (1990). Motivational and self-regulated learning components of classroom academic performance. *Journal of Educational Psychology, 82,* 33–40.

Pintrich, P.R., & Schunk, D.H. (1996). *Motivation in education: Theory, research and applications.* Englewood Cliffs, NJ: Prentice Hall Merrill.

Pintrich, P. R., & Schunk, D. H. (2002). *Motivation in education: Theory, research, and applications* (2nd ed.). Englewood Cliffs, NJ: Prentice Hall.

Raskind, M. H., Goldberg, R. J., Higgins, E. L., & Herman, K. L. (2002). Teaching "life lessons" to students with LD: Lessons learned from a 20-year study. *Intervention in School and Clinic, 37,* 201–208.

Reiff, H. B., Gerber, P. J., & Ginsberg, R. (1997). *Exceeding expectations: Successful adults with learning disabilities.* Austin, TX: Pro-Ed.

Reiff, H. B., Ginsberg, R., & Gerber, P. J. (1995). New perspectives on teaching from successful adults with learning disabilities. *Remedial and Special Education, 16,* 29–37.

Robertson, J. S. (2000). Is attribution training a worthwhile classroom intervention for K–12 students with learning difficulties? *Educational Psychology Review, 12,* 111–134.

Rock, M. L. (2004). Transfiguring it out: Converting disengaged learners to active participants. *Teaching Exceptional Children, 56*(5), 64–72.

Salend, S. J. (2001). *Creating inclusive classrooms: Effective and reflective practices* (4th ed.). Upper Saddle River, NJ: Merrill.

Salvia, J., & Ysseldyke, J. E. (2001). *Assessment* (8th ed.). Boston: Houghton Mifflin Company.

Schunk, D. H. (1999). Social-self interaction and achievement behavior. *Educational Psychologist, 34,* 219–227.

Schunk, D. H. (2001). Social cognitive theory and self-regulated learning. In B. J. Zimmerman & D. H. Schunk (Eds.), *Self-regulated learning and academic achievement: Theoretical perspectives* (pp. 125–151). Mahwah, NJ: Erlbaum.

Schunk, D. H. (2003). Self-efficacy for reading and writing: Influence of modeling, goal setting, and self-evaluation. *Reading & Writing Quarterly: Overcoming Learning Difficulties, 19,* 159–172.

Schunk, D. H., Hanson, A. R., & Cox, P. D. (1987). Peer-model attributes and children's achievement behaviors. *Journal of Educational Psychology, 79,* 54–61.

Schunk, D. H., & Zimmerman, B. J. (1997a). Developing self-efficacious readers and writers: The role of social and self-regulatory processes. In J. T. Guthrie & A. Wigfield (Eds.), *Reading engagement: Motivating readers through integrated instruction* (pp. 34–50). Newark, DE: International Reading Association.

Schunk, D. H., & Zimmerman, B. J. (1997b). Social origins of self-regulatory competence. *Educational Psychologist, 32,* 195–208.

Shimabukuro, S. M., Prater, M. A., Jenkins, A., & Edelen-Smth, P. (1999). The effects of self-monitoring of academic performance on students with learning disabilities and ADD/ADHD. *Education and Treatment of Children, 22,* 397–414.

Simmons, D. C., & Kameenui, E. T. (1996). A focus on curriculum design: When children fail. *Focus on Exceptional Children, 28*(7), 1–16.

Steinberg, L., Brown, B., & Dornbusch, S. (1996). *Beyond the classroom: Why school reform has failed and what parents need to do.* NY: Simon & Schuster..

Stipek, D. (1998). *Motivation to learn: From theory to practice* (3rd ed.). Boston: Allyn & Bacon.

Swanson, H. L. (2000). What instruction works for students with learning disabilities? Summarizing the results from a meta-analysis of intervention studies. In R. Gersten, E. P. Schiller, & S. Vaughn (Eds.), *Contemporary special education research: Synthesis of the knowledge base on critical instructional issues* (pp. 1–30). Mahwah, NJ: Lawrence Erlbaum.

Taylor, B., Harris, L.A., Pearson, P. D., & Garcia, G. (1995). *Reading difficulties: Instruction and assessment* (2nd ed.). NY: McGraw-Hill.

Torgesen, J. K. (1977a). Memorization processes in reading disabled children. *Journal of Educational Psychology, 69,* 571–578.

Torgesen, J. K. (1977b). The role of nonspecific factors in the task performance of learning disabled children: A theoretical assessment. *Journal of Learning Disabilities, 10,* 27–34.

Vaughn, S., Gersten, R., & Chard, D. J. (2000). The underlying message in LD intervention research: Findings from research syntheses. *Exceptional Children, 67,* 99–114.

Wagner, M., Blackorby, J., & Hebbeler, K. (1993). *Beyond the report card: The multiple dimensions of secondary school performance of students with disabilities. A report from the national longitudinal transition study of special education students.* Menlo Park, CA: SRI International.

Wehmeyer, M. (1996). Self-determination for youth with significant cognitive disabilities—From theory to practice. In L. E. Powers, G. H. S. Singer, & J. Sowers (Eds.), *Promoting self-competence in children and youth with disabilities: On the road to autonomy* (pp. 115–133). Baltimore: Paul H. Brookes.

Wehmeyer, M. L., & Lawrence, M. (1995). Whose future is it anyway? Promoting student involvement in transition planning. *Career Development for Exceptional Individuals, 18,* 69–83.

Wehmeyer, M. L., & Palmer, S. B. (2003). Adult outcomes for students with cognitive disabilities three-years after high school: The impact of self-determination. *Education and Training in Developmental Disabilities, 38,* 131–144.

Wehmeyer, M. L., Palmer, S. B., Agran, M., Mithaug, D. E., & Martin, J. E. (2000). Promoting causal agency: The self-determined model of instruction. *Exceptional Children, 66*(4), 439–453.

Wigfield, A. (2004). Motivation for reading during the early adolescent and adolescent years. In D. S. Strickland & D. E. Alvermann (Eds.), *Bridging the literacy achievement gap, grades 4–12* (pp. 56–69). NY: Teachers College Press.

Wigfield, A., Guthrie, J. T., Tonks, S., & Perencevich, K. C. (2004). Children's motivation for reading: Domain specificity and instructional influences. *The Journal of Educational Research, 97,* 299–309.

Willingham, D. T. (2004). Practice makes perfect—but only if you practice beyond the point of perfection. *American Educator, 28*(1), 31–33, 38–39.

Wilson, G. L., & Michaels, C. A. (2000). Competency and learning disabilities. In *Their world* (pp. 73–76). New York: National Center for Learning Disabilities.

Wong, B. Y. (1991). The relevance of metacognition to learning disabilities. In B. Y. Wong (Ed.), *Learning about learning disabilities* (pp. 232–258). San Diego, CA: Academic Press.

Wong, B. Y., & Wong, R. (1986). Study behavior as a function of metacognitive knowledge about critical task variables: An investigation of above average, average, and learning disabled readers. *Learning Disabilities Research, 1,* 101–111.

Zickel, J. P., & Arnold, E. (2001). Putting the I in IEP. *Educational Leadership, 59*(3), 71–73.

Zimmerman, B. J. (2000). Self-efficacy: An essential motive to learn. *Contemporary Educational Psychology, 25,* 82–91.

Zimmerman, B.J. (2001). Theories of self-regulated learning and academic achievement: An overview and analysis. In B. J. Zimmerman & D. H. Schunk (Eds.), *Self-regulated learning and academic achievement: Theoretical perspectives* (pp. 1–37). Mahwah, NJ: Lawrence Erlbaum.

Chapter Six

PEER-ASSISTED LEARNING STRATEGIES: AN EFFECTIVE INTERVENTION FOR YOUNG READERS

Paul L. Morgan, Ph.D.

The Pennsylvania State University

Caresa Young, Doctoral Candidate

Peabody College of Vanderbilt University

Douglas Fuchs, Ph.D.

Peabody College of Vanderbilt University

What Type of Reading Instruction Do Young Children Need?

There is an emerging consensus about the skills that young children need to become proficient readers (e.g., Adams, 1990; National Institute of Child Health and Human Development [NICHD], 2000; Pressley, 2002; Snow, Burns, & Griffin, 1998). These skills include acquiring phonological awareness, understanding the alphabetic principle, reading fluently, developing an adequate vocabulary, and gaining comprehension skills (NICHD). Mastering these skills quickly is considered critical. Indeed, children who enter first or second grade without them are often considered "at risk" both for continued reading failure and other undesirable long-range outcomes. For example, children displaying severe reading deficits by third grade are far more likely to grow up to be adjudicated, incarcerated, and poor (Adams; Smith, 1998; Snow et al.).

Two types of research point to the importance of these reading skills. First, many longitudinal studies indicate that children who fail to acquire critical reading skills soon after entering school grow up to be poor readers. For example, Juel (1988) reported a probability of .88 that a child who ended first grade with poor phonemic awareness remained a poor reader in fourth grade. Francis, Shaywitz, Stuebing, Shaywitz, and Fletcher (1996) reported a probability of .74 that a child who struggled with reading in third grade remained a poor reader in ninth grade. These longitudinal studies indicate that early reading difficulties often become chronic problems, particularly if they go undetected and unremediated more than a year or two after children start school. Although teachers sometimes feel that struggling readers will "catch up" after another year or two of formal instruction, this in fact rarely occurs (e.g., Vellutino, Scanlon, & Lyon, 2000).

Second, many experimental studies indicate that providing children with explicit instruction in these skills often helps them become better readers (e.g., O'Connor, Notari-Syverson, & Vadasy, 1996, 1998; Rashotte, MacPhee, & Torgesen, 2001; Torgesen & Davis, 1996; Torgesen et al., 1999; Uhry & Shepherd, 1997; Vellutino et al., 1996). Whereas the longitudinal studies show that most children without good decoding skills experience later reading failure, the experimental studies show that explicitly teaching such skills helps prevent it. Taken together, the longitudinal and experimental studies strongly suggest that poor decoding ability is the reason most children initially struggle with reading (Pressley, 2002).

This is not to say, however, that teachers need only to teach children how to decode. Decoding instruction works best when combined with classroom practices that help keep children interested in learning to read (e.g., Dahl & Freppon, 1995; Foorman, Francis, Fletcher, Schatschneider, & Mehta, 1998; Turner, 1995; Xue & Meisels, 2004). These practices are important because "word study is all too often a dull activity that does not sustain interest" (Baker, 2000, p. 29). For example, Foorman et al. found that students in phonics classes held more negative attitudes towards reading than those in whole-language classes. Hoffman et al. (1998) found that first grade teachers and students were less motivated when traditional basals with isolated skills instruction were used in beginning reading programs rather than high-quality literature. Palincsar and Klenk (1992) described children in special education classrooms who were "mired in materials that both children and teacher found to be uninteresting and largely irrelevant to their lives" (p. 218). Although it promotes critical skill development, decoding instruction alone sometimes fails to keep children's interest in reading from flagging. This is problematic because low levels of task-engagement lead to less academic growth. For example, Greenwood, Delquadri, and Hall (1989) found that students with learning disabilities "lost" about one month of instruction each year as a result of being less engaged in classroom activities.

Challenges to Providing the Instruction that Young Readers Need

Teaching children to decode in a way that remains engaging poses many challenges. There are at least three reasons for this. First, teachers increasingly lead classrooms of children displaying a wide range of ability levels. Such academic diversity makes it difficult to provide decoding instruction that engages all children equally (D. Fuchs, Fuchs, Mathes, & Simmons, 1997). Second, teachers sometimes lack a good grasp of either (a) the skills young children need to acquire to become readers (e.g., McCutchen et al., 2002; Moats & Lyon, 1996) or (b) the practices that help bolster children's interest in reading (e.g., Bogner, Raphael, & Pressley, 2002). Third, the experimental studies establishing the effectiveness of decoding instruction have often used interventions that teachers might find difficult to use in their classrooms. For example, these interventions typically have taken place in small groups or through one-to-one tutoring outside of the regular classroom (e.g., O'Connor et al., 1996; O'Connor 2000) for long amounts of time (e.g., Torgesen et al., 1999; Vellutino et al., 1996). Given these challenges, how can teachers effectively provide necessary decoding instruction that engages all their students and yet remains easy to implement and use?

The Development of Peer-Assisted Learning Strategies (PALS)

PALS is our attempt to help classroom teachers meet these challenges. Like the intervention that inspired it (i.e., Classwide Peer Tutoring [CWPT], Delquadri, Greenwood, Whorton, Carta, & Hall, 1986), PALS is a type of peer-mediated instruction. In both CWPT and PALS, teachers reorganize their class-rooms into pairs of students. These same-age pairs work together to master both basic skills and higher-order strategies. As a result, peer-tutoring helps "decenter" the classroom. Children actively collaborate with their peers rather than passive-ly watching and listening to their teacher lead the lessons. Increasing the num-ber of opportunities for children to interact while reading is thought to be a good way to bolster children's interest in word study (e.g., Baker, 2000). In addi-tion, by "loosening the straight-jacketed nature of traditional classrooms" (D. Fuchs et al., 1997, p. 178), peer-tutoring helps teachers better facilitate children's learning and more closely monitor their progress. These practices are also thought to help bolster task engagement (e.g., Bogner et al., 2002).

PALS was also developed to keep children's interest-level high. First, the activities require children to work on many different skills during any one les-son. For example, in First-Grade PALS, children work on letter-sound corre-spondence, word recognition, and fluency-building tasks. Thus, each PALS les-son is made up of several mini-lessons. Mini-lessons help maintain high levels of task engagement (e.g., Bogner et al., 2002). Second, each PALS activity is fast-paced and highly structured. During each mini-lesson, children are given fre-quent opportunities to (a) respond to prompts and queries by teachers and peers, (b) receive immediate praise and corrective feedback and (c) exchange tutoring responsibilities. Each of these practices is recognized as a way to increase chil-dren's engagement during instruction (e.g., Gambrell, Mazzoni, & Almasi, 2000; Pressley, 2002; Shunk & Zimmerman, 1997; Simmons, Fuchs, Fuchs, Hodge, & Mathes, 1994; Sutherland & Wehby, 2001; Wigfield, 2000). In short, the PALS lessons are structured to include as many practices as possible that promote task engagement. This reflects a key observation made by many researchers (e.g., Baker, 2000; Gambrell et al., 2000): Teachers who combine or bundle such practices help create classroom environments that are "massively motivational" (Bogner et al., 2002, p. 135) to children learning to read.

Research that Supports PALS

Research shows that PALS improves the decoding skills of young children. In one study of first grade students (D. Fuchs et al., 2001), PALS outperformed controls by about .50 standard deviations on both phonological awareness and word-level measures (i.e., measures involving spelling and reading both non-sense and real words). Children in PALS classrooms who regularly played a short fluency-building game also outperformed controls on fluency and com-prehension measures by .20 to .30 standard deviations. Moreover, PALS has often improved the reading skills of low-achieving, average-achieving, and high-achieving students, as well as students with disabilities (e.g., D. Fuchs et al., 1997; D. Fuchs et al., 2001; Mathes, Howard, Allen, & Fuchs, 1998). For example, in another study, PALS activities increased the reading fluency and comprehension skills of students with LD and both low- and average-achieving students (e.g., D. Fuchs et al., 1997). Although designed as a brief (i.e., about 1.5 hours per week for about 20 weeks) supplemental program, use of PALS can lead to educationally relevant effect sizes of .50 or higher in early reading skills for many different learner types (e.g., Mathes et al). Because the PALS activities help many different types of students, they help classroom teachers better meet the challenge of academic diversity.

These findings on the effectiveness of PALS conform to a best-evidence synthesis of studies assessing peer tutoring in reading with students with disabilities. The average effect size based on 11 studies was .36, with effect sizes ranging from .07 to .75 (Mathes & Fuchs, 1994). Another indication of PALS' effectiveness in improving children's reading skills is that the U. S. Department of Education's Program Effectiveness Panel certified it as a "best-practice."

We know less about how PALS affects children in non-academic ways. However, the initial findings are promising. Positive effects for CWPT on children's academic engagement have already been found (Mortweet et al., 1999). D. Fuchs, Fuchs, Mathes, and Martinez (2002) reported that children with LD participating in PALS classrooms were more socially accepted than their counterparts in no-PALS classrooms. Indeed, children with LD in PALS classrooms enjoyed the same social status as their non-disabled peers. These findings are encouraging because they suggest that PALS can help classroom peers view children with LD as involved, capable partners during reading activities. Informally, classroom teachers report that PALS helps create an engaging classroom environment (see D. Fuchs, Fuchs, & Burish, 2000, for one teacher's insights). L. S. Fuchs, Fuchs, & Kazdan (1999) reported that high school students with serious reading problems held more positive beliefs about working hard to improve their reading after participating in PALS. Other researchers already view PALS as a potential model intervention for bolstering children's motivation to learn to read (Gambrell et al., 2000).

Why PALS Works

As suggested above, we believe that at least two reasons account for PALS' effectiveness. First, PALS lessons help struggling readers master critical reading skills. The activities explicitly target children's phonological awareness, letter-sound knowledge, word recognition, fluency, and comprehension skills. Thus, depending on the grade, children in PALS classrooms learn and practice skills considered necessary (e.g., NICHD, 2000) to become readers. Second, we purposely bundle together many practices thought to maximize children's engagement. Specifically, PALS provides the children with frequent opportunities to: (a) work collaboratively with a peer who models skilled reading; (b) respond to frequent prompts; (c) receive immediate praise and corrective feedback from both their peers and teacher; (d) monitor their progress while mastering these reading skills; and (e) earn points and incentives for making progress in learning to read. PALS may work well because it allows children to learn and practice decoding skills in a way that both children and teachers see as fun.

What Children Do During PALS

Below we describe the PALS activities separately for preschool, kindergarten, and first grade. We focus on the PALS activities in these grades because they involve more decoding practice than the PALS activities used in second grade and beyond. We also highlight practices that keep children's task engagement high as they practice decoding.

Overall, PALS is structured so that young children of different reading levels work together in pairs to practice and master phonological awareness, letter-sound correspondence, decoding, sight-word recognition, and text reading skills. (PALS activities have also been developed for older readers, as well as for early math skills, e.g., L. S. Fuchs, Fuchs, & Karns, 2001.) These activities encourage frequent verbal interactions and feedback between the stronger and weaker readers. Lessons are typically practiced three times a week. For preschoolers, the lessons are shorter (about 15 minutes) and involve more teacher-direction. For kindergartners and first graders, the lessons are longer (about 20 and 35 minutes, respectively) and involve more peer-mediated activities. As noted above, PALS is designed to be a supplement to teachers' regular reading instruction.

For all three levels of PALS, the teacher follows the same general procedures for assigning the Coach and Reader. First, she rates students in the class from highest to lowest based on their reading ability or, for preschoolers, on their general academic readiness. Using this rank-ordered list, the teacher then splits the class in half. The highest-ranked student in the top half is placed with the highest-ranked student in the bottom half. The next-to-highest-ranked student in the top half is placed with the next-to-highest-ranked student in the lower half, and so on.

For each pair, the higher-ranked child is assigned the role of Coach. The lower-ranked partner is assigned the role of Reader. The Coach monitors the Reader and provides corrective feedback when necessary. The Reader reads and cooperates with the Coach. Throughout the PALS lesson, the children take turns being the Coach and Reader. The more highly-skilled reader in each pair is always the Coach first so that he or she can model each part of the lesson. Teachers are always free to reassign pairs who do not work well together. Teachers generally make up new pairs every four weeks to help keep the students' engagement high.

TEACHER-DIRECTED ACTIVITY (5 MIN.)
1. Flashcard review: Show card with 'a.' Say, What letter? Students respond 'a.' Repeat with card 'i.' Show card with apple and 'a.' Say, What sound? Students respond apple, /aaa/. Show igloo with, 'i' card and say, What sound? Students respond igloo, /i/. Show the card with 'p' and say, What letter? Students respond 'p.' Show card with pig and 'p.' Say, What sound? Students respond pig, /p/. Show card with 't.' Say, What letter? Students respond 't.' Show card with toe and 't.' Say, What sound? Students respond toe, /t/. Show card with 's.' Say, What letter? Students respond 's.' Show card with sun and 's.' Say, What sound? Students respond sun, /sss/. Show card with 'n.' Say, What letter? Students respond 'n.' Show card with nine and 'n.' Say, What sound? Students respond nine, /nnn/.
2. Say, You have already learned the letter 'p.' This is the letter 'p.' Display poster with a big 'p' at the top on the left and 't' on the right. Point to 'p' and say, What sound does the letter 'p' say? Students respond /p/.
3. Say, You have also learned the letter 't.' This is the letter 't.' Point to 't' and say, What sound does the letter 't' say? Students respond /t/.
4. Some of our pictures say /p/ and some say /t/. Show paper squares with pictures one at a time. Say, This is a pie. Students repeat pie, /p/. Does pie say /p/? Students respond. Yes, pie says /p/. Paste square on poster under 'p.'
5. Continue with other pictures. If it starts with /p/, say Yes, ___, /p/ ___says /p/. Paste square on poster. If it starts with /t/, say Yes, ___, /t/.___ says /t/. Paste square on poster.
GUIDED STUDENT PRACTICE ACTIVITY (5 MIN.)
1. The teacher gives each student a worksheet with four lines. Each line has a picture on the left and 'p' and 't' printed in large letters to the right.
2. Point to the picture of the pipe on the first line and say, Pipe. (Students repeat.) Then point to the letter 'p' to the right of the pipe and say 'p,' /p/. (Students repeat.) Next point to the letter 't' to the right and say, 't,' /t/. (Students repeat.) Point again to the pipe and say, Does "pipe" say /p/ or /t/? Students say /p/ and mark 'p.' Correct errors as needed.
3. Continue with the next three lines.
PEER-MEDIATED ACTIVITY (5 MIN.)
1. Pair the students and give a worksheet to each "Coach."
2. On the first line, the Coach points to the picture of the pig and says, Pig. Then, Coach points to 'p' and 't' in turn as he or she says, Does pig say /p/ or /t/? Reader says, /p/ and circles 'p.' Coach corrects the Reader as needed. Continue with the next three lines.
3. Students switch roles and teacher gives the new Coach a clean worksheet. The new Coach leads the Reader through the worksheet.

Figure 1. P-PALS teacher reference card

Preschool PALS (P-PALS). Children in P-PALS participate in 60 lessons. In the first 30 lessons, teachers introduce letter names and their respective sounds. In the next 12 lessons, children practice making discriminations among these letter names and letter sounds (e.g., "p" vs. "t" and /p/ vs. /t/). This is done in hopes of strengthening their conceptualization of the letters and sounds. In the final 18 lessons, word families (e.g., "-at," "-it," "-an,") are introduced, as well as onset-rime.

P-PALS teachers typically conduct the lessons during "center time." A teacher's aide often helps supervise the various center activities while the teacher implements P-PALS with four to six children at a time. On a typical day, the teacher works with between two and four groups in succession on the P-PALS lessons. Teachers are provided a reference card to assist with implementing the activities (see Figure 1).

The P-PALS lessons comprise three types of activities. Each lasts five minutes. The first is teacher directed; the second provides students with guided practice; the last is peer-mediated. To better illustrate these three types of activities, we describe how a teacher would use Lesson 11. The goal of Lesson 11 is to help children to discriminate among letter names and sounds.

The teacher-directed component begins with the teacher using flashcards to rehearse letter names and letter sounds with his or her students. The teacher asks, "What letter name?" Students say, "a." The teacher then shows another flashcard. On this card is both a picture of an apple and an "a." Pointing to the "a," the teacher says, "What sound?" Students respond, "apple, /a/." This teacher-student dialogue is repeated for the other letters (e.g., "i," "p," "t").

Next, the teacher helps the students learn to distinguish among different letter names and letter sounds. She presents a conventional paper-sized poster, at

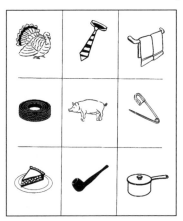

Figure 2. Example P-PALS teacher-directed picture cards

Figure 3. Example P-PALS guided practice worksheet

the top of which are the letters "p" and "t" printed side-by-side. She says, "You've already learned that this is the letter 'p.' What letter?" The students say, "p." The teacher responds, "What sound does 'p' make?" The students reply, "/p/." The teacher repeats this for the letter "t." Pointing to a handful of small squares with pictures of different objects on each (see Figure 2), the teacher then says, "Some of our pictures say /p/; others say /t/." She shows the pictures one at a time, beginning with a pie. She says, "This is a pie." Students say, "pie, /p/." The teacher posts the picture under the large "p" at the top of the poster and continues with the other pictures, placing them under the "p" or the "t."

The teacher also provides opportunities for guided practice. The teacher gives every student a worksheet with four lines (see Figure 3). Each line begins with a picture and a "p" and "t" printed in large letters to the right. The teacher points to the picture of a pipe on the first line and says "pipe." Students repeat the word. She then points to the letter "p" and says "'p,' /p/." Students repeat, "'p,' /p/." The teacher points to the "t," and says "'t,' /t/." Students repeat the letter name and sound. The teacher then points again to the pipe and says, "Does pipe say /p/ or /t/?" Students say, "/p/" and circle the "p." Teacher and students then proceed to the next line.

PHONOLOGICAL SKILL	SOUND PLAY GAME	COACH SAYS	READER SAYS	CORRECTION PROCEDURE	LESSONS
REFERENCE CARD FOR SOUND PLAY GAMES					
Segmentation	Clap the Syllables	"Clap mitten."	"mit (clap) ten (clap)"	Coach claps word correctly, "mit (clap) ten (clap)."	Intro 1, 2
First sound identification	First Sound A (forced choice of 2)	"apple /aaa/, alligator /aaa/, what starts with /a/: ax or hat?"	"ax /a/"	Coach says correct word and its first sound, "ax /a/."	Intro 3, 4 1-4 21-24
First sound identification	First Sound B (forced choice of 3)	"mat /m/, what starts with /m/: milk, table, or strawberry?"	"milk /m/"	Coach says correct word and its first sound, "milk /m/."	5-8 25-28 57-60
Rhyming	Rhyming	"cat, bat, what rhymes with cat and bat--carrot or rat?"	"rat"	Coach says correct word, "rat."	9-12 41-44
Segmentation and Blending	Guess My Word A (word families)	(Touch Coach's box at top of page) "/c/ /a/ /t/, guess my word."	(Touch Reader's boxes above each picture) "/c/ /a/ /t/, cat"	Coach touches Reader's boxes near picture and says, "/c/ /a/ /t/ cat."	13-16 29-32 45-47 65-68
Segmentation and Blending	Guess My Word B (words with same first letter)	(Touch Coach's box at top of page) "/b/ /u/ /s/, guess my word."	(Touch Reader's boxes above each picture) "/b/ /u/ /s/, bus"	Coach touches Reader's boxes near picture and says, "/b/ /u/ /s/ bus."	17-20 33-36
Segmentation and Blending	Guess My Word (mix of words)	(Touch Coach's box at top of page) "/b/ /u/ /s/, guess my word."	(Touch Reader's boxes above each picture) "/b/ /u/ /s/, bus"	Coach touches Reader's boxes near picture and says, "/b/ /u/ /s/ bus."	48-52 61-64
Last sound identification	Last Sound	"cat /t/, boat /t/, what ends with /t/, apple or foot?"	"foot /t/"	Coach says correct word and its last sound, "foot /t/"	37-40 53-56 69-72

Figure 4. K-PALS teacher reference card

To prepare their children for the peer-mediated activities, teachers spend the first several weeks of the P-PALS program assuming the role of Coach of the entire class who act as Readers. Teachers model and explain to their students how to perform as Coach and Reader and how to follow the P-PALS rules.

The peer-mediated segment of Lesson 11 begins by the teacher giving a worksheet to each Coach. The worksheets are very similar to those used in guided student practice. For example, the Coach points to the picture of a pig on the first line and says to her partner, "pig." Then she says, "Does pig say /p/ or /t/," pointing in turn to the "p" and "t." The Reader says, "/p/" and circles the "p." The Coach immediately provides corrective feedback to the Reader as necessary, continuing with the next three lines on the page. Finally, the partners switch roles and the teacher gives the new Coach an unmarked identical worksheet.

Kindergarten PALS (K-PALS). In K-PALS, children learn letter sounds, basic decoding skills, common sight words, and phonological awareness skills. Students are trained in the K-PALS procedures by completing eight lessons over the course

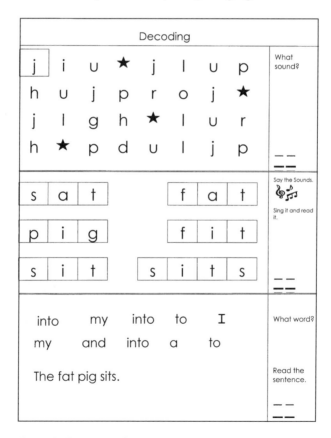

Figure 5. Example K-PALS lesson for sounds and words

Point Sheet
Group: _____

1 ☺	2 ☺	3 ☺	4 ☺	5 ☺	6 ☺	7 ☺	8 ☺	9 ☺	10 ☺
11 ☺	12 ☺	13 ☺	14 ☺	15 ☺	16 ☺	17 ☺	18 ☺	19 ☺	20 ☺
21 ☺	22 ☺	23 ☺	24 ☺	25 ☺	26 ☺	27 ☺	28 ☺	29 ☺	30 ☺
31 ☺	32 ☺	33 ☺	34 ☺	35 ☺	36 ☺	37 ☺	38 ☺	39 ☺	40 ☺
41 ☺	42 ☺	43 ☺	44 ☺	45 ☺	46 ☺	47 ☺	48 ☺	49 ☺	50 ✮

Figure 6. Example K-PALS point sheet

of two weeks. The teachers are given scripted lessons to help train the students. During the training, children practice as Coach and Reader. They also learn the standardized correction and modeling procedures. As in P-PALS, K-PALS teachers are given reference cards to help implement the activities (see Figure 4).

Each K-PALS lesson is divided into two sections. These are Sounds and Words and Sound Play. There are 30 lessons, each of which lasts two days. On the lesson's first day, the teacher introduces a new sound and reviews sounds already learned by the class. On the second day, the children play Sounds and Words and Sound Play. Figure 5 displays an example K-PALS lesson.

During the Sounds and Words day, each pair shares a printed lesson sheet. The first activity targets letter-sound correspondence. The Coach begins by pointing to each letter and asking the Reader, "What sound?" If the Reader responds correctly, the Coach moves on to the next letter. If the Reader responds incorrectly, the Coach says, "Stop. That sounds is /___/. What sound?" In this way, the Reader receives immediate corrective feedback. The Reader is then asked to start the line again. When the Reader finishes saying all of the sounds, he or she marks a smiley face and five points on the point sheet (see Figure 6). The Reader then takes on the role of the Coach and the Coach becomes the Reader.

The second Sounds and Words activity lets children practice segmenting and blending decodable words. The words are made up of only the sounds that have been learned in the current and previous lessons. The Coach asks the Reader to point to the letters in the boxes and to then do three things: (a) sound out the word; (b) sing the sounds; and (c) read the word. If the Reader responds correctly, the Coach moves on to the next word. If the Reader responds incorrectly, the Coach again provides immediate corrective feedback. For example, if the Reader makes a mistake reading "back," the Coach would say, "Stop. That word is b-a-ck, back. Say the sounds. Sing it. Read it." The Reader must then again segment and blend the word. When the pair finishes all the words, the Reader marks a smiley face and five points on the point sheet. The pair then switches jobs.

The third Sounds and Words activity lets children practice reading sight words. Unlike in the preceding activity, these words are not decodable. Consequently, the correction procedure is different. The Coach asks the Reader "What word?" If the Reader incorrectly reads a word, the Coach says, "Stop. That word is _____. What word?" The Reader is then asked to start the line again to provide additional practice on the missed word. When all the words are read, the Reader marks a smiley face and five points.

In the Sound Play segment, children practice phonological awareness in five different ways. Specifically, children practice (a) segmenting syllables, (b) isolating the first sound in a word, (c) recognizing rhymes, (d) blending sounds into words, and (e) isolating the last sound in a word. All Sound Play activities use common pictures of objects or animals. For example, the rhyming activity shows six sets of pictures. The first two pictures rhyme; the child has to pick which of the other two remaining pictures rhymes with the first two pictures. If the first two pictures were "pan" and "van," the Coach would ask the reader, "What rhymes, turkey or man?" The Reader would then reply "man."

First-Grade PALS. Each First-Grade PALS lesson lasts about 35 minutes. As with K-PALS, teachers train students in First-Grade PALS over eight lessons. These eight lessons take place over about two weeks. Teachers are provided with scripted lessons for the training. During training, children practice as both the Coach and the Reader. All students learn the correction and modeling procedures. After the training is completed, teachers implement First-Grade PALS three days each week using a reference card (see Figure 7). Teachers assign pairs using the same Coach and Reader procedures described above.

Each First-Grade PALS lesson has three parts. These are: (a) Teacher-directed Instruction, (b) Sounds and Words, and (c) Partner Reading. These activities are detailed below (see Figure 8 for an example lesson). As in both P- and K-PALS, we actively try to create a classroom atmosphere where students are trying to read quickly and accurately. First, teachers encourage this behavior during the training. Second, we ask teachers to use a countdown timer throughout the year to make sure each of the lesson's activities remain relatively brief. Students soon begin to notice that they are "working against the clock."

PALS REFERENCE CARD
(Weeks 11 to 22: Includes Partner Reading)

HELPFUL HINTS

- Keep a brisk pace.
- Model activities, correction procedures, and PALS rules as needed.
- Reinforce students with praise and points when they follow PALS rules, cooperate with their partners, and use correction procedures.
- Make sure lessons are at the appropriate level of difficulty for each pair. (i.e., Lower-performing student should miss no more than 2 sounds and 2 sight words.)
- Implement PALS Sounds and Words lessons with Partner Reading 3 times a week and Games once a week.

MATERIALS

Teacher:
1. Timer
2. Hearing Sounds lesson
3. Daily Reference card
4. Lesson Sequence
5. Folder with Star Charts and incentives

Students:
1. Folders with lessons, point sheets, Star Charts, book and pencil

- Students move quickly and quietly to PALS places and get materials ready.
- Teacher does "Hearing Sounds" with students (about 3 minutes).
- Teacher introduces new sound(s). See Lesson Sequence.
- Teacher introduces new sight word(s). See Lesson Sequence.
- Partners do: Saying Sounds   3 minutes
                Sounding Out   4 minutes
                Sight Words   3 minutes
- Teacher introduces new rocket words (bolded words on Lesson Sequence) and reviews old rocket words (underlined words on Lesson Sequence) and models reading the story quickly and correctly.
- Partners do: Reading Stories   5 minutes
- Students mark 5 points for each marked happy face.
- Partners do: Speed Game with Stories   6 minutes
- Partners do: Partner Reading   10 minutes
- Students mark 5 points each time they finish their Partner Reading book. Change books when a pair has read the same book four times in a row.
- Students put away materials and return to seats.

Figure 7. First-grade PALS teacher reference card

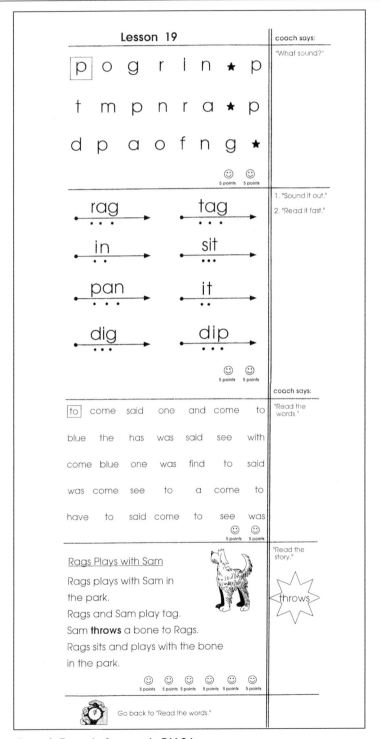

Figure 8. Example first–grade PALS lesson

Children also begin to notice that they can earn more points when they work together diligently.

For the first three minutes of each First-Grade PALS lesson, the teacher introduces new sounds and sight words to the students. The teacher also previews the eight to ten new and old decodable words encountered in the lesson. To increase phonological awareness, the teacher says each word (e.g., "cat") as students hold up a finger for each sound and say each sound that they hear in the word ("c/a/t"). To increase phonemic awareness, the teacher then holds up each word in print and points to each letter as students sound out the word and read it fast.

The Sounds and Words portion of the PALS lesson is printed on lesson sheets that each pair shares. Sounds and Words has four types of activities. Each activity promotes one of four critical reading skills: (a) learning letter-sound correspondence, (b) segmenting and blending words, (c) recognizing sight words, and (d) reading text. To promote automaticity (i.e., quick and accurate reading), we also train students to play a speed game while practicing recognizing sight words or reading text.

For letter-sound correspondence, the Coach points to each letter and asks the Reader, "What sound?" If the Reader responds correctly, the Coach moves on to the next letter. If the Reader responds incorrectly, the Coach says, "Stop. That sound is /___/. What sound?" As in P- and K-PALS, the Reader receives immediate corrective feedback. The Coach then asks the Reader to start the line again. When the Reader finishes all of the sounds, he marks a smiley face and gives himself five points on the point sheet. The Reader then takes on the role of the Coach and the Coach becomes the Reader. Students work together on this activity for three minutes.

In segmenting and blending, the Coach points to the word and tells the Reader, "Sound it out. Read it fast." The Reader points to the dots under the word's letters while sounding out the word and reading it fast. If the Reader responds correctly, the Coach moves on to the next word. If the Reader responds incorrectly, the Coach says, "Stop. That word is b-a-ck, back. Sound it out. Read it fast." The Reader then segments and blends the missed word again. When the pair finishes all the words, they mark a smiley face and five points on their point sheet. The Coach and Reader then switch roles. We introduce approximately 50 words across all of the lessons. For each lesson, students use the same 8 to 10 words that the teacher reviewed during the teacher-directed instruction. All of the words are controlled. That is, they are made up only of sounds learned in the current and previous lessons. The students practice this activity for ten minutes.

In recognizing sight words, the Coach tells the Reader to point and "Read the words." Because these words are not decodable, the Coach says, "Stop. That word is _____. What word?" when the Reader reads a word incorrectly. The Coach then asks the Reader to start the line again. After all the words are read, the pair marks a smiley face and five points. We introduce a total of 113 high frequency words from the 1st-grade Dolch list across the lessons. The students practice reading sight words for five minutes.

Students also play a speed game using the sight words. Each Reader has 30 seconds to read as many of the sight words as possible. The goal is to beat the initial score on one of two subsequent trials. If students beat their score, they color a star on a special chart. When a student completes a chart, he or she can trade the chart in for a small prize such as a pencil or pencil grip.

Lastly, pairs practice reading the decodable and sight words in connected text. The teacher introduces the day's "Rocket Words," which are printed in stars on the lesson sheet. Rocket Words are new words that help make the story more interesting. The teacher then models reading the story out-loud for students. The Coach tells the Reader to "Read the story." If the Reader makes a mistake, the Coach simply points to the missed word and models the correct response. The Reader repeats the missed word and continues reading the story. If the Reader pauses at a word, the Coach gives the Reader three seconds to identify the word before giving the correct answer. When the pair finishes reading the story, they mark a happy face, mark five points, and switch roles.

After about 12 weeks, children begin playing the speed game using text rather than sight words. The game is played in the same way as when students read sight words: Each Reader has 30 seconds to read as much of the story as possible. The Reader then tries to beat his or her score during two subsequent trials. If the student beats his or her score, a star on a special chart is colored. When a child completes a chart, he or she can trade the chart in for a small prize.

The last part of First-Grade PALS, Partner Reading, involves students reading stories appropriate for their reading level. Teachers train students to do Partner Reading in two 20-minute sessions about nine weeks into PALS. To begin Partner Reading, the Coach reads the title of the story and then the Reader reads the title. The Coach reads the next page and the Reader then reads the same page. The pair continues in the same manner—taking turns reading the same page of text—throughout the entire book. When the pair finishes a book, they mark five points on their point sheets. Each pair practices reading a book four times before receiving a new book. Pairs read the same page of text because doing so can be an effective way to increase reading skills and reading comprehension (Meyer & Felton, 1999). Partner Reading is conducted for 10 minutes at the end of the Sounds and Words activities.

DISCUSSION

Both longitudinal and experimental research point to poor decoding skills as a primary reason for children's struggles with learning to read (see Adams, 1990, NICHD, 2000; Pressley, 2002). Some research, however, also suggests that decoding instruction is often a "dull activity" that does not sustain children's interest (e.g., Baker, 2000). How then can teachers provide students with the necessary decoding skills in a way that remains highly engaging? Moreover, how can teachers—who themselves sometimes lack important information both on teaching decoding skills and promoting children's task engagement—meet this challenge while also leading classrooms of students displaying an increasingly wide range of abilities?

Meeting the Challenge with PALS

PALS is our attempt to help classroom teachers meet these challenges. PALS activities target early reading skills considered critical if children are to become proficient readers (e.g., NICHD, 2000). Specifically, children in PALS classrooms practice acquiring phonological awareness, understanding the alphabetic principle, learning to read fluently, acquiring an adequate vocabulary, and developing reading comprehension skills. We target these skills in an age-appropriate way. For example, whereas preschoolers use PALS to practice discriminating letters, first graders use it to practice reading text fluently. There is also a strong emphasis on teaching all young children to learn to decode. For example, children in P-PALS, K-PALS, and First-Grade PALS all learn and practice identifying the sounds that letters make.

To make word-study more engaging, we bundle together a number of practices thought to improve children's task engagement. First, rather than passively watching and listening to their teachers lead lessons, children actively collaborate with their peers to master decoding skills. This "decentering" helps teachers better facilitate children's learning and more closely monitor their progress. Second, PALS activities are put together so that children work on many different skills during any one lesson. For example, in First-Grade PALS, children work on letter-sound correspondence, word recognition, and fluency-building tasks. Thus, each PALS lesson is made up of several mini-lessons. Third, each mini-lesson is fast-paced and highly structured. Children are given frequent opportunities to (a) respond to prompts and queries by teachers and peers, (b) receive immediate praise and corrective feedback, and (c) exchange tutoring responsibilities. Researchers view each of these practices as a way to increase children's engagement during instruction (e.g., Gambrell et al., 2000; Pressley, 2002; Shunk & Zimmerman, 1997; Simmons et al., 1994; Sutherland & Wehby, 2001; Wigfield, 2000). In short, by bundling so many of these activities together, we hope to create "massively motivational" (Bogner et al., 2002, p. 135) classroom contexts where children learning to decode stay highly engaged in the tasks at hand.

There is a considerable amount of evidence suggesting PALS helps children become better readers. Repeated empirical evaluations have shown that PALS bolsters the reading skills of high-, average-, and low-achieving students, as well as students with disabilities (e.g., D. Fuchs et al., 1997; D. Fuchs et al., 2001; Mathes et al., 1998). Because PALS activities help many different types of students, they help classroom teachers better meet the challenge of academic diversity. Some initial findings also suggest that PALS successfully bolsters children's task engagement during reading activities. For example, children with LD working in PALS classrooms have been found to enjoy the same social status as their non-disabled counterparts (D. Fuchs et al., 2002). Other researchers already view PALS as a potential model intervention for bolstering children's motivation as they learn to read (Gambrell et al., 2000).

Concluding Thoughts

Through PALS, we attempt to couple the benefits of decoding instruction with instructional practices that help keep learning to read fun. We provide skills instruction through structured opportunities to practice decoding while also allowing students to interact with a partner offering immediate corrective feedback. Students receive frequent praise from their partners, receive reading-related prizes for completing the activities, and compete with others and themselves in an appropriate manner to promote success. These and the other practices we have described should help boost children's task engagement.

Our findings are quite promising in light of the positive outcomes associated with early success in learning to read (e.g., Adams, 1990). Children who develop reading skills early and who begin to enjoy reading in turn practice reading more, which spurs further skill development (Juel, 1988). These children grow up as increasingly motivated and competent readers. By coupling effective skills practice with activities designed to promote greater task engagement, we hope to prevent struggling readers from viewing reading as difficult, frustrating, and something to be avoided. This is an important aim. By making learning to read fun early on, we hope to ensure these children enjoy later success.

ACKNOWLEDGMENTS

Correspondence concerning this chapter should be addressed to Paul L. Morgan, 211 Cedar, University Park, Pennsylvania, 16802. E-mail: paulmorgan@psu.edu

PALS activities have been extended for both older readers and children struggling to acquire math skills. To learn more about PALS, or to purchase a training manual, please visit our website: http://kc.vanderbilt.edu/kennedy/pals or email us at pals@vanderbilt.com

REFERENCES

Adams, M. J. (1990). *Beginning to read: Thinking and learning about print.* Cambridge, MA: MIT Press.

Baker, L. (2000). Building the word-level foundation for engaged reading. In L. Baker, M. J. Dreher, & J. T. Guthrie (Eds.), *Engaging young readers: Promoting achievement and motivation* (pp. 17–42). New York: Guilford.

Bogner, K., Raphael, L., & Pressley, M. (2002). How grade 1 teachers motivate literate activity by their students. *Scientific Studies of Reading, 6,* 135–165.

Dahl, K. L., & Freppon, P. A. (1995). A comparison of innercity children's interpretations of reading and writing instruction in the early grades in skills-based and whole language classrooms. *Reading Research Quarterly, 30,* 50–74.

Delquadri, J., Greenwood, C. R., Whorton, D., Carta, J. J., & Hall, R. V. (1986). Classwide peer tutoring. *Exceptional Children, 52,* 535–542.

Foorman, B. R., Francis, D. J., Fletcher, J. M., Schatschneider, C., & Mehta, P. (1998). The role of instruction in learning to read: Preventing reading failure in at-risk children. *Journal of Educational Psychology, 90,* 37–55.

Francis, D. J., Shaywitz, S. E., Stuebing, K. K., Shaywitz, B. A., & Fletcher, J. M. (1996). Developmental lag versus deficits models of reading disability: A longitudinal, individual growth curve analysis. *Journal of Educational Psychology, 88,* 3–17.

Fuchs, D., Fuchs, L. S., & Burish, P. (2000). Peer-Assisted Learning Strategies: An evidence-based practice to promote reading achievement. *Learning Disabilities Research and Practice. 15,* 85–91.

Fuchs, D., Fuchs, L. S., Mathes, P. G., & Martinez, E. A. (2002). Preliminary evidence on the social standing of students with learning disabilities in PALS and no-PALS classes. *Learning Disabilities Research and Practice, 17,* 205–215.

Fuchs, D., Fuchs, L. S., Mathes, P. G., & Simmons, D. C. (1997). Peer-assisted learning strategies: Making classrooms more responsive to diversity. *American Educational Research Journal, 34,* 174–206.

Fuchs, D., Fuchs, L. S., Thompson, A., Svenson, E., Yen, L., Al Otaiba, S., et al. (2001). Peer-assisted learning strategies in reading: Extensions for kindergarten, first grade, and high school. *Remedial and Special Education, 22,* 15–21.

Fuchs, L. S., Fuchs, D., & Karns, K. (2001). Enhancing kindergartners' mathematical development: Effects of peer-assisted learning strategies. *Elementary School Journal, 101,* 495–510.

Fuchs, L. S., Fuchs, D., & Kazdan, S. (1999). Effects of peer-assisted learning strategies on high school students with serious reading problems. *Remedial and Special Education, 20,* 309–318.

Gambrell, L. B., Mazzoni, S. A., & Almasi, J. F. (2000). Promoting collaboration, social interaction, and engagement with text. In L. Baker, M. J. Dreher, & J. T. Guthrie (Eds.), *Engaging young readers: Promoting achievement and motivation* (pp. 119-139). New York: Guilford.

Greenwood, C. R., Delquadri, J. C., & Hall, V. R. (1989). Longitudinal effects of classwide peer tutoring. *Journal of Educational Psychology, 81,* 371–383.

Hoffman, J. V., McCarthey, S. J., Elliott, B., Bayles, D. L., Price, D. P., Ferree, A., et al. (1998). The literature-based basals in first-grade classrooms: Savior, Satan, or same-old same old? *Reading Research Quarterly, 33,* 168–197.

Juel, C. (1988). Learning to read and write: A longitudinal study of 54 children from first through fourth grades. *Journal of Educational Psychology, 80,* 437–447.

Mathes, P. G., & Fuchs, L. S. (1994). The efficacy of peer tutoring in reading for students with mild disabilities: A best-evidence synthesis. *School Psychology Review, 23,* 59–80.

Mathes, P. G., Howard, J. K., Allen, S. H., & Fuchs, D. (1998). Peer-Assisted Learning Strategies for first-grade readers: Responding to the needs of diversity. *Reading Research Quarterly, 33,* 62–94.

McCutchen, D., Harry, D. R., Cunningham, A. E., Cox, S., Sidman, S., & Covill. A. E. (2002). Reading teachers' knowledge of children's literature and English phonology. *Annals of Dyslexia, 52,* 207–228.

Meyer, M. S., & Felton, R. H. (1999). Repeated reading to enhance fluency: Old approaches and new directions. *Annals of Dyslexia, 49,* 283–206.

Moats, L. C., & Lyon, G. R. (1996). Wanted: Teachers with knowledge of language. *Topics in Language Disorders, 16,* 73–86.

Mortweet, S. L., Utley, C. A., Walker, D., Dawson, H. L., Dequadri, J. C., Reddy, S. S., et al. (1999). Classwide peer tutoring: Teaching students with mild mental retardation in inclusive classrooms. *Exceptional Children, 65,* 524–536.

National Institute of Child Health and Human Development (2000). *Report of the National Reading Panel. Teaching children to read: An evidence-based assessment of the scientific research literature on reading and its implications for reading instruction: Reports of the subgroups* (NIH Publication No. 00–4754). Washington, DC: U.S. Government Printing Office.

O'Connor, R. E. (2000). Increasing the intensity of intervention in kindergarten and first grade. *Learning Disabilities Research and Practice, 15,* 43–54.

O'Connor, R. E., Notari-Syverson, A., & Vadasy, P. F. (1996). Ladders to Literacy: The effects of teacher-led phonological activities in kindergarten for children with and without mild disabilities. *Exceptional Children, 63,* 117–130.

O'Connor, R. E., Notari-Syverson, A., & Vadasy, P. F. (1998). First-grade effects of teacher-led phonological activities in kindergarten for children with mild disabilities: A follow-up study. *Learning Disabilities Research and Practice, 13,* 43–52.

Palincsar, A., & Klenk, L. (1992). Fostering literacy learning in supportive context. *Journal of Learning Disabilities, 25,* 211–225.

Pressley, M. (2002). *Reading instruction that works: The case for balanced teaching* (2nd ed.). New York: Guilford.

Rashotte, C. A., MacPhee, K., & Torgesen, J. K. (2001). The effectiveness of a group reading instruction program with poor readers in multiple grades. *Learning Disabilities Quarterly, 24,* 119–134.

Shunk, D. H., & Zimmerman, B. J. (1997). Developing self-efficacious readers and writers: The role of social and self-regulatory processes. In J. T. Guthrie & A. Wigfield (Eds.), *Reading engagement: Motivating readers through integrated instruction* (pp. 34–50). Newark, DE: International Reading Association.

Simmons, D. C., Fuchs, D., Fuchs, L. S., Hodge, J. P., & Mathes, P. G. (1994). Importance of instructional complexity and role reciprocity to classwide peer tutoring. *Learning Disabilities Research and Practice. 9,* 203–212.

Smith, M. C. (1998). *Literacy for the twenty-first century: Research, policy, practices, and the National Adult Literacy Survey.* Westport, CT: Praeger.

Snow, C. E., Burns, M. S., & Griffin, P. (1998). *Preventing reading difficulties in young children.* Washington, D.C.: National Academic Press.

Sutherland, K. S., & Wehby, J. H. (2001). Exploring the relationship between increased opportunities to respond to academic requests and the academic behavioral outcomes of students with EBD: A review. *Remedial and Special Education, 22,* 113–121.

Torgesen, J. K., & Davis, C. (1996). Individual difference variables that predict response to training in phonological awareness. *Journal of Experimental Child Psychology, 63,* 1–21.

Torgesen, J. K., Wagner, R. K., Rashotte, C. A., Lindamood, P., Rose, E., Conway, T., et al. (1999). Preventing reading failure in young children with phonological processing disabilities: Group and individual responses to instruction. *Journal of Educational Psychology, 91,* 579–593.

Turner, J. C. (1995). The influence of classroom contexts on young children's motivation for literacy. *Reading Research Quarterly, 30,* 410–441.

Uhry, J. K., & Shepherd, M. J. (1997). Teaching phonological recoding to young children with phonological processing deficits: The effect on sight-vocabulary acquisition. *Learning Disabilities Quarterly, 20,* 104–125.

Vellutino, F. R., Scanlon, D. M., & Lyon, G. R (2000). Differentiating between difficult-to-remediate and readily remediated poor readers: More evidence against the IQ-achievement discrepancy definition of reading disability. *Journal of Learning Disabilities, 33,* 223–238.

Vellutino, F., Scanlon, D. M., Sipay, E., Small, S., Pratt, A., Chen, R., et al. (1996). Cognitive profiles of difficult-to-remediate and readily remediated poor readers: Early intervention as a vehicle for distinguishing between cognitive and experiential deficits as basic causes of specific reading disability. *Journal of Educational Psychology, 88,* 601–638.

Wigfield, A. (2000). Facilitating children's reading motivation. In L. Baker, M. J. Dreher, & J. T. Guthrie (Eds.), *Engaging young readers: Promoting achievement and motivation* (pp. 140–158). New York: Guilford.

Xue, Y., & Meisels, S. J. (2004). Early literacy instruction and learning in kindergarten: Evidence from the Early Childhood Longitudinal Study—Kindergarten Class of 1998–1999. *American Educational Research Journal, 41,* 191–229.

Chapter Seven

CURRICULUM-BASED MEASUREMENT: USING PROGRESS MONITORING TO INFLUENCE INSTRUCTION

Erica S. Lembke, Ph.D.
University of Missouri

Christine A. Espin, Ph.D.
University of Minnesota

DTT — is set up this way
1st BSL

INTRODUCTION

Curriculum-Based Measurement (CBM) is a simple method of repeated measurement toward long-range instructional goals (Deno, 1985). CBM can be used by teachers to monitor progress and evaluate and improve instructional programs for students. CBM can be used for students with learning disabilities in special or general education settings, and can be used to identify and assist students at-risk.

When using CBM, teachers set annual goals, administer and score short assessments on a frequent basis, graph the scores, and use the data to make decisions about instructional effectiveness. Figure 1 shows a sample graph of student performance in the area of reading. This graph demonstrates what a picture of performance might look like for a given student, Jennifer. The teacher collects baseline data to establish Jennifer's present level of performance, sets a long-range goal, and then collects and graphs weekly data on Jennifer's performance. The teacher inspects the graph on a regular basis to evaluate Jennifer's progress, and the effectiveness of Jennifer's instructional program. If Jennifer's performance consistently falls below her goal, the teacher makes a change in instruction, and continues to collect data to examine the effects of

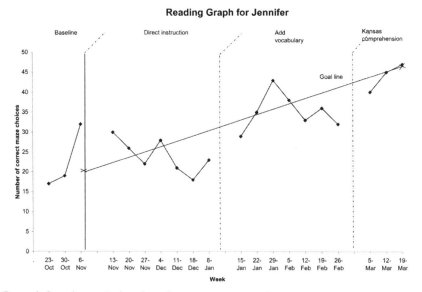

Figure 1. Sample curriculum-based measurement graph

the instructional change. If Jennifer's performance is consistently above her goal, Jennifer's teacher raises the goal.

A *curriculum-based measurement* approach to ongoing evaluation can be contrasted with a *curriculum-based assessment* approach to ongoing evaluation (see L. S. Fuchs & Deno, 1991 for an in-depth discussion of the two approaches). Curriculum-based Assessment or CBA is a method of collecting direct and frequent measures of a student's performance on a series of objectives that are from the classroom curriculum and are arranged in hierarchal order by difficulty (Blankenship, 1985; Idol-Maestas, 1983). In a CBA approach to ongoing assessment, the skill that is being taught is measured. When that skill changes, the measure changes. In contrast to CBA, CBM is a method of measuring ongoing progress toward a long-range goal that represents improvement in a general academic area, such as improvement in reading. In a CBM approach to ongoing assessment, general proficiency is sampled throughout the year using indicators of performance. The measurement system in CBM remains constant over time.

Critical features of CBM that make it useful to teachers are (a) the measures are reliable and valid indicators of performance, (b) the measures are easy and inexpensive to develop, (c) the CBM procedure is easy to learn and does not take a lot of class time to implement, (d) the graphed data provide valuable information to teachers about students' performance on a regular basis, and (e) the measures have been developed and researched in many subject areas, and at both elementary and secondary levels.

Increasingly, teachers are under pressure from school districts to provide evidence of student improvement. CBM gives teachers the opportunity to display evidence of student progress and teachers' instruction in response to that progress. Parents and administrators alike can see the efforts of students and teachers as they work together to improve performance.

CBM can be used to aid in instructional decision making at an individual, school, or district level. CBM was originally developed for use at the individual student level to allow teachers to monitor student progress and evaluate instructional programs. In special education, this type of individual progress monitoring has fit well with the conceptualization of the IEP where a student's progress toward an IEP goal needs to be systematically assessed. On the school or district level, CBM can be used as a screening instrument to help identify students in need of additional help and frequent monitoring.

In this chapter, we describe the research on, and explain the implementation of, CBM at individual and school-wide levels. We focus on two academic areas: reading and mathematics.

RESEARCH ON CBM

Research on the effectiveness of Curriculum-Based Measurement has been conducted in several academic areas including reading, math, spelling, written expression, and content areas such as science and social studies. Initial research on CBM conducted at the University of Minnesota in the Institute on Research for Learning Disabilities (IRLD) sought to identify short, efficient measures of academic performance that would serve as indicators of overall academic performance for elementary-age students. This initial research identified reliable and valid measures in reading (Deno, Mirkin, & Chiang, 1982), math (Skiba, Magnusson, Marston, & Erickson, 1986), spelling (Deno, Mirkin, Lowry, & Kuehnle, 1980), and written expression (Deno, Mirkin, & Marston, 1980). These measures were reliable in that they could be used to consistently monitor students' progress over time. They were valid in that they served as indicators of overall proficiency in each academic area. The initial work at the IRLD sought to identify measures that special education teachers could use to evaluate the effectiveness of students' instructional programs. Subsequent research replicated and expanded the original research to address CBM development for older students and in other academic areas (see Busch & Espin, 2003; Espin & Tindal, 1998; Espin, Weissenburger, & Benson, in press). In addition, research has addressed the effects of CBM use on student achievement (e.g., L. S. Fuchs & Fuchs, 1997), its use in a prereferral intervention process (e.g., Shinn, 1989), and its use as a component in a responsiveness-to-intervention (RTI) approach to identifying students with learning disabilities (e.g., D. Fuchs, Mock, Morgan, & Young, 2003).

To understand the research on CBM, it is necessary to understand the concepts of validity and reliability as they apply to progress monitoring. In CBM terms, reliability refers to the relationship between scores on alternate forms of the same measure, between scores on the same measure given two different times, or between different administrations of each probe. Reliability must be high if teachers are to have confidence that a change in score reflects a real change in performance rather than a change in the measure itself. Validity in a CBM approach refers to the extent to which the CBM measure is an indicator of general proficiency in an academic area. CBM measures are not important in and of themselves, but only insofar as they reflect general growth and progress in an academic area. For example, in reading, the number of words read correctly in one minute is used as an *indicator* of general reading proficiency, not a *measure* of reading fluency. As students improve in the number of words they read aloud in one minute, it is a good indicator that they are improving in reading in general. The validity of the reading aloud measure as an indicator of general reading proficiency is supported through research that shows the measure is related to other measures of reading proficiency, including reading comprehension. Reliability and validity are usually expressed as a number between 0 and 1. The closer the number is to 1, the more reliable and valid a measure is.

In the following section, we describe the research on CBM in reading and mathematics. We first describe research on the validity and reliability of the measures used in CBM reading and math, and then describe the research on the effects of CBM progress monitoring on student achievement. Due to the extensive literature in the area of CBM, it is not possible to discuss all academic areas in this chapter; there are however, many resources available for those interested in other areas, including written expression at the elementary-school level (Deno, Marston, & Mirkin, 1982; Deno, Mirkin, & Marston, 1980; Gansle, Noell, Van Der Heyden, Naquin, & Slider, 2002; Marston, 1989; Tindal & Parker, 1991; Videen, Deno, & Marston, 1982), written expression at the secondary-school level (Espin, De La Paz, Scierka, & Roelofs, in press; Espin, Scierka, Skare, & Halverson, 1999; Espin, Shin, Deno, Skare, Robinson, et al., 2000; Parker, Tindal, & Hasbrouck, 1991a, 1991b; Tindal & Parker, 1989), spelling (Deno, Mirkin, Lowry, et al., 1980; Shinn & Marston, 1985; Shinn, Ysseldyke, Deno, & Tindal, 1986; Tindal, Germann, & Deno, 1983) and content-area learning (Espin, Busch, Shin, & Kruschwitz, 2001; Espin & Deno, 1993; Espin & Foegen, 1996; Espin, Shinn, & Busch, in press; Nolet & Tindal, 1995; Tindal & Nolet, 1995).

CBM Research in Reading

Research in the area of reading has been particularly abundant, with the majority of studies examining two tasks: reading aloud and maze selection. In reading aloud, students are given a passage of text, usually at their instructional level, and are asked to read aloud for one minute (see Appendix A for administration and scoring directions). Teachers mark words that are read incorrectly as the student reads. At the end of the minute, teachers score and graph the number of words read correctly. Reliability for the reading aloud measure is usually quite strong, with coefficients ranging from .82 to .97 (Marston, 1989). Validity correlations between the reading aloud measures and other measures of reading proficiency, including standardized tests and teacher ratings of reading performance, generally range from .63 to .90, with the majority of correlations above .80 for elementary school students (see Marston for a review). Research in reading at the secondary-school level, has been sparse; validity coefficients, however, between oral reading and comprehension questions on expository material have been found to range from .52 to .57 (Espin & Foegen, 1996).

In the maze task, students are given a passage in which every seventh word is deleted and replaced by the correct word and two distracters (Deno & Espin, 1989; L. S. Fuchs & Fuchs, 1992; L. S. Fuchs, Fuchs, Hamlett, & Ferguson, 1992). Students read along silently, selecting correct word choices. A benefit of maze is that it can be group administered, so teachers have the freedom to give it to their entire class, if they so choose. An example of administration and scoring directions, a sample maze task, and a scored maze task can be found in Appendices A, B, and C. At the elementary level, correlations between the maze task and scores on the reading comprehension and total reading subtests of standardized achievement tests range from .80 to .89 (Jenkins & Jewell, 1993; L. S. Fuchs & Fuchs). At the secondary level, correlations between maze and comprehension questions, daily test scores, and a comprehensive posttest on expository material range from .56 to .62 (Espin & Foegen, 1996).

Although in this chapter, we do not focus on pre-reading, we wish to alert the reader to the fact that for students who are emergent readers, there is a system of progress measurement called the Dynamic Indicators of Basic Early Literacy Skills or DIBELS (Good & Kaminski, 2002). DIBELS measures include initial sound fluency, phoneme reading fluency, nonsense word fluency, and letter naming fluency. Those who wish more information on these pre-reading measures can refer to the DIBELS website (http://dibels.uoregon.edu/) which has technical adequacy reports, descriptions of the measures, and measures available for download.

CBM Research in Math

Research in math has been more limited than in reading, but several studies have identified measures that are reliable and valid indicators of general math proficiency. CBM math probes usually consist of problems that are representative of those that the students might encounter during the school year. For example, if a teacher were monitoring a student in third grade, CBM math probes might include single digit multiplication, double digit multiplication, and addition and subtraction with regrouping problems on each probe. Initial research in math (Skiba et al., 1986) identified the number of digits correct in two minutes on grade level probes with mixed basic facts as a technically adequate measure of math proficiency for students in grades 1 to 6. Reliability was found to range from .48 to .93 (Tindal et al., 1983) and validity with the Metropolitan Achievement Test (MAT) from .26 to .67 (Skiba et al.). These initial correlations were somewhat lower than the correlations for the CBM reading measure; subsequent research, however, further developed and improved the math measures. Fuchs, Fuchs and colleagues developed computation and concepts and applications measures that sampled curriculum in grades 1 through 6 (L. S. Fuchs, Fuchs, Hamlett, & Stecker, 1990; L. S. Fuchs et al., 1994). The Math Operations Test-Revised, provided students 50 problems in addition, subtraction, multiplication, and division and 10 minutes to complete the problems. Problems were scored according to the number of digits correct. Reliability for the measures was .87, and criterion validity with two math subtests of the Stanford Achievement Test (SAT) ranged from .78 to .80. The Math Concepts and Applications Test provided students with problems that included number concepts, numeration, geometry, measurement, charts and graphs and word problems. Reliability for the Concepts and Applications Test ranged from .94 to .98 and criterion validity with three math subtests of the Comprehensive Test of Basic Skills (CTBS) ranged from .64 to .81.

At the secondary-school level, Foegen and Deno have examined the use of basic facts measures and estimation tasks (Foegen & Deno, 2001; Foegen, 2000). Estimation tasks provide students with either number or word sentences (e.g., 915 – 320 = ? or "Each month I earn $56. How much will I earn in 3 months?", in Foegen & Deno) and three choices for the correct answer. Students in grades 7 and 8 were given one minute to complete the basic facts measures or three minutes to complete the estimation measures. Reliability for the basic facts measure ranged from .79 to .92. Correlations between basic facts and math standardized tests ranged from .44 to .63 and correlations with students' grades ranged from .44 to .62. Reliability for the estimation measures ranged from .67 to .93. Correlations between estimation and math standardized tests and course grades ranged from .22 to .56. Ongoing research is being conducted to examine measures in secondary math areas such as algebra (Foegen, 2004).

Effects of progress monitoring using CBM on student achievement

Previous sections have addressed the validity and reliability of the reading and math CBM measures, but does teacher use of CBM lead to improved student performance? There are some specific ways in which CBM can enhance student performance. These include helping teachers set ambitious goals, assisting teachers as they determine when instructional changes are necessary, and providing data to aid teachers as they choose instructional changes (L. S. Fuchs & Fuchs, 1997).

In a study designed to examine how changes in goal-setting can affect student achievement in math, L. S. Fuchs, Fuchs, and Hamlett (1989a) randomly assigned special education teachers to either a static or dynamic goal condition. In the static condition, teachers could choose whether or not to raise the student's goal when data were consistently above the goal line. In the dynamic condition, teachers were *prompted* to raise the goal when data were consistently above the goal line. Teachers in the dynamic condition made significantly more changes in the students' goals and obtained higher levels of achievement for their students than did teachers in the static goal group.

Another area in which CBM can enhance the effects of instruction is assisting teachers in determining when instructional changes are needed. Teachers can look at the slope or trend of the student's data and compare it to the goal line to determine when students are struggling and when changes in instruction need to be made. Alternatively, teachers can use decision-making rules to implement changes (i.e., if a student has three consecutive data points below the goal line, implement a change; if a student has six consecutive data points above the goal line, raise the goal). L. S. Fuchs, Fuchs, and Hamlett (1989b) compared reading achievement for students whose teachers: (a) measured student performance using CBM and implemented changes based on the data or (b) measured student performance using CBM and did not implement changes based on the data. Students in the group whose teachers changed instruction in response to the data performed better than students in the no-change group. This study indicated that simply collecting data does not enhance educational achievement: The use of the data for instructional decision making is important. When implementing interventions, CBM data can be used to determine what type of intervention might be necessary. Computerized CBM procedures that provide diagnostic information have been developed and tested in the areas of math (L. S. Fuchs, Fuchs, Hamett, & Sticker, 1991) and reading (L. S. Fuchs, Fuchs, & Hamlett, 1989c). In each of these studies, teachers who had access to diagnostic information about student performance designed more varied instruction and obtained higher rates of achievement than teachers who did not have access to diagnostic information.. Even if teachers do not have access to computer programs that provide diagnostic data, CBM can aid in providing diagnostic information as teachers examine student probes on a regular basis and look for patterns of errors.

Areas for future research

We have discussed the reliability and validity of the CBM reading and math measures with respect to the technical adequacy of the measures themselves, and with respect to enhancing student instruction. Even with the abundance of work that has been completed in the area of CBM, there is still much to be done. The majority of research has been done in reading and for students in grades 2 through 6. Research is currently being extended to examine and develop measures for different academic areas, for students of different ages and skill levels, and for students who are non-native English speakers.

There has been little work done in the areas of spelling and writing, and these are areas where further research should be pursued. In addition, initial work on measures for emergent learners in math and writing has recently been completed (Clarke, 2002; Lembke, Deno, & Hall, 2003), but continued work in those areas is essential for early identification and treatment of learning difficulties.

For secondary-school students, research needs to extend the existing work in the content areas of social studies (Espin et al., 2001) and science (Espin, Busch, Lembke, & Seo, 2004). Recent research has also examined the use of CBM to predict performance on high stakes assessments (Espin, Wallace, Lembke, & Campbell, 2004) and this work needs to persist as demands on students continue to increase with respect to performance outcomes. Finally, continued examination of computerized systems of CBM needs to be conducted, to identify administration, scoring, and graphing techniques that are more time-efficient for teachers.

Thus far, we have provided a summary of the research on a progress monitoring system referred to as CBM. We will now describe how teachers might implement CBM with an individual student. We describe how to create and administer the measures, how to score the tasks, how to set a goal for a student, and how to graph the student's progress. We also describe how CBM might be utilized on a school-wide level.

IMPLEMENTATION OF CBM

Individual Progress Monitoring

Students who are identified as the lowest performers in their general education classrooms, students in Title I programs, students in special education, or other students at-risk are good candidates for individual progress monitoring. Progress monitoring can be done with individual students once or twice a week. Collecting data on a frequent basis helps the teacher to be sensitive to small changes in student performance. Data can be collected by a teacher, a volunteer, or a paraprofessional who is trained in the administration procedures. Using the data for instructional decision-making is the most important and valuable part of CBM. Thus, it is important that the professional who is delivering instruction to the student graph and use the data to make changes in the student's instruction. The following is a description of how a teacher might implement a CBM system of progress monitoring in his/her classroom.

Measure Creation. Measures can be developed by the teacher, downloaded for free from a website, or purchased. Several CBM resources are listed in Appendix D. Reading aloud (see Appendix E) and maze (see Appendix B) passages can be developed from any reading material that is novel to the student. Passages should be 200–300 words in length (long enough so that the student cannot finish in the allotted time), should be roughly at the student's instructional level and should be text that the student has not encountered. Maze passages can be created from reading passages, leaving the first sentence of the story intact and thereafter, deleting every seventh word and replacing the deleted word with the correct word and two distracters. Typically, the distracters are within one letter in length of the correct choice and are clearly incorrect. See Appendix F for more detail on creating reading aloud and maze passages.

In math, the most common measures for elementary students have been basic facts or computation and concepts and applications. In the area of computation, probes can be created either with facts from one basic skill area (e.g., addition) or across several basic skill areas (i.e., addition, subtraction, multiplication, division). Teachers can create the probes by typing facts on each probe sheet in a random order, can download probes for free from the internet (e.g., www.interventioncentral.org), or can purchase them from a published source (e.g., L. S. Fuchs, Hamlett, & Fuchs, Monitoring Basic Skills Progress, 1998). See Appendix F for more detail on creating math basic facts probes. Probes that contain problems in the areas of concepts and applications, such as money, time, fractions, etc., have also been developed by L. S. Fuchs, Hamlett, and Fuchs.

At the secondary level, work by Foegen and Deno (2001) has explored the use of basic estimation and modified estimation tasks. More information on constructing these tasks, including sample problems can be found in Foegen and Deno.

Administration. Administration of all of the CBM measures involves the same basic procedures. The teacher provides a student with a copy of the probe and then asks the student to work for a specified time (often only one to five minutes). After the student has completed the probe, the teacher collects the probe, scores it, and graphs the student's score. Oral reading probes must be individually administered, while maze probes and math probes can be group administered. A sample of administration directions for the reading aloud, maze, and math tasks can be found in Appendix A. At the beginning of the year, the teacher administers several probes (e.g., three to seven) to establish the student's present level of performance or baseline data. The baseline data are graphed and the median or middle score of the three data points serves as the starting point for the goal that will be established.

Scoring. Each curriculum-based measurement task is scored using methods that have been determined to be technically adequate with respect to criterion validity. An example of a scored reading probe can be seen in Appendix E. As a teacher listens to the student read aloud, the teacher marks the words that the student reads incorrectly. These incorrectly read words might include words that the student skips, pronounces incorrectly, or does not know. At the end of one minute, the teacher totals the number of words that the student has read correctly and graphs that score.

For the maze task, the student completes the probe independently, and the teacher corrects it afterward. The teacher reads through the student's maze task, marking incorrect choices that the student has made. If a student makes three, consecutive incorrect choices, the teacher stops scoring, and goes back to the student's last correctly chosen word. The teacher places a bracket after the final correctly chosen word, and counts all correct choices up to and including the final correct choice. The score that is graphed is the number of correct choices made. An example of a scored maze passage can be found in Appendix C.

In math, students' probes are scored according to the number of digits correct or the number of problems correct. The method of scoring varies according to the student's age and the type of probe given. An example of a math basic facts probe scored according to number of digits correct and problems correct, can be found in Appendix G.

Graphing and Goal Setting. After collecting baseline data the teacher must determine the amount of growth that he/she hopes the student will make during the monitoring period. This growth trajectory can be determined by deciding on a weekly criterion (e.g., one to two words per week is a common criterion for reading aloud), multiplying this criterion by the number of monitoring weeks, and adding this to the median baseline score to determine an ending goal. An X is placed on this score on the horizontal line that specifies the final week of data collection. A line is then drawn between the median baseline point and the X that specifies the end goal.

Alternatively, the teacher can decide on an end goal by examining the performance level of the monitored student's peers or district-wide norms for a particular grade level. As with the first method for goal setting, an X is placed on the horizontal line that represents the final week of data collection at the point where the teacher hypothesizes student performance will be at that time. The median baseline data point is connected with this end goal to establish the student's goal line.

When looking at Jennifer's graph in Figure 1, one can see that her three baseline data points were approximately 17, 18, and 32. Her median or middle point was 18, so this was the beginning point for her goal. Jennifer's teacher hoped that she would be reading 45 words per minute by the end of the monitoring period, so Jennifer's end goal was set at 45 for the week of March 19th.

School-wide progress monitoring

Although originally designed to monitor the progress of individual students, CBM can also be used on a school-wide basis. Most commonly, schools organize school-wide testing of all students in the fall, winter, and spring. Teachers, paraprofessionals, and other volunteers work together to conduct the assessments. Each student is administered three probes at each assessment period. For example, each student might do three, one-minute reading aloud probes in the fall, and then again in the winter and spring. The median or middle score from the three is recorded for each testing session. The median is used because it is less sensitive to very high or very low scores. The median scores are then averaged across students in the school to create normative data. This information can be valuable to special education teachers as they determine how their students are performing compared to peers. It can also be helpful to general education teachers as they seek to determine which students are the lowest performers in their class in order to provide preventive instruction to these students.

Data can also be collected across schools and over a period of years to establish district-wide norms. These norms can serve as benchmarks for incoming students. Because these norms are established *locally,* they have enhanced educational validity when used for decision-making. After each screening (fall, winter, and spring), districts can determine what type of preventive instruction or monitoring they will provide to students who are the lowest performing. For example, a district might decide that students in the lowest 20th percentile will be monitored on a weekly basis. For a more-detailed example of school-wide screening, see Howe, Scierka, Gibbons, and Silberglitt (2003).

Case Study: Use of CBM for individual progress monitoring and decision making

Using CBM procedures on an ongoing basis to monitor progress and evaluate instruction can be an effective intervention for a student with learning disabilities. Progress monitoring in the form of CBM provides a way for teachers to reliably and validly examine instructional effects on student performance on an ongoing basis. Moreover, by setting academic goals for students, teachers are challenging their students to achieve at higher rates.

We present here a case study to illustrate how CBM can be used to enhance a student's academic performance. Examination of Jennifer's graph (Figure 1) reveals that Jennifer's teacher first implemented a Direct Instruction curriculum for Jennifer. Her teacher adopted a decision-making rule that if three consecutive data points fell below the goal line, the teacher would implement an instructional change. On January 8th, three consecutive data points fell below the goal line, so Jennifer's teacher changed instruction by adding vocabulary instruction to the instructional program. Following implementation of this change, Jennifer's performance improved, but on February 26th, another change was indicated on the graph. This time, Jennifer's teacher added comprehension strategy instruction to the instructional program. The teacher continued to collect data on Jennifer's academic performance, implementing instruction changes when the data indicated the need.

CONCLUSION

This chapter has provided an overview of Curriculum-Based Measurement, a system of progress monitoring that teachers can use to collect data on students' academic progress. CBM is unique from other methods of progress monitoring because technically adequate indicators of academic performance are used to monitor students' progress. The indicators serve as general outcome measures (L. S. Fuchs & Deno, 1991) of students' overall proficiency in academic areas such as reading and math. A teacher sets a goal for the student, administers a short probe, graphs the student's performance, and then uses the graphed data to make decisions about the effectiveness of the teacher's instruction. If the student's data indicate that he or she is not on track to meet the goal, then an intervention is implemented for that student.

CBM is an important and useful intervention for teachers who work with students with learning disabilities because it is easy and inexpensive to develop, and takes a short amount of class time to implement. Individual and school-wide data can be collected for students. Significant achievement effects have been realized for students that are in classrooms where teachers are using CBM (L. S. Fuchs, Fuchs, & Hamlett,1989a; L. S. Fuchs, Fuchs, & Hamlett, 1989b; L. S. Fuchs et al., 1991).

REFERENCES

Blankenship, C. S. (1985). Using curriculum-based assessment data to make instructional decisions. *Exceptional Children, 52*(3), 233–238.

Busch, T., & Espin, C. A. (2003). Using curriculum-based measurement to prevent failure and assess learning in content areas. *Assessment for Effective Intervention, 28,* 49–58.

Clarke, B. S. (2002). *The identification, development, and investigation of early mathematics curriculum-based measurement.* Doctoral dissertation: University of Oregon.

Deno, S. L. (1985). Curriculum-based measurement: The emerging alternative. *Exceptional Children, 52,* 219–232.

Deno, S. L., & Espin, C. A. (1989). *The Basic Academic Skills Samples: An instrument for screening and identifying children at risk for failure in the regular education classroom.* Paper presented at the American Educational Research Association, San Francisco, CA.

Deno, S. L., Marston, D., & Mirkin, P. K. (1982). Valid measurement procedures for continuous evaluation of written expression. *Exceptional Children, 48,* 368–371.

Deno, S. L., Mirkin, P. K., & Chiang, B. (1982). Identifying valid measures of reading. *Exceptional Children, 49,* 36–45.

Deno, S. L., Mirkin, P. K., Lowry, L., & Kuehnle, K. (1980). *Relationships among simple measures of spelling and performance on standardized achievement tests* (Research Report No. 21). Minneapolis: University of Minnesota, Institute for Research on Learning Disabilities.

Deno, S. L., Mirkin, P. K., & Marston, D. (1980). *Relationships among simple measures of written expression and performance on standardized achievement tests* (Research Report No. 22). Minneapolis: University of Minnesota, Institute for Research on Learning Disabilities.

Espin, C. A., Busch, T. W., Lembke, E., & Seo, K. (2003). *Curriculum-based measurement in science: Progress monitoring for students at-risk.* Presentation at the National Conference of the Council for Exceptional Children, Seattle, WA.

Espin, C. A., Busch, T. W., Shin, J., & Kruschwitz, R. (2001). Curriculum-based measurement in the content areas: Validity of vocabulary-matching as an indicator of performance in social studies. *Learning Disabilities Research and Practice, 16*(3), 142–151.

Espin, C. A., De La Paz, S., Scierka, B. J., & Roelofs, L. (in press). Relation between curriculum-based measures in written expression and quality and completeness of expository writing for middle-school students. *Journal of Special Education.*

Espin, C. A., & Deno, S. L. (1993). Performance in reading from content-area text as an indicator of achievement. *Remedial and Special Education, 14*(6), 47–59.

Espin, C. A., & Foegen, A. (1996). Validity of three general outcome measures for predicting secondary students' performance on content-area tasks. *Exceptional Children, 62,* 497–514.

Espin, C. A., Scierka, B. J., Skare, S., & Halverson, N. (1999). Curriculum-based measures in writing for secondary students. *Reading and Writing Quarterly, 15,* 5–27.

Espin, C. A., Shin, J., & Busch, T. W. (in press). Curriculum-based measurement in the content areas: Vocabulary-matching as an indicator of social studies learning. *Journal of Learning Disabilities.*

Espin, C. A., Shin, J., Deno, S. L., Skare, S., Robinson, S., & Benner, B. (2000). Identifying indicators of written expression proficiency for middle school students. *The Journal of Special Education, 34,* 140–153.

Espin, C. A., & Tindal, G. (1998). Curriculum-based measurement for secondary students. In M. R. Shinn (Ed.), *Advanced applications of curriculum-based measurement* (pp. 214–253). New York: Guilford.

Espin, C. A., Wallace, T., Lembke, E. S., & Campbell, H. (2004). *Preparing secondary students for state standards tests: Monitoring reading with curriculum-based measures.* Presentation at the National Conference of the Council for Exceptional Children, New Orleans, LA.

Espin, C. A., Weissenburger, J. W., & Benson, B. J. (in press). Assessing the writing performance of students in special education. *Exceptionality.*

Foegen, A. (2000). Technical adequacy of general outcome measures for middle school mathematics. *Diagnostique, 25,* 175–203.

Foegen, A. (2004). *Algebra instruction and assessment for students with disabilities: First steps in a three-year project.* Presented at the annual Pacific Coast Research Conference, San Diego, CA.

Foegen, A., & Deno, S. L. (2001). Identifying growth indicators for low-achieving students in middle school mathematics. *Journal of Special Education, 35*(1), 4–16.

Fuchs, D., Mock, D., Morgan, P. L., & Young, C. L. (2003). Responsiveness-to-intervention: Definitions, evidence, and implications for the learning disabilities construct. *Learning Disabilities Research and Practice, 18*(3), 157–171.

Fuchs, L. S., & Deno, S. L. (1991). Paradigmatic distinctions between instructionally relevant measurement models. *Exceptional Children 57,* 488–499.

Fuchs, L. S., & Deno, S. L. (1994) Must instructionally useful performance assessment be based in the curriculum? *Exceptional Children, 61*(1), 15–24.

Fuchs, L. S., & Fuchs, D. (1992). Identifying a measure for monitoring student reading progress. *School Psychology Review, 21*(1), 45–58.

Fuchs, L. S., & Fuchs, D. (1997). Use of curriculum-based measurement in identifying students with disabilities. *Focus on Exceptional Children, 30*(3), 1–16.

Fuchs, L. S., Fuchs, D., & Hamlett, C. L. (1989a). Effects of alternative goal structures within curriculum-based measurement. *Exceptional Children, 55,* 429–438.

Fuchs, L. S., Fuchs, D., & Hamlett, C. L. (1989b). Effects of instrumental use of curriculum-based measurement to enhance instructional programs. *Remedial and Special Education, 10*(2), 43–52.

Fuchs, L. S., Fuchs, D., & Hamlett, C. L. (1989c). Monitoring reading growth using student recalls: Effects of two teacher feedback systems. *Journal of Educational Research, 83*, 103–111.

Fuchs, L. S., Fuchs, D., Hamlett, C. L., & Ferguson, C. (1992). Effects of expert system consultation within curriculum-based measurement using a reading maze task. *Exceptional Children, 58*, 436–450.

Fuchs, L. S., Fuchs, D., Hamlett, C. L., & Stecker, P. M. (1990). The role of skills analysis in curriculum-based measurement in math. *School Psychology Review, 19*, 6–22.

Fuchs, L. S., Fuchs, D., Hamlett, C. L., & Stecker, P. M. (1991). Effects of curriculum-based measurement and consultation on teacher planning and student achievement in mathematics operations. *American Educational Research Journal, 28*, 617–641.

Fuchs, L. S., Fuchs, D., Hamlett, C. L., Thompson, A., Roberts, P. H., Kubek, P., et al. (1994). Technical features of a mathematics concepts and applications curriculum-based measurement system. *Diagnostique, 19*(4), 23–49.

Fuchs, L. S., Hamlett, C. L., & Fuchs, D. (1998). *Monitoring basic skills progress: Basic math computational manual* (2nd ed.). Austin, TX: PRO-ED.

Gansle, K. A., Noell, G. H., Van Der Heyden, A. M., Naquin, G. M., & Slider, N. J. (2002). Moving beyond total words written: The reliability, criterion validity, and time cost of alternative measure for curriculum-based measurement in writing. *School Psychology Review, 31*(4), 477–497.

Good, R. H., & Kaminski, R. A. (Eds.). (2002). *Dynamic Indicators of Basic Early Literacy Skills* (6th ed.). Eugene, OR: Institute for the Development of Education Achievement. (Available from http://dibels.uoregon.edu/).

Howe, K. B., Scierka, B. J., Gibbons, K. A., & Silberglitt, B. (2003). A schoolwide organization system for raising reading achievement using general outcome measures and evidence-based instruction: One education district's experience. *Assessment for Effective Intervention, 28*(3–4), 59–71.

Idol-Maestas, L. (1983). A model for direct, data-based reading instruction. *Journal of Special Education Technology, 6*(3), 61–77.

Jenkins, J. R., & Jewell, M. (1993). Examining the validity of two measures for formative teaching: Reading aloud and maze. *Exceptional Children, 59*(5), 421–432.

Lembke, E., Deno, S. L., & Hall, K. (2003). Identifying an indicator of growth in early writing proficiency for elementary students. *Assessment for Effective Intervention, 28*(3–4), 23–25.

Marston, D. (1989). A curriculum-based measurement approach to assessing academic performance: What it is and why to do it. In M. Shinn (Ed.), *Curriculum-based measurement: Assessing special children* (pp. 18–78). New York: Guilford.

Nolet, V., & Tindal, G. (1995). Essays as valid measures of learning in middle-school science classes. *Learning Disabilities Quarterly, 18*(4), 311–324.

Parker, R., Tindal, G., & Hasbrouck, J. (1991a). Countable indices of writing quality: Their suitability for screening-eligibility decisions. *Exceptionality, 2*, 1–17.

Parker, R., Tindal, G., & Hasbrouck, J. (1991b). Progress monitoring with objective measures of writing performance for students with mild disabilities. *Exceptional Children, 58*, 61–73.

Shinn, M. R. (1989). Identifying and defining academic problems: CBM screening and eligibility procedures. In M. Shinn (Ed.), *Curriculum-based measurement: Assessing special children* (pp. 90–129). New York: Guilford.

Shinn, M. R., & Marston, D. (1985). Differentiating mildly handicapped, low-achieving and regular education students: A curriculum-based measurement approach. *Remedial and Special Education, 6,* 31–45.

Shinn, M. R., Ysseldyke, J. E., Deno, S. L., & Tindal, G. (1986). A comparison of differences between students labeled learning disabled and low achieving on measures of classroom performance. *Journal of Learning Disabilities, 19,* 545–552.

Skiba, R., Magnusson, D., Marston, D., & Erickson, K. (1986). *The assessment of mathematics performance in special education: Achievement tests, proficiency tests, or formative evaluation?* Minneapolis: Special Services, Minneapolis Public Schools.

Tindal, G., Germann, G., & Deno, S. L. (1983). *Descriptive research on the Pine County norms: A compilation of findings* (Research Report No. 132). Minneapolis: University of Minnesota, Institute for Research on Learning Disabilities.

Tindal, G., & Nolet, V. (1995). Curriculum-based measurement in middle and high schools: Critical thinking skills in content areas. *Focus on Exceptional Children, 27* (7), 1–22.

Tindal, G., & Parker, R. (1989). Assessment of written expression for students in compensatory and special education programs. *The Journal of Special Education, 23,* 169–183.

Tindal, G., & Parker, R. (1991). Identifying measures for evaluating written expression. *Learning Disabilities Research and Practice, 6,* 211–218.

Tindal, G., & Nolet, V. (1995). Curriculum-based measurement in middle and high schools: Critical thinking skills in content areas. *Focus on Exceptional Children, 27* (7), 1–22.

Videen, J., Deno, S. L., & Marston, D. (1982). *Correct word sequences: A valid indicator of proficiency in written expression* (Research Report No. 84). Minneapolis: University of Minnesota, Institute for Research on Learning Disabilities.

why maze passage?

APPENDIX A

CBM Administration and Scoring Directions

READING ALOUD

MATERIALS:

Teacher copy (numbered) of the passage on a clipboard

Student copy (unnumbered) of the passage

Pencil

Stop watch

Directions:

1. Place the unnumbered copy in front of the student.
2. Place the clipboard with the numbered copy in front of you, but shielded so that the student cannot see what you record.
3. Say to the student: **"When I say begin, I want you to read this story out loud to me. Start here** (point to the first word in the passage) and read across the page (demonstrate by moving finger along the first line of text) **trying to read each word. If you come to a word that you don't know, I will help you. Be sure to do your best reading. Do you have any questions?** (Pause.) **Ready, begin."** (Start your stop watch.)
4. If the student does not say the first word within 3 seconds, supply the word, mark it as incorrect, and continue scoring.
5. Mark any words that the student reads incorrectly on your teacher copy. For more information on what constitutes an error, see Scoring Rules.
6. If a student does not say a word within 3 seconds, supply the word and mark it as incorrect on your teacher copy.
7. At the end of 1 minute, place a bracket after the last word read and say to the student **"Stop. Thank you."**
8. Calculate the number of words that the student read correctly and write this at the top of the page.

Scoring:

As the student reads aloud, put a slash mark through any word that the student says incorrectly. This might include words that the student mispronounces, leaves out, or words you have to supply for the student. Repetitions, self-corrections, and words that are added are not counted as errors. At the end of one minute, place a bracket (]) around the last word that the student read and then count all of the words that the student read correctly. This will be the score that you graph.

CBM Maze

Materials:

Teacher copy of maze passage with correct answers circled to use as a key

Student copy of the passage

Pencil

Stop watch

DIRECTIONS:

Say to the students: **"Read the passage, and whenever you come to three word choices, circle the word that belongs in the sentence. Circle a word even if you're not sure of the answer. Continue working until I tell you to stop. Remember to do the best you can. Ready? Begin."**

After 1 to 3 minutes say: **"Stop. Thank you. Put your pencils down."**

Appendix A
CBM Administration and Scoring Directions (continued)

NOTE:
- If students ask you to identify a word, remind them to just do the best they can.
- In order to maintain reliability, please keep a close watch on the timing of the test. Have a back-up (clock or watch) available in case your stop watch doesn't work.

SCORING
1. Mark a line through any incorrect choice the student has made. Skips are counted as incorrect. If two answers are circled, score the item as incorrect. If you are unsure of the student's choice, score the item as incorrect.
2. Once the student has made three errors in a row, stop scoring.
3. Return to the last correctly chosen word.
4. Count the number of correct choices selected prior to the first of the three consecutive errors. Do not count any choices made after the first of the three consecutive errors.

CBM MATH, BASIC FACTS
MATERIALS:
Teacher copy of math probe with correct answers written to use as a key
Student copy of the problems
Pencil
Stop watch

DIRECTIONS:
1. Place the math probe in front of the student.
2. Say to the student: "**When I say begin, I want you to write the correct answers to the math problems on the sheet in front of you. Start here** (point to problem in upper left hand corner) **and work across the page** (demonstrate by moving finger across the page), **trying each problem. If you come to a problem that you don't know, put an X on it and move on to the next problem Do you have any questions?** (Pause.) **Ready, begin.**" (Start your stop watch.)
3. At the end of 2 minutes, place a bracket after the last problem solved and say to the student "**Stop. Thank you.**"

SCORING:
Score the probe, putting a slash over either any problems that the student did not get correct or any digits that the student did not get correct. Count either the number of problems or the number of digits the student got correct. This is the number that you will graph.

Appendix B
Maze Example

One morning, Jimmy and his mother decided to go to the grocery store.

Jimmy went into his bedroom and **too / got / real** some money out of his piggy

bank / are / onto. He was excited to get himself **I / to / a** treat! Jimmy's mother

walked and Jimmy **paper / rode / tie** his bike. When he would ride **too / line / us**

far ahead, Jimmy's mother would call **to / can / as** him, "Slow down!" They finally

got **be / is / to** the store. Jimmy locked his bike **she / and / to** the bike rack and he

and **his / name / on** mother went inside.

Jimmy walked around **zero / the / of** store, looking for something to buy.

By / No / He only had fifty cents, so he **had / for / type** to choose wisely. He

looked at **fit / the / make** gum and candy, but he did **not / has / if** want to waste his

money on **than / those / showed** things. He looked at the pencils **and / gone / have**

notepads, but he already had some **top / in / of** those at home. Then he saw

size / what / can he wanted.

On a small shelf **in / a / no** the back of the store, there **all / might / were**

items that were on sale. On **for / use / the** shelf, he saw a small vase

with / best / most silk flowers in it. This would **can / be / of** perfect for his

mother! But Jimmy **addition / different / wondered** how much would the vase

cost? Surely **he / no / are** would not have enough money.

Appendix C
Scored Maze Passage

One morning, Jimmy and his mother decided to go to the grocery store. Jimmy

went into his bedroom and **too / got / real** some money out of his piggy

bank / are / onto. He was excited to get himself **I / to / a** treat! Jimmy's mother

walked and Jimmy **paper / rode / tie** his bike. When he rode **too / line / us** far

ahead, Jimmy's mother called **to / can / as** him, "Slow down!" They finally got

be / is / to the store. Jimmy locked his bike **she / an / to** the bike rack and he and

his / name / on mother went inside.

Jimmy walked around **zero / the / of** store, looking for something to buy.

By / No / He only had fifty cents, so he **had / for / type** to choose wisely. He

looked at **it / the / make** gum and candy, but he did **not / has / if** want to waste his

money on **than / those / showed** things. He looked at the pencils **and / gone / have**

notepads, but he already had some **top / in / of** those at home. Then he saw

size / what / can he wanted.

On a small shelf **in / a / no** the back of the store, there **all / might / were**

items that were on sale. On **for / use / the** shelf, he saw a small vase

with / best / most silk flowers in it. This would **can / be / of** perfect for his

mother! But Jimmy **addition / different / wondered** how much would the vase

cost? Surely **he / no / are** would not have enough money.

Number graphed—8 correct word choices

Appendix D
Websites Where You Can Find Additional Information on Progress Monitoring[1]

EdCheckup—www.edcheckup.com
   A website where individuals can access CBM probes and can graph students' data on the computer (fee-based).

Intervention central—www.interventioncentral.org
   A website developed by Jim Wright, a school psychologist from Syracuse, NY. This site contains numerous tools for creation, administration, and graphing of CBM measures, and includes ideas for research-based interventions (free).

Aimsweb, from Edformation—www.aimsweb.com
   Provides an online progress monitoring and graphing program, including measures to download (fee-based).

Yearly Progress Pro from McGraw-Hill Digital Learning— http://www.bredex.com/index.jsp
   Provides assessment tools, instructional feedback, and data reports and analysis in math (fee-based).

[1] Because websites are frequently updated and URLs change, the listed websites are available at the time of this publication, but may not be available in the future.

Appendix E
Scored Reading Probe

One morning, Jimmy and his mother decided to go to the grocery   12

store. Jimmy went into his bedroom and got some money out of his piggy   26

bank. He was excited to get himself a treat! Jimmy's mother walked and   39

Jimmy rode his bike. When he would ride too far ahead, Jimmy's mother   52

would call to him,"Slow down!" They finally got to the store. Jimmy   65

locked his bike to the bike rack and he and his mother went inside.   79

Jimmy walked around the store, looking for something to buy. He   90

only had fifty cents, so he had to choose wisely. He looked at the gum and 106

candy, but he did not want to waste his money on those things. He looked 121

at the pencils and notepads, but he already had some of those at home. Then 136

he saw what he wanted.   141

On a small shelf in the back of the store, there were items that were   156

on sale. On the shelf, he saw a small vase with silk flowers in it. This 172

would be perfect for his mother! But Jimmy wondered how much the   184

vase would cost? Surely he would not have enough money.   194

Number of words attempted—129 , number of words incorrect—10, Number of words correct

(graphed score)—119

Appendix F

Directions for Probe Development

READING ALOUD

   Step 1—Determine what material you will use for your reading probes.
Options include using content from a basal reader that the student is no longer reading or
getting pre-made probes from a website. Sources for probes on-line are listed in Appendix
D.[1] The text used for the probes should be novel, in that the student has not read the text
before. Keep the difficulty of the text constant across the entire year. We suggest selecting
text at the student's instructional level so that it is neither too difficult nor too easy.

   [1] Research has determined that selecting reading passages from the local curriculum is not
   essential to meeting the measurement or instructional goals of CBM (L. S. Fuchs & Deno,
   1994).

   Step 2—Develop probes. For each probe, you will develop a student and a teacher
copy. If you are using your own material, go through the basal reader or other material that you
are using and randomly select pages of text. Choose pages that do not have pictures on them,
so that there are no distractions for the student and try not to pick passages that have many difficult pronouns. Each probe should be approximately 200–300 words in length, or long enough
so that the student will not be able to finish the passage in one minute. The student copy will be
unnumbered, while the teacher copy will have the cumulative number of words at the end of
each line of text down the right-hand side of the page. Initially, develop 25 to 30 probes. You may
need to develop more depending on how long you decide to monitor the student.

MAZE

   Follow the guidelines for creating reading aloud passages (Steps 1 and 2 above). Next,
leave the first sentence intact and go through the passage, circling every 7th word. Replace
each word with the correct word and two distracters. The distracters should be within one
letter in length of the correct word and should be easily identifiable (is a different part of
speech, does not rhyme with the correct word, does not begin with the same letter as the
correct word). Leave the final sentence intact.

Additional construction suggestions might include:
   • Put correct choices and distracters in bold and underlined
   • Keep the maze selections intact, rather than splitting at the end of lines
   • If the seventh word is a proper noun, move one word forward or back
   • Vary the placement of the correct maze choice
   • If the 7th word is the first word in the sentence, capitalize correct choice and
     distracters

MATH—BASIC FACTS PROBES

   Step 1—Decide which skills will be included. Include all math skills that will be
encountered by the student during the school year. For example, if the student will be learning single and double-digit addition and subtraction during the school year, include samples of
each of these problems on each probe. It is often helpful in constructing the math probes to
select problems from end of chapter or unit tests in a grade-level textbook.

   Step 2—Randomly sample facts for the probes. Place one problem each on a
notecard. Mix the notecards and then randomly select 25–60 problems to put on each
probe. The number of problems will vary according to the student's ability. There should
be enough problems so that the student does not finish in 2 minutes. Each time you create a new probe, put all the cards back in the pile, shuffle them, and select 25–60 once
again. Create a minimum of 25–30 probes to begin.

Appendix G.
Scored Math Basic Facts Probe

```
   14              23              36
+  35            - 19           +  45
  21              22              81


   51              79              40
-   9            + 41           -  13
  60             110              27


   38              90              16
-   9            + 25           +  57
 187             105              73


   50              91              71
-  14            + 34           -  56
```

Number graphed—10 digits correct or 3 problems correct

Chapter Eight

PROVIDING INTERVENTION TO INFANTS AND TODDLERS THROUGH
FAMILY-GUIDED ROUTINES BASED INTERVENTION (FGRBI):
IMPLICATIONS FOR LEARNING DISABILITIES

Kere Hughes, Ph.D.
Iowa State University

The recognition that families provide the primary context for infant and toddler development has greatly influenced the provision of early intervention in the United States. Part C of the Individuals with Disabilities Education Act (IDEA, 1997; PL 105-17) mandates the participation of family members in all phases of the intervention process including determining priorities and outcomes and training parents (and others) regarding the provision of services within natural environments. Although children are not typically diagnosed as having a specific learning disability (LD) until they reach school-age when their difficulty with reading, writing, and often times math becomes apparent, there are several early warning signs that arise during the toddler years that often lead to toddlers receiving early interventions under the provisions for developmental delays and other risk factors such as low birth weight.

Relating Infant and Toddler Experience to Learning Disabilities

In their seminal study of the onset of language, Hart and Risley (1995) intensively followed 42 families over the first two years of their children's lives. They concluded that children need hundreds of thousands of experiences with positive, encouraging language over the first four years of life, more than any child care center or intervention program alone could provide. Although their study did not focus specifically on children with LD, because it was a prospective study, it did compare children on welfare with children from working class, and professional families. Children living in poverty received far fewer encouraging language experiences and far more discouraging language experiences.

Children of low socioeconomic status (SES) are at greater risk for having a learning disability placement by age 12 to 14 (Blair & Scott, 2002). It can be argued that although LD is primarily thought of as a neurological disorder (Steele, 2004), the early experiences with language studied by Hart and Risley (1995), may mediate the relationship between low SES and later identified LD. In fact, it has been suggested that identification and intervention occur as early as possible in order to prevent the need for more intensive special education in the future (Taylor, Anselmo, Foreman, Schatschneider, & Angelopoulos, 2000) and decrease the likelihood of secondary problems associated with LD, such as anxiety, frustration, and low self-esteem (Lowenthal, 1998). It is not, however, necessary that children wait until they have a labeled diagnosis before receiving intervention (Steele, 2004). Certainly early intervention strategies that drastically increase the quantity of positive early language and social experiences for infants and toddlers with developmental delays will also help reduce the number of children identified with LD later or at the very least, decrease the extensiveness of later intervention.

Family Guided Routines Based Intervention

Family-guided routines based intervention (FGRBI) is an intervention approach designed specifically for use with infants and toddlers with a wide range of special needs. This approach can be effectively used by practitioners from all specialty areas, including speech/hearing therapists, occupational therapists, early childhood special educators and others. FGRBI focuses on empowering families through family-centered practices, and providing frequent and meaningful learning opportunities to infants and toddlers within natural environments and daily routines. The implications of using FGRBI for intervening with infants and toddlers at risk for LD are that children will receive many positive language and social interactions that cross contexts and routines allowing for multiple modes of learning and generalization.

In essence, FGRBI defines the interventionist as a facilitator of parent-child interaction in a way that supports the developmental outcomes of the child. Figure 1 is a visual depiction of this relationship. Evaluation studies of FGRBI are just now being conducted and disseminated so the empirical support for this approach is limited. Empirical evidence, however, supporting family-centered practice, natural environments and embedded learning, which provide the overarching framework for FGRBI, have been well documented and are presented here. Subsequently, there will be a thorough description of the key components of FGRBI along with useful tools to aid in implementation. The chapter will also provide a discussion of potential barriers to quality implementation.

Family Empowerment and Family-Centered Practices

Empowering caregivers to support their child's developmental outcomes is the underlying goal of FGRBI. According to Dunst and Trivette (1987), there are three components necessary for empowering families: (a) high quality technical assistance, (b) interventionist traits and attributions, and (c) participatory involvement of caregivers. High quality technical assistance is associated with the interventionist's training in his/her field. This expertise can be viewed as the content and skills that need to be transferred to caregivers.

The attitudes practitioners have toward the caregivers' ability to provide for their child, interest in their child's development, and ability to implement intervention strategies are directly related to the interventionist's ability to engage family members in the intervention process and to be effective collaborators. Beliefs that caregivers would be burdened with the intervention, that they may be unable to implement intervention strategies, or that families don't

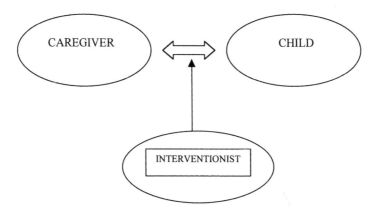

The interventionist's role is to facilitate the development-enhancing interactions between the caregiver and child.

Figure 1. Visual of the interventionist role in FGRBI

have "routines" (many practitioners confused routines with family schedules) have been found to be significant barriers to FGRBI (Hughes, Summers, Carta, & Woods, 2004). ~~Phrase~~

Caregiver engagement in the intervention process is a critical element to successful outcomes. Multiple studies covering many types of intervention programs have identified parent or caregiver engagement as the critical factor associated with intervention effectiveness (Gomby, Culross, & Behrman, 1999; Roggman, Boyce, Cook, & Jump, 2001). Although caregiver characteristics and preferences have an effect on engagement, it is not uncommon for practitioners to be untrained in adult learning strategies and inexperienced in the area of facilitating engagement resulting in missed opportunities. In fact, Hughes et al. (2004) documented many instances where caregivers were observed showing signs of engagement during the home visit (leaning forward, attending to what was happening and asking questions etc . . .) but practitioners did not invite the caregiver to be an active participant in the intervention. Practitioners need to be aware of the verbal and nonverbal signs caregivers give indicating that they are willing participants. Appendix A contains the Adult Learning Checklist from TaCTICS (Therapists as Collaborative Team members for Infants/Toddlers Community Services) which is a training and support outreach project, in the area of adult learning strategies (TaCTICS, 2004). This checklist can help practitioners set up the intervention process in a way that promotes caregiver engagement.

Caregivers with a history of non-participation under more traditional teacher-directed models can be difficult to engage. Therefore it is essential that practitioners help caregivers recognize their roles as active team members and interventionists from the beginning of the intervention process.

Natural Environments and Embedded Learning

Empowering caregivers to build and expand skills related to parenting a child with special needs is largely an effort to improve the quantity and quality of learning opportunities they provide to their child. Providing naturalistic intervention has been shown to be more effective than traditional teacher-directed therapy (Losardo & Bricker, 1994, McLean & Cripe, 1997; McWilliam, 1996; Warren, 1992). Naturalistic intervention takes place within the everyday environments of children and their families.

Natural environments are the places, activities and experiences where children typically find themselves. Three main contexts of natural environments for young children have been identified: (a) family life, (b) community life, and (c) early childhood programs (Bruder & Dunst, 1999-2000). Environments refer to the locations where children find themselves i.e., at home, child care, grocery store, neighbor's house, or church. Children's activities within these locations may or may not provide developmentally supportive learning opportunities. The term "activity settings" refers to the experiences that promote learning and are the focus for intervention. (Bruder & Dunst; Dunst et al., 2001; Dunst, Hamby, Trivette, Raab, & Bruder, 2000).

An activity setting has been formally defined as "a situation-specific experience, opportunity, or event that involves a child's interaction with people, the physical environment, or both, and provides a context for a child to learn about his or her own abilities and capabilities as well as the propensities and proclivities of others" (Dunst et al., 2001, p. 70). Dunst, Bruder, Trivette, Raab, and McLean (1998) documented 134 children participating in 87 different activity settings at 15 locations. Within these activity settings, an average of 113 kinds of learning opportunities were identified. This study supports the idea that the places and activities that make up the natural every day life of children can provide an important context for developmentally supportive learning opportunities.

Bronfenbrenner (1995) contends that maximal development occurs when children participate in developmentally supportive activities repeatedly and over long periods of time. Specifically, activity settings have been shown to be most effective at promoting new skill development and skill mastery if: (a) they are varied, (b) they are repeated often, (c) they are engaging to the child, (d) they afford opportunities for the child to manifest targeted behaviors, (e) they provide opportunities for exploration, and (f) competencies are reinforced by adults

(Dunst et al., 2001). These development enhancing characteristics identified by Dunst and colleagues have been well documented by others (Bronfenbrenner, 1993; Faver, 1999; Nelson, 1999; Wachs, 2000). In addition to these development enhancing characteristics, learning skills within the very environments where children need to use them increases the probability of skill maintenance and generalization (Shumway-Cook & Woollacott, 1995).

By the process of embedding, learning opportunities can be strategically placed into activity settings within natural environments in a way that can lead to maximal developmental gains and generalization for very young children. Embedding refers to the "procedure in which children are given opportunities to practice individual goals and objectives that are included within an activity or event in a manner that expands, modifies, or adapts the activity/event while remaining meaningful and interesting to children" (Bricker, Pretti-Frontczak, & McComas, 1998, p. 13).

By facilitating the caregiver's ability to embed learning opportunities that have development-enhancing characteristics within the family's natural environments, practitioners engage in recommended practice for infants and toddlers with special needs. Family-guided routines based intervention focuses recommended practice on a functional skills approach that is considered developmentally appropriate practice for early childhood educators (Bredekamp & Copple, 1997).

KEY STRATEGIES AND TOOLS OF FGRBI

Defining routines as the context for intervention

By their very nature, family and caregiving routines have many of the specific development supporting characteristics (as defined above by Dunst et al., 2001) that make them amenable to embedding intervention strategies. Routines are repeated, have a predictable sequence, and have a meaningful outcome for participants (Cripe & Venn, 1997). An important distinction must be made between *routines* and *schedules*. Routines are events that occur within schedules, but are not defined by them. For example, a diaper changing routine may happen on a very flexible and as-needed basis by a family, or on a more predictable, every 45 minute schedule, in a child care center. Either way, routines can be identified in any caregiving situation because the functional outcomes are required for the care of infants and toddlers. The first step is to identify which routines are best suited for embedding learning strategies that are tied to the outcomes identified by caregivers and practitioners on the Individualized Family Service Plan (IFSP). Routines that are short, flexible, predictable, and contain repetitive actions should be among the preferred routines (Cripe, Hanline, & Daley, 1997).

Routines that practitioners identify as optimal for embedding particular learning strategies may not be appropriate for a particular family. On paper, meal-time may appear to be a perfect routine for embedding communication strategies, such as signing and time delay, however the family may find meal times already very hurried and stressful, or they may not want to alter an already very enjoyable activity. What is critical here is that practitioners work with caregivers to identify targeted routines. This will help ensure that caregivers will be comfortable with implementing the intervention.

Several helpful tools have been developed to help families and practitioners identify appropriate routines for intervention. The Routines Based Interview (RBI) provides a structure for conversation with caregivers about their routines (McWilliam, 1992). The recording form for this interview is in Appendix B and comprehensive instructions can be obtained from the author. Caregivers are asked to describe their typical day. The interventionist helps guide the discussion around daily routines gathering critical information about child engagement, independence, and social interactions during each routine. The interventionist also helps the caregiver determine if the routine would be a "good fit" for embedding intervention strategies for various developmental domains. In addition to identifying targeted routines, this conversation gives the interventionist valuable information about the caregivers' attitudes and feelings about their daily life with their child.

Another useful interview tool for targeting routines has been developed by Woods and colleagues for Project TaCTICS. Appendix C contains the Identifying Family Activities and Routines Conversation Starters (TaCTICS, 2004). Either of these interview tools can help caregivers and practitioners identify routines that would be especially suited for embedding learning opportunities on a frequent basis.

Conducting a FGRBI Home Visit

Using a FGRBI approach during home visits drastically changes the role of the interventionist from being the child's primary interventionist to being an adult model, teacher, and collaborator. A recent study of implementation suggests that there are some attitudinal barriers that keep practitioners from providing quality FGRBI services. In addition, there are administrative barriers to intervention when programs are set up under traditional service provision (Hughes et al., 2004). If practitioners, however, are willing to expand their skills and step out in a new direction, children and families can benefit greatly from their services. A helpful tool to use during home visits is the Self Evaluation of Family-guided/Routines Based Intervention Form (TaCTICS, 2004). This form is located in Appendix D and helps practitioners document and organize their observations of routines and identify specific strategies to model and communicate to parents during routines.

Another useful self-evaluation tool was developed for research purposes and is contained in Appendix E. The Fidelity Checklist was used in a recent project of FGRBI implementation. Items were identified in consultation with Dr. Juliann Woods from Project TaCTICS (2004). Of the 22 items listed, 14 were identified as positive teaching strategies that have been shown to be effective teaching strategies. Eight items were identified as being key elements that separate FGRBI from these other, more general strategies. When used together, these 22 strategies promote the use of daily routines for embedding learning opportunities within infant and toddler natural environments. Recent research indicates that most practitioners engage in positive teaching strategies with relative consistency and quality, that the strategies specific to FGRBI are new to most practitioners, and therefore that these strategies are typically more difficult to implement (Hughes et al., 2004). These eight strategies are:

1. requesting data from the caregiver,
2. joining in routines and activities with the caregiver and child,
3. talking about how to incorporate child outcomes into a variety of routines/locations during the visit,
4. working with the child in a variety of non-play related routines,
5. using everyday materials appropriate to families' routines,
6. doing routines in their natural setting,
7. signaling the beginning and end of routines, and
8. incorporating IFSP objectives into daily living routines.

Requesting data from the caregiver. This strategy involves gathering data about the process of embedding learning opportunities within routines since the last visit. Practitioners should provide specific instructions to caregivers about what information to document, i.e., how the routine went, how engaged the child was in the routine, what kinds of problems or accomplishments were made, and what general feelings they had about how the process is going. Practitioners can design fun data collection forms to go on the family's refrigerator or anywhere that is convenient for quick and easy documentation. This will help the interventionist and family member identify any needs for modifications and reinforce progress made since the last visit. This is a great time for the interventionist to encourage caregivers and provide reinforcement for the good things they are doing to support their child's development. It is important that feedback to family members be concrete and specific. For example an interventionist might say, "You provided many opportunities for Mindy to practice bringing her arms to midline during the diapering routines this past week."

Joining in routines and activities with the caregiver and child. When conducting a FGRBI home visit it is imperative that the interventionist become a collaborator instead of the director. With some prior discussion of the agenda for the visit, the interventionist should join in the routines or activities that the caregivers are doing with the child. This strategy is called Triadic Interaction (caregiver, child, and interventionist). In this way, the interventionist's role becomes that of a consultant which changes the focus of the visit from interventionist-child interaction to caregiver-child interaction. Joining caregivers in their own routines also helps the interventionist understand the nature of interactions within the family. Many times during home visits with infants and toddlers, diapers need to be changed, or children need to be fed. Typically practitioners will stop the visit while the caregiver and child complete the routine alone. From a FGRBI approach, however, the interventionist would observe and provide specific information to caregivers about how to embed learning strategies into the routine or just provide information on how to make it more enjoyable and efficient. The interventionist may also model teaching strategies or provide other kinds of physical assistance.

Strategies that support the triadic relationship between parent-child and interventionist include (a) establishing a supportive context (one that promotes playful interaction), (b) acknowledging caregiver competence, (c) focusing attention on the particular competencies or actions to be enhanced, (d) modeling the competencies or actions to be learned, and (e) suggesting specific strategies for use with the child (McCollum & Yates, 1994). The strategies are ordered from the most open-ended and least directive to the most directive. The interventionist's job is to determine the most appropriate starting point with the particular caregiver and then adjust the use of the strategies based on following the caregiver's lead (McCollum & Yates). By utilizing these strategies, the interventionist changes the focus of intervention from teacher-child to parent-child interactions.

Talking about how to incorporate child outcomes into a variety of routines/locations during the visit. As suggested by the research presented from Dunst and colleagues (Dunst et al., 2000; Dunst et al., 2001), opportunities to practice specific skills can be embedded across many different activity settings (routines in this case). And within each routine, many different skills can be practiced. Hence, primary functions of the interventionist are to be creative and to talk to caregivers about how to provide learning opportunities that are related to their child's outcomes across a variety of routines. This strategy will increase both the frequency of practice and the generalization of skills.

As caregivers become more accustomed to planning intervention, they will be able to contribute more and more to the conversation about locations and times for routines and embedding. Practitioners should be aware of the growing awareness and competence of caregivers as they progress through the intervention process.

Working with the child in a variety of non-play related routines. The inclusion of this strategy is not intended to diminish the importance of play related activities, but to emphasize the importance of daily caregiving routines in the lives of infants and toddlers. In fact, several excellent resources are available on Activity Based Intervention (ABI), a system which focuses on child initiated and play-based activities as a context for intervention (e.g., Pretti-Frontczak & Bricker, 2001). What distinguishes FGRBI from ABI is the significance of family routines (particularly caregiving routines) in the lives of infants and toddlers and their families. Therefore, it is essential that practitioners devote a significant amount of time during home visits to modeling and supporting the parent within identified routines.

Practitioners and caregivers need to plan when to conduct home visits and to schedule ahead of time so that children and caregivers can be supported while routines are actually happening. It may be the case that schedules need to be modified by either the interventionist or the family to accommodate the home visit. For instance, a bath time routine may be conducted when the family normally gives the baby a bath (potentially restructuring the interventionist's typical schedule), or it may be altered slightly to accommodate the intervention visit. These decisions should be made jointly with the preference given to accommodating family schedules whenever possible.

Using everyday materials appropriate to families' routines. Under traditional models of service provision, practitioners come to homes with bags and trunks full of materials that may not be at all familiar or meaningful to families. Steering practitioners away from the use of specialized play materials to those things within the families' natural environments is perhaps one of the most difficult barriers to implementing FGRBI. Several reasons exist for the continued use of toy bags even after training in FGRBI occurs. During our study of home visiting, practitioners mentioned that they liked their toys bags because: (a) many of the families did not have appropriate materials for intervention, (b) the materials provided a sense of security in that the interventionist could "fall back" on activities with the toys, and (c) the children liked the toys and their novelty engaged the children. From a practical standpoint, these reasons seem to support the use of toy bags (Hughes et al., 2004). These reasons, however, run counter to the FGRBI approach.

Based on what we know about how children learn through natural environments, the use of the families' own materials is imperative for several reasons. First, the family's materials are familiar. Thus, infants and toddlers are likely to have a preliminary understanding of how to manipulate these objects. Second, caregivers will be more comfortable using their own materials rather than using borrowed materials or materials that seem intimidating. Third, the use of the family's own materials during routines increases the likelihood that modeled strategies will be embedded when the practitioners (and toy bags) leave the home. Finally, specialized toys and equipment (other than physically adaptive equipment needed to support children's involvement in routines) are an expensive and unnecessary program expense.

To help practitioners decrease and eventually eliminate the use of toy bags, TaCTICS uses a 10 Step Program to Decrease Toy Bag Dependence (TaCTICS, 2004). This program, described in Appendix F, outlines several strategies for choosing alternate materials, gaining child acceptance of toy baglessness, and preparing for home visits based on family routines and materials.

Doing routines in their natural setting. The majority of activities conducted during home visits occur in the family's front room or living room. Most infant/toddler caregiving routines, however, do not regularly take place in this room. Conducting routines during the home visit, where the routines are likely to occur between visits, is essential if caregivers are to gain information about what materials to use and exactly how to embed learning strategies during routines. Many practitioners have identified this as a particularly difficult strategy since it is often uncomfortable to move into other rooms of the family's house. It is therefore crucial that practitioners work to build rapport and a sense of trust with caregivers. In the planning stages, caregivers and practitioners need to discuss which routines and related locations are the most comfortable for intervention.

Signaling the beginning and end of routines. Although many practitioners provide signals to children that activities are about to begin or that they are ending, the importance of using this strategy is particularly relevant to routines. The sequential nature and outcome focus of routines make it especially important for children to understand when a routine is beginning and when it is ending. A signal can be verbal or non-verbal, but must give the child a clear clue that the routine is beginning or ending. This signal also helps caregivers focus in on routines between intervention visits by having a repetitive way of opening and ending the routine with the child.

Incorporating IFSP objectives into daily living routines. The focus of intervention strategies for infants and toddlers needs to be directly related to the priorities identified by family members. Goals and objectives related to these priorities should be documented in the child's Individualized Family Service Plan (IFSP). Without clearly defined goals and outcomes, practitioners and caregivers lack the required information to determine if progress is being made. Goals and outcomes need to be action statements that relate to the family's priorities for their child's development. A recommended strategy for identifying appropriate goals and outcomes is for the family members to visualize what their child's behavior would look like once the outcome has been met (Cripe et al., 1997). For example, their child will be able to eat finger foods independently. The outcomes need to be clearly distinguished from the services. In other words, an appropriate outcome is not "monitoring the child's progress or occupational therapy." The strategies used to obtain the outcomes also need to be clearly delineated _and observable_. Specifying the strategies to be embedded within routines (including who, how, where, when and with what materials) needs to be clearly articulated in the IFSP document. For example, "Mom will provide multiple daily opportunities for Callie to pick up and eat food independently during mealtimes in the dining area and during snack time in the living room (location of snack was identified by caregiver). Mom will provide finger foods that Callie likes, such as raisins and cereal and will place Callie in a supported position in her high chair during each eating routine." As intervention progresses, these strategies need to be continually monitored and adapted to provide the best fit for families and the greatest improvement in children's skills.

The process of creating the IFSP document empowers families by allowing them to make choices about their priorities and the direction intervention will take. Writing goals, objectives and strategies in the family's own words can also help practitioners determine if caregivers fully understand how to incorporate these strategies into routines.

BARRIERS TO EFFECTIVE FGRBI IMPLEMENTATION

There are several important barriers that need to be addressed in order to effectively transition early intervention programs from more traditional models of service provision to FGRBI. They include ensuring practitioners receive training and on-site support for implementing the approach, working to give families flexibility in scheduling visits at times that are natural to their routines, and adjusting caseloads and evaluation strategies to support outcomes-based practice as opposed to outputs-based practice.

Training and Support

To provide quality FGRBI, practitioners need a specific set of tools beyond the positive teaching strategies that many have obtained through their education and experience prior to FGRBI. These positive strategies for teaching children may include such things as contingent responsiveness, following the child's lead, positive interactions, and strategies specific to their areas of expertise. Nevertheless, training and support in the areas of adult education, collaboration and coaching are essential if practitioners are to move from a teacher directed approach to FGRBI. It is also essential that support be provided on-site. Just as practitioners provide modeling and support for parents during the natural course of routines, practitioners making this paradigm shift need direct support. It cannot be stressed enough that providing on-site technical assistance to practitioners is a critical component for obtaining quality intervention practices.

Flexibility for Families

One of the central barriers to implementing a FGRBI approach is having an intervention schedule that does not provide flexibility to families. If family, community, and program routines are to be the basis for intervention, then modeling and support need to be provided at times when routines are occurring (or at least when they can be easily scheduled to occur). Having an intervention schedule that is limited to 9:00 a.m. through 3:00 p.m. does not provide the flexibility required for families. Programs need to identify how to schedule interventionist work hours in a way that promotes natural daily routines with infants and toddlers.

Outcomes vs. Outputs

In order to effectively implement FGRBI, interventionist caseloads and evaluation strategies must be determined not only by how many contacts are made but by how much support the parents need. From this approach, family members are providing the direct intervention. Practitioners are providing modeling, support, and planning. Because of this shifted role, practitioners can still serve several families. Their time, however, has to be allocated according to the amount of support a particular family needs. In addition, evaluation strategies need to focus not on the number of hours per family but by the actual progress families are making at providing learning opportunities to their infants and toddlers. Depending on how states and agencies conduct business, this shift may be an extremely difficult one. Evidence, however, suggests that if our ultimate goal is to empower families to provide development-enhancing experiences to their children, it's a shift that needs to take place.

Good luck to you. As a provider of early intervention services to infants and toddlers, you have a wonderful opportunity to directly impact the lives of families. Promoting caregiver-child interactions that are positive, that facilitate the child's developmental goals, and that produce competencies in parents that otherwise may never be known is an incredibly rewarding experience!

Address correspondence for this chapter to Kere Hughes, Ph.D. Iowa State University, Human Development and Family Studies, 2362 Palmer, Ames, IA 50011. Email: kereh@iastate.edu

REFERENCES

Blair, C., & Scott, K. G. (2002). Proportion of LD placements associated with low socioeconomic status: Evidence for a gradient? *The Journal of Special Education 36*(1), 14–22.

Bredekamp, S., & Copple, C. (1997). *Developmentally appropriate practice in early childhood programs,* (Rev. ed.). Washington, DC: National Association for the Education of Young Children.

Bricker, D. D., Pretti-Frontczak, K. L., & McComas, N. R. (1998). *An activity-based approach to early intervention* (2nd ed.). Baltimore, MD: Brookes.

Bronfenbrenner, U. (1993). The ecology of cognitive development: Research models and fugitive findings. In R. H. Wozniak & K. W. Fischer (Eds.), *Development in context: Acting and thinking in specific environments* (pp. 3–44). Hillsdale, NJ: Erlbaum.

Bronfenbrenner, U. (1995). Developmental ecology through space and time: A future perspective. In P. Moen, G. H. Elder, Jr., & K. Luscher (Eds.), *Examining lives in context: Perspectives on the ecology of human development* (pp. 619–647). Washington, DC: American Psychological Association.

Bruder, M. B. & Dunst, C. J. Expanding learning opportunities for infants and toddlers in natural environments: A chance to reconceptualize early intervention. *Zero to Three,* December 1999/January 2000, 34–36.

Cripe, J. W., Hanline, M. F., & Daley, S. E. (1997). Preparing practitioners for planning intervention for natural environments. In P. J. Winton, J. A. McColllum, & C. Catlett, (Eds.), *Reforming personnel preparation in early intervention: Issues models and practical strategies.* Baltimore, MD: Brookes.

Cripe, J. W., & Venn, M. L. (1997). Family-guided routines for early intervention services. *Young Exceptional Children, 1*(1), 18–26.

Dunst, C. J., Bruder, M. B. Trivette, C. M., Hamby, D., Raab, M., & McLean, M. (2001). Characteristics and consequences of everyday natural learning opportunities. *Topics in Early Childhood Special Education, 21*(2), 68–92.

Dunst, C. J., Bruder, M. B., Trivette, C. M., Raab, M., & McLean, M. (1998, May). *Increasing children's learning opportunities through families and communities early childhood research institute: Year 2 progress report.* Asheville, NC: Orelena Hawks Puckett Institute.

Dunst, C. J., Hamby, D., Trivette, C. M., Raab, M., & Bruder, M. B. (2000). Everyday family and community life and children's naturally occurring learning opportunities. *Journal of Early Intervention, 23*(3), 151–164.

Dunst, C. J., & Trivette, C. M. (1987). Enabling and empowering families: Conceptual and intervention issues. *School Psychology Review, 16*(4), 443–456.

Faver, J. A. M. (1999). Activity setting analysis: A model for examining the role of culture in development. In A. Goncu (Ed.), *Children's engagement in the world: Sociocultural perspectives* (pp. 99–127). Cambridge, England: Cambridge University Press.

Gomby, D. S., Culross, P. L., & Behrman, R. E. (1999). Home visiting: Recent program evaluations-analysis and recommendations. *Future of Children, 9*(1), 4–26.

Hart, B., & Risley, T. R. (1995). *Meaningful differences in the everyday experience of young American children.* Baltimore, MD: Brookes.

Hughes, K. P., Summers, J. A., Carta, J. J., & Woods, J. C., (2004). *Defining and measuring the implementation of routines based intervention.* Manuscript submitted for publication.

Losardo, A., & Bricker, D. (1994). Activity-based intervention and direct instruction: A comparison study. *American Journal on Mental Retardation, 98*(6), 744–765.

Lowenthal, B. (1998). Precursors of learning disabilities in the inclusive preschool. *Learning Disabilities: A Multidisciplinary Journal, 9*(2), 25–31.

McCollum, J. A., & Yates, T. J. (1994). Dyad as focus, triad as means: A family-centered approach to supporting parent-child interactions. *Infants and Young Children, 6*(4), 54–63.

McLean, L. K. & Cripe, J. W. (1997). The effectiveness of early intervention for children with communication disorders. In M. J. Guralnick (Ed.), *The effectiveness of early intervention* (pp 349–428). Baltimore, MD: Brookes.

McWilliam, P. J. (1996). Collaborative consultation across seven disciplines: Challenges and solutions. In R. A. McWilliam (Ed.), *Rethinking pull-out services in early intervention* (pp. 49–69). Baltimore, MD: Brookes.

McWilliam, R. A. (1992). *The family-centered intervention plan: A guide for classroom-based early intervention* (pp. 349-428). Tucson, AZ: Communication Skill Builders. (Out of print. Available from author R. A. McWilliam, Ph.D., Director, Vanderbilt Center for Child Development, 415 Medical Center South, Vanderbilt University Medical Center, 2100 Pierce Avenue, Nashville, TN 37232–3573).

Nelson, K. (1999, Winter). Making sense: Language and thought in development. *Developmental Psychologist, 1*–10.

Pretti-Frontczak, K. & Bricker, D. (2001). Use of the embedding strategy during daily activities by early childhood education and early childhood special education teachers. *Infant-Toddler Intervention, 11*(2), 111–128.

Roggman, L. A., Boyce, L. K., Cook, G. A., & Jump, V. K. (2001). Inside home visits: A collaborative look at process and quality. *Early Childhood Research Quarterly, 16*(1), 53–71.

Shumway-Cook A. & Woolacott M. (1995). *Motor control: Theory and practical applications.* Baltimore, MD: Williams & Wilkins.

Steele, M. M. (2004). Making the case for early identification and intervention for young children at risk for learning disabilities. *Early Childhood Education Journal, 32*(2), 75–79.

TaCTICS, (2004). *Therapists as Collaborative Team members for Infants/Toddlers Community Services.* Retrieved November 19, 2004, from Florida State University Web Site: http://tactics.fsu.edu

Taylor, H. G., Anselmo, M., Foreman, A. L., Schatschneider, C., & Angelopoulos, J. (2000). Utility of kindergarten teacher judgments in identifying early learning problems. *Journal of Learning Disabilities, 33*(2), 200–210.

Wachs, T. D. (2000). *Necessary but not sufficient: The respective roles of single and multiple influences on individual development.* Washington, DC: American Psychological Association.

Warren, S. F. (1992). Facilitating basic vocabulary acquisition with milieu teaching procedures. *Journal of Early Intervention, 16*(3), 235–251.

Appendix A
Adult Learning Checklist

Therapists as Collaborative Team members for Infant/Toddler Community Services

Implementing Information About Adult Learners in Family-guided Activity Based Intervention:
A Checklist

Yes	No	
❑	❑	1. Are family members comfortable in the environment in which we work together? Have they identified the environment as preferred for the child and themselves? Have they had input into the time, materials, and participants in the activity? Is the environment non- threatening?
❑	❑	2. Am I aware and respectful of the cultural and structural makeup of the family? Do I listen for the family's values and priorities? Do I accommodate the family's concerns and activities in our planning and implementation? Are family members who care for the child included? Do I promote interactions in which family members feel comfortable sharing their thoughts, beliefs, and ideas?
❑	❑	3. Do I use effective communication strategies? Is there always "time just to talk"? Do I seek family observations/information in assessment? In monitoring? Do family members have opportunities to ask questions or seek clarification? Do I present information at a time and in a format preferred by the family members? Do I keep my work with family members respectful, yet informal, and free of professionally precious jargon?
❑	❑	4. Am I aware and do I make use of the positive and negative experiences that affect family members as adult learners? Do I listen and respond to family members' comments that reflect their perceptions and histories of teaching and learning opportunities for their child? Were the intervention strategies already used by family members identified and incorporated into the routine? Were strategies reviewed with family members and options offered? Did the family make the choice of where, when, and how often to intervene?
❑	❑	5. Do family members feel that the goals of the teaching and learning experience are their goals? Are family priorities the basis for the plan? Are family members' recommendations identified as strategies? Are family members assured that plans are flexible and can be modified as the need arises?
❑	❑	6. Do I provide opportunities for collaborative problem solving? Do family members have the opportunity to "brainstorm" concerns and issues with team members? Is information available and offered to families to assist them in generating ideas? Are they encouraged to discuss alternatives before deciding on the best solution? Does the team respect and support the family's plan?
❑	❑	7. Can the content be immediately applied by the family member to a real situation? Did the family identify the routines? Did the service provider observe family members engage in routines with the child? Did the family members have the opportunity to practice within the context of the routines and receive feedback?
❑	❑	8. In planning intervention, do I take into account the various other commitments of family members? Are variables identified and negotiated during planning? Do I seek to involve multiple care providers? Do family members have the opportunity to make final decisions in determining appropriateness?

Note. From "Therapists as Collaborative Team Members for Infant/Toddler Community Services (TaCTICS)," by J. Woods, 2004, Florida State University Website: http://tactics. fsu.edu Reprinted with permission of the author.

183

Appendix B
Routines Based Interview (RBI) Form

RBI Report Form

Routines-Based Interview

October 03
R. A. McWilliam
2003
Vanderbilt Center for Child Development

Directions:

This form is designed to be used to report the findings from the McWilliam model of conducting a routines-based interview. A second person (e.g., someone assisting the lead interviewer) can use the form to summarize the discussion during the interview, or it can be filled out at the end of the interview.

1. Complete the information below.
2. For each routine, write a short phrase defining the routine (e.g., *waking up, breakfast, hanging out, circle, snack, centers*).
3. Write brief descriptions about the child's engagement in the Engagement box (e.g., *Participates with breakfast routine, banging spoon on the high chair* or *Pays attention to the teacher; names songs when asked; often leaves circle before it has ended*).
4. If the interview revealed no information about one of the three domains, circle *No information* in that domain for that routine.
5. Write brief descriptions about the child's independence in the Independence box (e.g., *Feeds herself with a spoon; drinks from a cup but spills a lot* or *Sings all the songs with the group, but needs prompting to speak loudly enough*).
6. Write brief descriptions about the child's communication and social competence in the Social Relationships box (e.g., *Looks parent in the eye when pointing to things in the kitchen* or *Pays attention to the teacher at circle but can't stand touching other children*).

Child's Name	
Date of birth	
Who is being interviewed	
Interviewer	
Date of interview	

Routine		Concern? ☐
Engagement		No information
Independence		No information
Social Relationships		No information

Appendix B
Routines Based Interview (RBI) Form (continued)

Home: Satisfaction with routine (CIRCLE ONE)		Classroom: Fit of routine and child (CIRCLE ONE)
1. Not at all satisfied		1. Poor goodness of fit
2.		2.
3. Satisfied		3. Average goodness of fit
4.		4.
5. Very satisfied		5. Excellent goodness of fit
Domains addressed (CIRCLE ALL THAT APPLY):		
Physical Cognitive Communication Social or emotional Adaptive		
Routine		
Engagement		No information
Independence		No information
Social Relationships		No information
Home: Satisfaction with routine (CIRCLE ONE)		Classroom: Fit of routine and child (CIRCLE ONE)
1. Not at all satisfied		1. Poor goodness of fit
2.		2.
3. Satisfied		3. Average goodness of fit
4.		4.
5. Very satisfied		5. Excellent goodness of fit
Domains addressed (CIRCLE ALL THAT APPLY):		
Physical Cognitive Communication Social or emotional Adaptive		

RBI Report Form   McWilliam 2003   2

Note. Adapted from "The family-centered intervention plan: A guide for classroom-based early intervention," by R. A. McWilliam, 1992, pp. 349–428. Copyright 1992 by Communication Skill Builders. Reprinted with permission of the author.

Appendix C
Indentifying Family Activities and Routines Conversation Starters

---

Therapists as Collaborative Team members for Infant/Toddler Community Services

Identifying Family Activities and Routines Conversation Starters

Consider using some of these comments or questions to open a dialog about the child's and family's activities, environments, and routines.

★   We'd like to learn about some of your child's daily routines and activities for teaching and learning. By sharing your daily activities and routines, you are identifying potential times and places for your child's intervention.

★   Tell me about your day. What are the routines/activities or places that you go that most often occur for you and your child?

★   What types of things happen on most:
Mornings?   Afternoons?   Nights?   Weekends?

★   Life with children usually makes us be pretty flexible. Can you give me some ideas about what usually happens before or after _____? (Use some event the careprovider mentions-- "One Life to Live." Systematically identify events, and then proceed.)

★   If the careprovider is having difficulty identifying activities or routines, ask some specific questions about some of the following: dressing, breakfast, watching TV, car travel, preparing meals, household chores, nap, lunch and evening meals, yard work, bath, bedtime stories, or hanging out.

Possible follow-up questions to consider:

★   Are there any activities or places that you go (e.g., shopping, doctor's appointments) that occur on a less than regular basis (e.g., once a week, every few days)?

★   Are there other events that occur fairly regularly or during the weekend (e.g., sport events for siblings)?

★   Who are the important people who participate in your child's life? Who are helpful in your child's care, and who may also have activities and routines for teaching and learning (e.g., grandparents, big brother, neighbor, friend)?

6/13/00   TaCTICS is a project of Florida State University

Appendix C
Indentifying Family Activities and Routines Conversation Starters (continued)

Therapist as Collaborative Team members for Infant/Toddler Community Service

★   What routines/activities does _____ (child's name) _____ enjoy doing?

  • What makes this routine(s) enjoyable to _____?

  • What does_____usually do during the routine/activity?

  • What do you (or the other careproviders) do during the routine/activity?

  • How long does it take?

★   Are there opportunities for your child to interact with other children?

  • How many other children participate in this routine/activity?

★   What routine/activity(s) does_____not like?

  • What makes this routine/activity difficult or uncomfortable for_____?

  • What does_____usually do during the routine/activity?

★   What are your (family's) expectations of the children during the routine/activity?

  • What do you do during the routine/activity?

  • How do you let the child know what is expected in this routine/activity?

★   Are there better times for you during the day or locations that are more comfortable for intervention routines?

SUMMARY INFORMATION

Potential Outcomes	Careprovider & Child Routines		Good Times & Places	
What to do	Who	Which Routine	When	Where

(Adapted from Woods Cripe; Woods Cripe & Venn)

Note. From "Therapists as Collaborative Team Members for Infant/Toddler Community Services (TaCTICS)," by J. Woods, 2004, Florida State University Website: http://tactics.fsu.edu Reprinted with permission of the author.

Appendix D
Self Evaluation of Family-guided/Routines Based Intervention Form

Therapists as Collaborative Team members for Infant/Toddler Community Services

Self Evaluation of Family-guided/Routines Based Intervention

Family guided features

Did I support/enhance:	YES	SOME	NO
1. caregiver's sharing about the child and/or family throughout the visit?	❏	❏	❏
2. caregiver's knowledge of linkage between IFSP outcomes and activities?	❏	❏	❏
3. caregiver's sharing information about child participation and progress since last visit?	❏	❏	❏
4. caregiver's knowledge about development, child progress, next steps, etc.?	❏	❏	❏
5. communication with careprovider through data collection and development of new plans?	❏	❏	❏

Responsive teaching and learning interactions between careprovider and child

Did I support/enhance:	YES	SOME	NO
6. positioning for positive interaction to occur between caregiver and child?	❏	❏	❏
7. child access to developmentally appropriate materials?	❏	❏	❏
8. joint attention to objects and/or action between child and caregiver?	❏	❏	❏
9. positive interactions between child and caregiver?	❏	❏	❏
10. the matching of pace to temperament (mood) of the child; and matching of complexity to temperment (mood) of the child?	❏	❏	❏
11. contingent responding to child's actions or initiations by the caregiver?	❏	❏	❏
12. joining the child and caregiver in the child's activity of interest?	❏	❏	❏
13. child initiations and the caregiver's knowledge of the child's actions?	❏	❏	❏
14. raising the expectation or "upping the ante" (as appropriate) by caregiver?	❏	❏	❏

5/30/03   TaCTICS is a project of Florida State University

Appendix D
Self Evaluation of Family-guided/Routines Based Intervention Form (Continued)

Therapists as Collaborative Team members for Infant/Toddler Community Services

Routines Based Intervention

Did I support/enhance:	YES	SOME	NO
15. a logical or predictable sequence to routine or activity?	❑	❑	❑
16. repetition (where appropriate)/sufficiency of opportunities for learning within routine?	❑	❑	❑
17. consequences logical to the routine?	❑	❑	❑
18. variations within routine/activity?	❑	❑	❑
19. embedding intervention into multiple routines?	❑	❑	❑
20. use of new skills in familiar routines and new routines for generalization of acquired skills? plans?	❑	❑	❑

Family-guided Routines Based Intervention

Did I support/enhance:	YES	SOME	NO
21. caregiver's identification of preferred routines and activities?	❑	❑	❑
22. caregiver's participation in routines and activities with child?	❑	❑	❑
23. caregiver's confidence in use of strategies in routines and activities by observing and giving supportive feedback?	❑	❑	❑
24. caregiver's participation and decision making in agenda or routine planning?	❑	❑	❑
25. active engagement of child and caregiver within the routine or activity?	❑	❑	❑
26. the use of appropriate intervention strategies by modeling, demonstrating or reinforcing caregiver's use?	❑	❑	❑
27. the reduction of support/cues (as appropriate) by caregiver?	❑	❑	❑
28. elaborations (new, different, model, suggest) of careprovider strategies?	❑	❑	❑
29. the identification and explanation of strategies caregiver uses within routines to enhance caregiver knowledge and reinforce occurance?	❑	❑	❑
30. embedding targets without interfering with caregiver's preferred sequence of routine?	❑	❑	❑

Note. From "Therapists as Collaborative Team Members for Infant/Toddler Community Services (TaCTICS)," by J. Woods, 2004, Florida State University Website: http://tactics. fsu.edu Reprinted with permission of the author.

Appendix E
Fidelity Checklist

Fidelity Checklist
Developed at Juniper Gardens Children's Project
University of Kansas
Judith Carta, Kere Hughes, & Juliann Woods

Child ID# _____ **Respondent's Rel. to Child** _____

Interventionist_____ **Date of IFSP**_____
Location_____

OBSERVER_____ **Date**_____ **Observation #:**_____

Listing of Child IFSP Outcomes	Check off which ones were addressed in this home visit

NOTE: If providing feedback, circle the number next to the item(s) for which feedback was given.

Observation Impressions:

Based on the IFSP and past observations of this child, please indicate for each of the following items: (1) No evidence of occurrence; (2) Occurred occasionally, (3) Occurred with consistent high quality, (4) You were not able to judge.

DID YOU SEE THE INTERVENTIONIST...	No evidence of occurrence	Occurred occasionally	High Quality	Not able to judge
1. gather information about the child				
2. request caregiver data on routines				
3. join in routines and activities with caregiver and child				
4. talk about ways to incorporate child outcomes into a variety of routines/locations during the visit'				
5. model, or support the parent instead of simply doing routine for the parent'				
6. provide information about the child's progress or participation'				
7. focus on family strengths/point out the ways they're supporting their child's development				
8. summarize and synthesize plans for caregiver				
9. identify agenda for next session				
DID THE PARENT OR CAREPROVIDER...				
1. appear to be engaged in the visit'				
2. discuss outcomes implemented within routines since last visit'				

Circle areas in which routines were observed: SNACK/   DRESSING   CLEAN-UP TOYS   TOILETING
PLAY FAMILY CHORES MEALS OUTDOOR PLAY   BATHTIME   SHOPPING   READING FAMILY
OUTING   WATCHING TV/VIDEOS   SINGING OTHER_____

Appendix E
Fidelity Checklist (continued)

Total Number of Routines Observed _____   Did routines occur in more than one room during visit?   Yes   No

Did the Parent (Careprovider) Perform? (1, 2, 3 or NA)	Scores mean the following: (1) No evidence of occurrence; (2) Occurred occasionally, (3) Occurred with consistent high quality, (NA) You were not able to judge.	Did the Primary Interventionist Perform? (1, 2, 3 or NA)	Did Another Interventionist Perform? (1, 2, 3 or NA)
	1. Work with child in a variety of routines/not just play		
	2. Use everyday materials appropriate to families' routines		
	3. Do routines in their "natural" setting		
	4. Promote child's access to materials		
	5. Promote child's participation or initiation in the routine		
	6. Focus on object of child's attention/follows child's lead		
	7. Allow for repetition or sufficiency of opportunities		
	8. Engage in positive interactions		
	9. Use appropriate intervention strategies (e.g., minimal assistance, wait time)		
	10. Incorporate logical consequences for the routine		
	11. Respond contingently		
	12. Signal beginning and end of routines		
	13. Incorporate IFSP objectives into routines		
Total Possible		Total Possible	
Total Score:		Total Score:	Total:

OVERALL IMPRESSION: Do the scores today reflect the overall fidelity of implementation?   YES NO
IF NOT, Please explain briefly.

_____
_____

Appendix F
Self Evaluation of Family-guided/Routines Based Intervention Form

Family-guided **A**pproaches to **C**ollaborative **E**arly-intervention **T**raining and **S**ervices

10 Step Program
to Decrease
Toy Bag Dependence

1. Functional Assessment:
   Identify materials and toys already available and likely to be engaging while visiting. Plan ahead to incorporate those materials/routines into next visit.

2. Using Existing Social and Daily Routines:
   Join careprovider and child in activities occurring throughout the household/center when you arrive.

3. Futures Planning:
   Plan activities/routines for your next visit before leaving. Joint identification supports problem solving, partnerships, and allows selective choice of any necessary materials.

4. Community Based Training:
   Plan a special activity with careprovider - a trip to the park, a walk around the block, gardening, making pudding.

5. Peer Mediation:
   Organize a play date with other children and careproviders.

6. Milieu Strategies:
   With permission of family, ask the child to show or get toys or preferred objects in bedroom, toy room, or another area of the house where child's things are and routines occur. Follow child's lead and move into other areas.

7. Fading Strategy:
   Decrease the size of bag. Choose 1 to 2 toys that support acquisition or generalization of specific outcomes to include in the bag for the visit.

8. Systematic Desensitization:
   Leave toy bag by the door. Join the child's activities. Use the toy bag only when and if needed. (The next step is to leave the bag outside and then in trunk or under seat in car.)

9. Hybrid Approaches:

   - Forgetfulness:
     Walk in empty handed. Ask child, "What's wrong?" Wait.
     When child responds, ask, "I forgot. What else should we do? What do we need?"
   - Choice Making:
     Put materials common to household in toy bag. Ask child (careprovider), "Isn't this like yours? Should we use yours or mine? Show me how you do it?"
   - Sabotage:
     If child really likes toy bag approach, take in an empty bag and fill it with child preferred objects of interest/toys.

10. Generalization:
    Demonstrate use of a toy that includes opportunities to practice a skill such as putting objects in small spaces (e.g. putting pieces into Mr. Potato Head). Then look around the home for toys or other materials that could provide additional practice for the same skill.

1/26/99   FACETS is a joint project of Kansas University Affiliated Program and Valdosta State University

Note. From "Therapists as Collaborative Team Members for Infant/Toddler Community Services (TaCTICS)," by J. Woods, 2004, Florida State University Website: http://tactics. fsu.edu Reprinted with permission of the author.

Chapter Nine

GOAL ORIENTATIONS, CLASSROOM GOAL STRUCTURES, AND REGULATION IN STUDENTS WITH AND WITHOUT LEARNING DISABILITIES: SHOULD WE ALTER STUDENT'S MOTIVATION, A CLASSROOM'S GOAL STRUCTURE, OR BOTH?

Georgios D. Sideridis, Ph.D.
University of Crete

"Genius is only the power of making continuous efforts. The line between failure and success is so fine that we scarcely know when we pass it: so fine that we are often on the line and do not know it. How many times a man has thrown up his hands at a time when a little more effort, a little more patience, would have achieved success."

Elbert Hubbard

I strongly believe that one significant missing element in past as well as present research in learning disabilities (LD) pertains to the contribution of motivational and emotional factors. Those characteristics belong to the inner self but are cultivated within a classroom's environment. Unraveling this reciprocal relationship, may be the most important advancement in educational research. My purpose in this chapter is twofold: (a) to present research evidence supporting the contribution of motivation in achievement for students with and without LD using the achievement goal theory framework, and (b) to describe how our knowledge of achievement goal orientations can be used toward modifying classroom environments to be conducive to learning. In my effort to accomplish these objectives I draw heavily from my personal line of research to present current findings linking achievement goals to academic and emotional variables, highlighting their salient role in student's regulation of their behavior in achievement situations.

Motivation is not new to the field of learning disabilities. In fact, throughout the past three decades, researchers have strongly advocated for motivation as an explanatory variable in the low achievement of students with LD (e.g., Deci, Hodges, Pierson, & Tomassone, 1992), and that academic interventions should incorporate elements of motivation (Adelman & Taylor, 1983). Further, after advocating the importance of motivation for the field of learning disabilities for twenty years, Taylor and Adelman (1999) concluded that it is ironic that although most teachers recognize the key role of motivation in accounting for poor instructional outcomes, they still do not incorporate it in their teaching.

So far, learning disabilities have been linked to neuropsychological and cognitive deficiencies only. Various definitions of learning disabilities systematically ignore motivational and emotional factors. Unfortunately, when you ignore something, it does not go away! For example, in a recent meta-analysis, I found that the prevalence of depression in learning disabilities has gone up to 88%!

(Sideridis, in press-d). If we compare that rate to the 5% rate in the general population, one can understand how striking this finding is. If depression is present in individuals with learning disabilities, should we expect them to function as if they were fine? Similarly, one cannot ignore that in most comparisons between typical student groups and those with LD, the latter group has displayed helplessness (Sabatino, 1982; Thomas, 1979; Valas, 2001), hopelessness (Sideridis, 2003), lowered motivation (Dunn & Shapiro, 1999; Olivier & Steenkamp, 2004; Pintrich, Anderman, & Klobucar, 1994), lowered persistence (Sideridis, in press-c) depression (Colbert, Newman, Ney, & Young, 1982; Dalley & Bolocofsky, 1992; Heath & Ross, 2000), anxiety (Hoy et al., 1997; Rodriguez & Routh, 1989), lowered self-esteem or self-concept (Chapman & Tunmer, 1995; Riddick, Sterling, Farmer, & Morgan, 1999; Stanovich, Jordan, & Perot, 1998), loneliness (Valas, 1999), external locus of control (Rogers & Saklofski, 1985), lowered goal commitment (Bouffard & Couture, 2003), lowered goal importance (Sideridis, 2002; Sideridis & Padeliadu, 2001), lowered intention to pursue goals (Sideridis, 2005), psychological disturbances (Greenway & Milne, 1999, Gregg, Hoy, King, Moreland, & Jagota, 1992), psychological maladjustment (Grolnick & Ryan, 1990), emotional disregulation (Masi, Brovedani, & Poli, 1998), metacognitive deficits (Botsas & Padeliadu, 2003; Palladino, Poli, Masi, & Marcheschi, 2000), self-regulation failure (Fulk, Brigham, & Lohman, 1998), and cognitive impairments (Chapman, 1988). Despite these salient between-group differences, no studies have explored how strongly these factors serve as identifying or core (rather than comorbid) characteristics of students with LD.

The above research findings suggest a very unfortunate profile for students with LD. These students seem to be "attacked" by various sources, thus, disabling the regulation of their behavior to achieve positive learning outcomes. Addressing the issue of "the chicken and the egg", my colleagues and I have argued that motivation, psychopathology, and emotions may not just be characteristics of students with LD but core identifying features (Sideridis, Morgan, Botsas, Padeliadu, & Fuchs, in press). We argued that those variables need to be included in the taxonomy of features characterizing students with LD because their predictive validity proved to be high (even higher) compared to cognitive variables alone (e.g., Watkins, 1996). For example, metacognitive variables such as "planning the task" and "monitoring their performance" proved to be poor predictors in identifying students as having learning problems. On the contrary, motivational and psychopathological variables were strong predictors in identifying students as having learning problems (see Figure 1).

As Figure 1 shows, the use of Receiver Operating Characteristic (ROC) curves, suggested that student motivation for writing, individualism, and

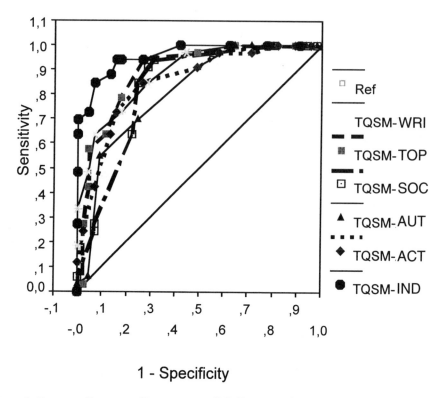

Figure 1. Receiver Operating Characteristic (ROC) curves showing the discriminant ability of motivational variables to account for the correct classification of students into LD vs. typical student groups.
Note: Variables were: individual (IND), activity (ACT), autonomy (AUT), social (SOC), topic (TOP), and writing (WRI). From "Prediction of students with LD based on metacognition, motivation, emotions, and psychopathology: A ROC analysis by G.D. Sideridis, P. Morgan, G. Botsas, S. Padeliadu and D. Fuchs—in press. *Journal of Learning Disabilities.* Reprinted with permission of the authors.

autonomy were significant predictors of the presence of learning disabilities. The further the ROC curves from the diagonal, the higher the classification accuracy[1]. In Figure 1, all curves were far apart from the diagonal suggesting non-chance classification. Thus, motivation may be "a lot more" than what previously thought of, regarding its presence and function in learning disabilities. Below, I describe goal theory, and how its constructs can assist us toward understanding underachievement in students with LD.

---

1. The ROC plot contrasts false positive rates to true positive rates. The diagonal line indicates chance classification (50:50) and the curve shows correct classification. The larger the area under the curve the better the classification (Hsu, 2002). Typical conventions of non-chance classification are: 90-99% = excellent; 80-89% = good, 70-79% = fair, and 60-69% = poor. Between 50 and 60% classification is considered at chance levels (Gallop, Crits-Christoph, Muenz, & Tu, 2003).

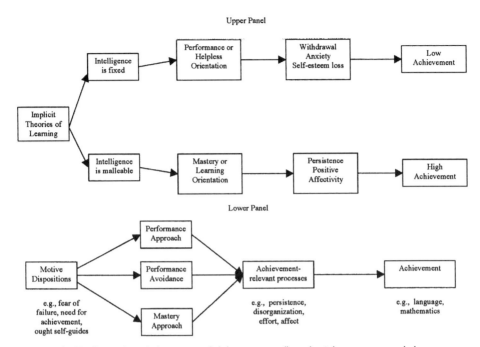

Figure 2. Traditional goal theory model (upper panel) and trichotomous goal theory model (lower panel)

Goal Orientations and Academic Achievement

A recent advancement of motivational theories is achievement goal theory (Figure 2). Achievement goals or goal orientations have been considered a "dynamic force," which directs and regulates student's actions (Maehr & Anderman, 1993). The basic premise of goal theory is that *how* one approaches a task is associated with a unique network of self-regulatory behaviors and subsequent goal-attainment. Dweck and Legget (1988) distinguished two types of goal orientations: *performance,* in which individuals are concerned with gaining favorable judgments regarding their ability, and *mastery,* in which individuals are concerned with increasing their skills and competencies for the sake of learning[2] (see Figure 2, upper panel). Dweck and Leggett added that a mastery orientation[3] involves the seeking of challenges, the ability to regulate one's

---

2. What distinguishes performance from mastery goal orientations is student's *conception of ability.* Mastery oriented students believe that intelligence is an entity that changes through the life course whereas performance oriented students believe it is a fixed attribute. Dweck and Leggett proposed that this conception is responsible for the variability observed in persistence.

3. Goal orientations have been termed in various ways in the past, but there is agreement that all these terms refer to the same conceptual ideas. So, a "learning" orientation has also been termed in the literature as "task" (Nicholls, 1984), "mastery" (Elliot, 1997), whereas a "performance" orientation has also been termed an "ego" (Nicholls, 1984), "helpless" (Dweck & Leggett, 1988), "performance approach-avoidance" (Elliot & Harackiewicz, 1996), or "self-enhancing/defeating" (Skaalvik, 1997).

strategies and be successful in the face of difficulty, the investment of large amounts of effort, the ability to persist in the face of difficulty, and the presence of joy and interest from being involved in challenging tasks. Following the dichotomization of performance goals into approach and avoidance (i.e., to show competence or avoid showing incompetence), a performance approach orientation (i.e., the orientation to outperform others) has been hypothesized to involve a range of processes (involving affective dimensions) which eventually facilitate optimal task engagement (Elliot & Harackiewicz, 1996), whereas previously a generalized performance orientation was conceptualized to elicit anxiety and self-worth threats (see Figure 2, lower panel).

Although a mastery orientation has always been considered adaptive and a performance orientation maladaptive, recent research has consistently linked a performance approach orientation to positive achievement outcomes (e.g., enhanced effort and persistence, Elliot, McGregor, & Gable, 1999). In fact, research findings have been so compelling regarding the positive role of a performance-approach orientation that several researchers have asked for a reconceptualization of the original theory that would explicitly state that positive role (Harackiewicz, Barron, & Elliot, 1998; Harackiewicz, Barron, Pintrich, Elliot, & Thrash, 2002; Kaplan & Middleton, 2002; Midgley, Kaplan, & Middleton, 2001; Sideridis in press-b). For example, Harackiewicz et al., (2002) reported 11 recent studies[4] in which a performance-approach orientation was significantly more predictive of academic achievement, compared to a mastery orientation. Similarly, across studies, a mastery orientation has consistently been found to be positively associated with achievement and achievement related outcomes such as adaptive learning strategies and positive affectivity (e.g., Ames, 1992).

Goal Orientations and Regulation in Learning Disabilities

Regulation of student behaviors. Given recent research findings suggesting the positive effects of both mastery and performance-approach goals with typical students, one interesting question is how goal orientation affects the performance of students with LD. The results have been unequivocal; Pintrich et al. (1994) reported that LD students were high on mastery and Carlson, Booth, Shin, and Canu (2002) found that they were low on a mastery orientation. Additionally, the relationship between mastery and performance orientations and achievement (in particular for students with LD) has not been frequently examined. For example,

---

4. The following studies formed the basis for the Harackiewicz et al. (2002) suggestions to revise goal theory (Barron & Harackiewicz, 2001; Barron, Schwab, & Harackiewicz, 1999; Church, Elliot, & Gable, 2001; Elliot & Church, 1997; Elliot & McGregor, 1999; Elliot & McGregor, 2001; Elliot, McGregor, & Gable, 1999; Harackiewicz, Barron, Carter, Lehto, & Elliot, 1997; Harackiewicz, Barron, Tauer, Carter, & Elliot, 2000; Harackiewicz, Barron, Tauer, & Elliot, 2002). More previous studies reported similar findings (e.g., Middleton & Midgley, 1997).

Sideridis (in press-c) reported that students with LD would benefit by either the presence of a high mastery or performance-approach orientation with the effects from the latter being slightly more pronounced. A performance-approach orientation had significant positive standardized weights associated with both academic achievement and important cognitive variables. One unit of change in student's performance orientation was associated with between .25 and .65 unit changes in student achievement and their intention to achieve and mathematics achievement. These findings strengthen the importance of the role of motivation in the achievement of students with LD, a role that has been underestimated throughout the years. In earlier studies, Sideridis (2002, 2005) and Sideridis and Padeliadu (2001) had indicated that affective variables incorporating the valence dimension of a performance orientation (i.e., goal importance) were positively associated with achievement outcomes for students with LD. Given recent evidence in favor of a performance-approach orientation, it is suggested that this orientation may be particularly more adaptive for students with LD (because of their strong desire to take their achievement to the level of their peers). Thus, preliminary recent evidence supports the notion that goal orientations are very influential in the achievement of students with LD.

Giving up in the face of challenges was a typical characteristic of students with LD. In a recent study, (Sideridis, 2003) attempted to evaluate both the academic and emotional regulation of students with and without LD. Participants were 132 students with LD and 705 typical 5th and 6th graders who were given a set of easy or challenging math exercises. Through a series of regression-type analyses, results indicated that mastery goals were positive predictors of (a) "time students spent engaged with the math exercises" ($b = .234$), (b) positive affect ($b = .354$), (c) math achievement ($b = .185$), and self-esteem ($b = .113$). The respective effects from adopting performance-approach goals were approximately null with the exception of self-esteem ($b = .149$). Furthermore, mastery goals had negative effects on (a) negative affect ($b = -.146$), and (b) feelings of hopelessness ($b = -.350$). Once again, the effects of performance-approach goals were miniscule with the exception of negative affect ($b = -.140$). Thus, mastery goals appear to possess the positive attributes, consistently reported with typical student groups, for students with LD as well.

In another study, (Sideridis & Tsorbatzoudis, 2003) examined the association of the multiplicative mastery and performance goals construct with cognitive, motivational, affective processes, and academic achievement. The presence of a synergy in goals (Barron & Harackiewicz, 2001) has been linked to specific or specialized outcomes as well as enhanced achievement compared to the operation of one set of goals [5] (i.e., when one is motivated by mastery or performance goals only). The study involved 58 students, 29 with and 29 without LD and investigators attempted to create achievement profiles of students based on a combination of cognitive, affective, and motivational variables. Results showed the existence of a parsimonious 3-cluster solution with the students with LD representing clusters 1 and 3 (i.e., amotivated-disengaged, and avoidant-uncommitted). In the two clusters in which students with LD belonged, the average goal orientations were well below the grand mean. Thus, a defining feature of low achievement (and of students with LD membership) was low levels of mastery and performance goals. Those differences reached statistical significance across all comparisons with the typical student group. For cluster 2 students (mostly typical students) the combination of mastery and performance goals ($z = .412$) was associated with the most positive academic outcomes compared to either a mastery ($z = .355$) or performance-approach ($z = .128$) orientation alone, indicating that both goals may interact with each other to produce enhanced achievement outcomes.

Regulation of student affective behaviors. The basic premises of goal theory state that mastery oriented students are challenged by a difficult task and view it as a way to learn and improve. On the contrary, performance-oriented students seek to establish that their ability is adequate and to avoid showing incompetence. So any achievement situation is viewed as a test of their ability and eventually as an evaluation of their self-worth (or a threat to self-worth). Thus, it is inevitable, that anxiety will be present, both before and after a performance evaluation. Anxiety prior to performance is hypothesized to be a function of appraising the event as threatening. Anxiety after the event has been associated with the individual's appraisal of their performance. Anxiety is a significant factor in the model although it operates differently for the two goal orientation groups. For example, for mastery oriented students, the view that the situation is an opportunity to learn, master new material, and exploit their ability, is likely to elicit low levels of anxiety. On the contrary, for performance-oriented students the threat to self-worth may be deleterious to their performance due to the manifestations of anxiety.

---

5. Barron and Harackiewicz (2001) and Pintrich, Conley and Kempler (2003) suggested that goals are not independent of each other, and the presence of one set of goals does not preclude the existence of others. In this vein, they proposed four patterns of multiple goal combinations. In the first pattern, the *additive goal hypothesis,* goal orientations exert independent, combined effects on the same outcomes (i.e., are orthogonal). It is suggested that it may be more adaptive to have two forces operating compared to one. The *selective goal hypothesis* states that individuals adopt different goals in different situations. Thus, a student may pursue performance goals in P.E. classes (to show off) but mastery goals in subjects he/she finds interesting to work with (e.g., algebra) (Barron & Harackiewicz, 2003). Based on the *interactive goal hypothesis,* individuals may like the material of a course but also wish to receive high grades. This interactive motivational form may be associated with unique gains, *over and above* those produced from the pursuit of mastery or performance goals alone. Lastly, the *specialized goal hypothesis* states that goal orientations exert different effects on different outcomes. For example, mastery goals may predict creative behaviors while performance goals may predict anxiety outcomes.

Table I

Qualitative Analysis by Goal Orientation During Engagement with an Insolvable Puzzle

GOAL ORIENTATION	QUALITATIVE COMMENTS
Performance	"These are stupid puzzles." "I can't solve them, I am tired, and besides, I've been sick this week." "Others will think I am dumb. Did Carol solve them? Will you tell me at the end how well I did?" "Are you kidding me, I am either stupid or those are insolvable. If I could take them at home I am sure I could solve them." "It's difficult, can't do it, what am I going to do? I don't know . . ." "If I had chosen a different folder I would move on but since I chose that one for comparisons, I will stick with it . . . " "Are there time limits?" "Have other students solved those before?" "Great, all of them are wrong, can't do them" "I am afraid I am going to be the worst among those who tried them." "Are you sure these puzzles can be solved?" "Can you show me how to do one?" "If you solve this one for me, I will think very highly of you."
Mastery	"I would like to try them again." "I'm going to solve them, are you sure there is a solution?" "I will stay here until I solve them." One mastery-oriented student asked if he had the opportunity to go back and change things he had done earlier in a certain way. He did not verbalize at all until the end of the task. At the end he was asked to respond as to how he felt and he added that: "You got to be very smart to solve those puzzles and you need lots and lots of practice". Then the experimenter asked that student: "What do you think is more important, to be smart or to practice?" The mastery student responded: "To practice." Regarding nonverbal behaviors, this mastery student was calm and effortful during the task, concentrated and focused, displaying a 'flow-like' experience, despite the fact that he had a broken arm, which prohibited his range of movement.

In two unpublished studies, we presented to college students (n = 96) and adolescents (n = 40) five puzzles, which were insolvable (Sideridis & Kaplan, 2005). Our purpose was to evaluate whether different goal groups would behave differently in an impossible task and we examined two outcomes (a) withdrawal of effort, and (b) emotional reactions. Table 1, shows some of the qualitative comments produced in both studies, based on student goal orientation grouping (mastery vs. performance-approach).

Research assistants recorded the verbalizations and non-verbal behaviors that took place during the task. Those responses were summarized to provide a qualitative picture of the experience of students motivated by various goal orientations. Student responses were summarized across three major classes of behaviors: (a) negative affect—frustration, (b) positive affect – energization, and, (c) calmness-relief, when the task was over. Seventeen students provided qualitative responses and were classified as follows: three were classified as calm, four expressed positive affect, and nine expressed negative affect during task engagement. Interestingly, 78% of the negative affect/frustration comments came from performance-oriented students (approach or avoidance), whereas 0% of the mastery students expressed negative affect. The respective percentages for positive affect/energization were 75% for mastery oriented students and 0% for performance oriented students.

As shown in Table 1, most of the mastery oriented students were not particularly distressed or disappointed by the difficulty of the task. Overall, they appeared more calm, focused, and joyful, enjoying the task rather than being stressed by it. On the contrary, performance-oriented students were highly anxious, especially as time went by. One typical example was George who attempted the puzzles at a medical lounge (his father was an M.D.). During the task, the teenager showed signs of distress and frustration. "I want to see how my friend Jim will do," he said. George's father provided us with additional information. "George did not do that well. I can understand that and I can tell when he does not do well because he usually comes to me saying, 'I won.'" He added that George was upset the whole evening and said that he did not like the puzzles and he thought they were stupid. Thus, the distressing experience stayed with the child that whole evening.

Summary of Research Findings from Goal Orientation Research

When putting together empirical evidence regarding the adaptiveness of goal orientations one can conclude the following:

1. Motivated by mastery goals is associated with acts of persistence (Patrick, 2004)

2. Motivated by mastery goals is associated with high achievement (Elliot et al., 1999)

3. Motivated by mastery goals is associated with positive affect when one engages in an academic task (Linnenbrink, 2004).

4. Motivated by mastery goals is associated with a 'flow-like' experience in which a student is absorbed in the task, loosing the sense of time. Fatigue is also experienced to a lesser degree (Turner et al., 2002).

5. Motivated by performance-approach goals can be adaptive to achievement outcomes (Harackiewicz et al., 2002).

6. Motivated by performance-approach goals is associated with elevations in anxiety and negative affect (Dykman, 1998; Pintrich et al., 2003).

7. Motivated by performance-approach goals is adaptive when a person also has high intrinsic interest, for example when a student pursues multiple goals (both mastery and performance) (Barron & Harackiewicz, 2001).

Potential Benefits from Adopting a Goal Orientation Approach in Learning Disabilities

Adopting a goal orientation approach may allow students with LD easier access to the general education curriculum since achievement goal theory has been proven to be very beneficial to achievement outcomes (Harackiewicz et al., 2002). Beckman (2001), suggested that successful student access to the general education curriculum is most likely when the teacher: (a) helps the students to set up their goals, (b) capitalizes on the strengths of the students, (c) values collaboration, (d) sets high expectations, and (e) varies instruction with regard to activities, assessment, etc. All five principles of successful student access to the general education curriculum are elements of mastery or performance goal environments. Thus, a goal orientation intervention may greatly facilitate that access.

A secondary implication of adopting a goal orientation approach into teaching pertains to the presence of *high stakes testing* for students with disabilities: According to a recent report by the American Educational Research Association (AERA), "for individual students, high scores (in high-stakes testing) may bring a special diploma attesting to exceptional academic accomplishment; low scores may result in . . . public embarrassment or students being held back in grade or denied a high school diploma." In achievement goal theory terms, high stakes testing is a property of a performance-oriented classroom environment that highly values normative assessments and this approach may, under certain circumstances be beneficial to student achievement. It may be, however, that given the presence of high stakes testing, it is more appropriate to examine the benefits of such an orientation (as the most important element of that orientation, normative evaluation, is mandated by the State). If a mastery-oriented intervention is more beneficial to learning, this finding will have important implications for even the existence of high stakes testing. For example, if the outcomes of high stakes testing are increased anxiety, threat appraisals, low self-esteem, negative affectivity, and even depression, maybe the concept of high stakes testing needs to be reconsidered.

Various aspects of motivation have already been embedded at the policy level (e.g., high stakes testing), in teaching (e.g., assessments emphasizing normative comparisons), and in student behaviors (e.g., avoidance or approach behaviors, etc). Most of the policy decisions have links to motivation and there may be great potential in enhancing student academic achievement by incorporating motivational elements into our instruction. Proper use of motivational principles in the classroom (at both the teacher and student level) may result in great student gains in achievement, particularly for students with learning disabilities who fit the learned helpless student profile (e.g., Sabatino, 1982; Sideridis, 2003). Of importance then is to examine how one can structure the classroom environment to be conducive for achievement purposes.

Classroom Goal Structures: Description and Empirical Evidence

Research examining the effects that classroom environments have on student behavior and achievement is scarce. This research area is pioneering and novel because it adds to our understanding of student behavior variables beyond those of the individual (student characteristics), teacher, family, and peers. The hypothesis is that in this interplay of classroom variables the instructor may play a role beyond that of the person who just delivers instruction. Elements of instructor's behavior have implications on students' engagement, boredom, support, reinforcement, motivation, affect, and eventually achievement.

Recently goal theory has been expanded suggesting that student's motivated behavior is influenced by both the person's dispositions and beliefs and also by the classroom environment (Patrick, 2004). This classroom context is hypothesized to shape the student's goal orientations but also other learning related outcomes (Linnenbrink, 2004; Turner et al., 2002). Based on goal theory, three types of classroom environments can be created: (a) mastery, (b) performance, and (c) combination mastery and performance. A mastery classroom structure is hypothesized to be associated with effective learning strategies, and a wide range of affective, cognitive, and motivational outcomes (Kaplan, Middleton, Urdan, & Midgley, 2002). Such outcomes are adaptive coping, enhanced self-efficacy and positive affect (Kaplan & Midgley, 1999).

Performance goal structures have a strong emphasis on external rewards and student success is defined as surpassing normative standards. As mentioned earlier, little research examined how classroom contexts affect student behavior and achievement. Recent research findings suggest that classrooms in which the emphasis is on performance goals are not conducive to learning. In those classroom students are reportedly more avoidant and withdrawing (Turner, Thorpe, & Meyer, 1998; Turner et al., 2002), avoid seeking help (Karabenick, 2004), are more disruptive (Kaplan, Gheen, & Midgley, 2002), and use self-handicapping as a strategy to compensate for low achievement (Urdan, 2004).

In a very recent study my colleagues and I examined how goal structures influence student behavior and affect in the inclusive classroom. Participants were 120 students, 60 with learning problems and 60 typical peers. Students were asked about their engagement and behavior following instruction in language arts. Their behaviors were recorded using a structured interview on five consecutive days. The classroom goal structure was assessed using an observation protocol which assessed various elements of teacher behavior (see Table 2). Teacher behaviors that had an emphasis on competition were classified as performance whereas those that emphasized cooperation were classified as mastery. Using the nested structure of the data, the analyses were run using Hierarchical Linear Modeling (HLM, Bryk & Raudenbush, 1992). For the purposes of the present chapter I will present the ability of mastery and performance goal structures to predict everyday school behaviors, in and out of the classroom.

Five different outcomes were assessed: (a) teacher's reinforcement as perceived by students, (b) teacher's punishment as perceived by students, (c) student affect (positive or negative), (d) student engagement, (e) student boredom, and (f) student behavior during the break. Our purpose was to examine whether student perceptions of their classroom goal structures could predict their everyday behaviors, anxieties, and perceptions of their teacher's behaviors. Results pointed to salient differences across goal oriented classrooms with regard to reinforcement, engagement and out-of-class behaviors (i.e., during the break). As Figures 3 and 4 show, students in mastery-oriented classrooms thought their teachers were more reinforcing compared to students in performance-oriented classrooms. Subsequently, the students in the mastery-oriented classrooms were engaged with the subject matter (language arts) substantially more time compared to the students in performance-oriented classrooms. Although no significant differences were observed in affect, students in performance-oriented classrooms reported being significantly more lonely during the break (in-between lessons). These recent findings provide empirical support with regard to the appropriateness of a mastery or performance goal structure. Because this line of research is novel, these findings should be regarded as preliminary regarding the effects of classroom goal structures on student behaviors at school. At present, it is premature to consider mastery goal structures as more adaptive compared to performance goal structures. Below I present the elements that describe the two goal structures, that if manipulated in specific ways, could produce mastery or performance classroom climates with their associated benefits and/or drawbacks.

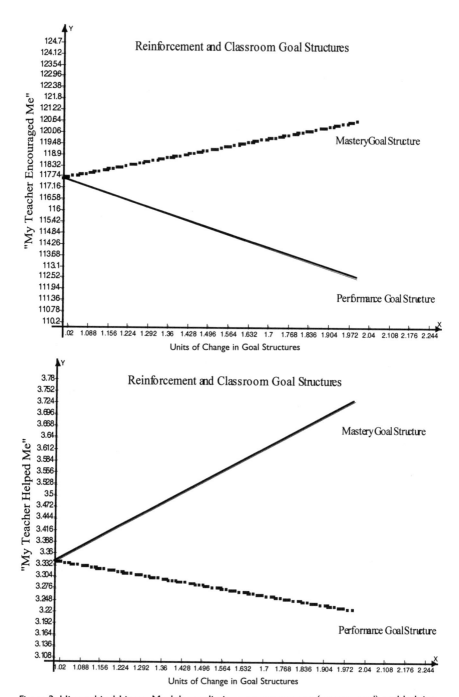

Figure 3. Hierarchical Linear Models predicting encouragement (upper panel) and helping behavior (lower panel) as a function of classroom motivation (mastery or performance goal structures).

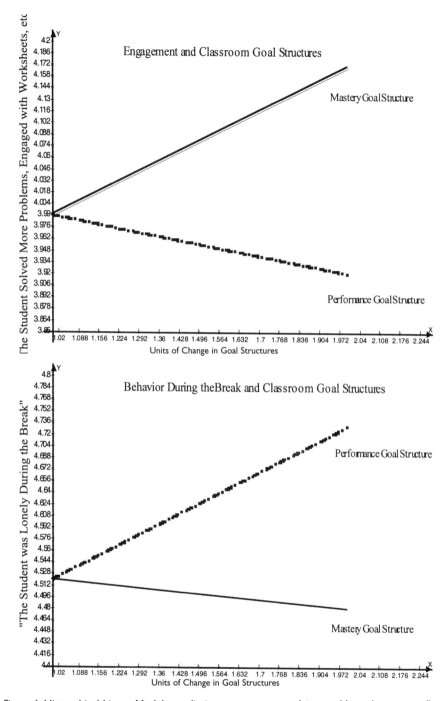

Figure 4. Hierarchical Linear Models predicting engagement—solving problems (upper panel) and behavior during the break (lower panel) as a function of classroom motivation (mastery or performance goal structures).

Table 2

Instructional Elements Manipulated to Create a Mastery or Performance Oriented Classroom Environment

Instructional Element	Mastery Goal Structure	Performance Goal Structure
1. Attitudes toward task	Understand process	Solve many math problem
2. Interest	Interesting word problems	Plain word problems
3. Reinforcement	For effort	For performance
4. Learning focus	Understanding	Performing well
5. Instructional emphasis	Cooperation	Competition
6. Help seeking	Encouraged, help cards	Not encouraged
7. Effort	Encouraged	Encouraged
8. Attitudes toward mistakes	Natural, part of learning	Threats, obstacles to achieving goals
9. Feedback	On understanding	On doing well, compared to others
10. Autonomy	Present	Absent
11. Goal setting	Master material	Perform better than others
12. Performance evaluation	Personal best	Public posting
13. Mood-affect	Positive, when mastering	Positive, when performing well

Goal Oriented Environments: Manipulated Variables

Table 2 presents the motivational elements of mastery and performance-approach oriented environments (Ames, 1992; Maehr & Anderman, 1993) that, if manipulated, may be associated with different student behaviors and achievement outcomes. Although, each instructional element is hypothesized to play a different role within each motivational climate, their potential contribution to achievement has been well demonstrated in past research (e.g., Butler, 1992). A brief description of these classroom elements is shown below:

1. *Attitudes toward task:* Positive attitudes toward an academic task have been found to be significant determinants of academic achievement for both typical students and students with LD. For example, Sideridis (2005) found that students with LD had significantly weaker attitudes toward spelling compared to typical students. Those findings were also replicated in language and math (see Sideridis 2002; Sideridis & Padeliadu, 2001). In a subsequent study, Sideridis (in press-c) investigated antecedents of

attitudes and reported that, for typical students, a mastery orientation was strongly associated with positive attitudes whereas for LD students, a performance-approach orientation was associated with both positive attitudes and academic achievement. Thus, both orientations have been considered important antecedents of academic achievement (in different populations).

2. *Interest:* Sansone, Weir, Harpster, and Morgan (1992) highlighted the importance of interest when they found that if a task is sufficiently interesting, individuals are more likely to continue being engaged; if not, boredom may lead to discontinuing the activity. The powerful effects of interest have been demonstrated in a mathematics intervention by Tobias and Everson (2000). They assigned students to a "high interest" condition in which math word problems were supplemented with familiar-to-the-student characters and fun scenarios. The results were dramatic; the group assigned to the high interest condition demonstrated significantly higher gains in mathematics (up to 30% more), compared to the control group (who were exposed to traditional math instruction). Given the importance of interest in academic achievement, it is unfortunate that students with LD have been reportedly lacking interest in an activity (oftentimes demonstrated with low engagement and task-avoidant behaviors) (e.g., Butler, 1992; Sideridis & Tsorbatzoudis, 2003).

3. *Reinforcement:* The effects of reinforcement on academic achievement, when rewards are incorporated into teaching, have been well documented in the literature (e.g., Meece & Miller, 1999). Reinforcement has been found to be effective, both if used in relevance to normative comparisons (e.g., for outperforming others) or for personal bests. The effects of reinforcement with special populations and across settings (integrated vs. segregated) have been well documented in the empirical literature (e.g., Hitchcock, Prater, & Dorwick, 2004; Kastner, Gottlieb, Gottlieb, & Kastner, 1995; Noell et al., 1998).

4. *Learning focus:* Focusing on understanding the concepts or on outperforming fellow students have been beneficial to student learning for both typical students and students with LD (e.g., Dunn & Shapiro, 1999). Thus, manipulating the learning focus may have important implications for student learning.

5. *Instructional emphasis:* Whether an emphasis is placed on cooperation or competition, results have indicated significant academic gains for both typical students (Turner et al., 1998) and students with LD (Sideridis, Utley, Greenwood, Dawson, & Delquadri, 1998; Sideridis et al., 1997). The style of learning, however, is more impersonal in performance-oriented classrooms. Given research findings, which suggest that performance goals are

more anxiety-eliciting, it is wiser to suggest an emphasis on mastering the material, rather than on performing well (e.g., Daly, Martens, Dool, & Hintze, 1998; Daly, Martens, Hamler, Dool, & Eckert, 1999; Daly, Martens, Kilmer, & Massie, 1996). In support of this proposition, there is ample evidence that high achievement and positive affect are present in cooperative structures (Wehby, Falk, Barton-Arwood, Lane, & Cooley, 2003).

6. _Help seeking:_ Avoiding help seeking has been characterized as an attribute of low achievement and students with LD have been reported to not seek help in the face of challenging and difficult conditions (e.g., Butler, 1993). Help seeking is a property of a mastery oriented classroom. Turner at al. (2002) described an example of this supportive motivational discourse. For example a student said: "I don't understand this" and the teacher replied: "You know what? That's why we are going to keep working on it today and tomorrow. You'll get it, Okay? We're just now starting it, April, so I don't expect you to fully understand it right away" (p. 93).

7. _Effort:_ The positive effects of increased effort and persistence on academic achievement have been consistently reported in the literature and, both mastery and performance orientations have been considered as antecedents of effort for both students with and without LD (e.g., Elliot et al., 1999; Sideridis, 2003).

8. _Attitudes toward mistakes:_ When mistakes are viewed as a natural part of learning, it is likely that they will not evoke anxiety, and performance will not be hindered by the effects of negative affectivity (e.g., Butler, 1993). The focus on avoiding mistakes and on performing to high normative standards however, has also been associated with positive academic gains (e.g., Elliot et al., 1999). For example, in a mastery-oriented classroom, Turner et al. (2002) presented an example of a student who gave an incorrect answer. The teacher responded: "Okay he's probably just checking to see if I was awake" (p. 93). Thus, the presence of humor by the teacher "softens" the fact that the student made a mistake and suggests that mistakes are not only natural, but a necessary condition for effective learning.

9. _Feedback:_ Feedback that is relevant to achievement has consistently been found to be positively associated with achievement outcomes for typical students (e.g., Elliot & Harackiewicz, 1996). Feedback, however, can be positive or negative. When feedback accompanies goal setting, with the students receiving feedback with regard to goal attainment, the academic outcomes for students with LD can be dramatically improved (Eckert, Ardoin, Daisey, & Scarola, 2000).

10. *Autonomy:* Students' flexibility in designing their own learning course within classroom instruction has been considered adaptive for learning, for both typical students and those with LD (e.g., Deci, Hodges, Pierson, & Tomassone, 1992). Several studies indicated that students feel more autonomous and are more self-regulating when they also believe they are competent to attain academic outcomes (Gagne, 2003; Levesque, Zuehlke, Stanek, & Ryan, 2004; Pelletier, Fortier, Vallerand, & Briere 2001; Reeve, Jang, Carrell, Jeon, & Barch, 2004; Reeve, Jang, Hardre, & Omura, 2002). Self-regulation of academic behaviors tends to "fail" when students feel pressured or controlled by important, to their life, adults (Grolnick, Ryan, & Deci, 1991; Sideridis in press-a). In correlational studies, autonomy was related positively to student's self-worth ($r = .36$) and negatively with anxiety ($r = -.32$) (Deci et al.). The opposite (a rigidly structured environment) has also been associated with positive academic gains as has been direct instruction (e.g., Engelman, Becker, & Carnine, 1988). For example, in the behavioral modification tradition, the focus is on highly controlling student behavior through manipulating contingencies of reinforcement or punishment. Those "controlled" environments have been associated with substantial academic benefits (Bonfiglio, Daly, Martens, Lin, & Corsaut, 2004). Deci et al., however, cautioned that: "although controlling contexts may have some benefits such as reducing confusion and increasing on-task behavior in the classroom, they could also have some unintended costs, namely, interfering with the students' developing greater self-regulation and leading to poorer achievement and adjustment in the classroom" (p. 470).

11. *Goal setting:* Goal setting has resulted in positive gains for both motivation and achievement (Page-Voth & Graham, 1999). The results have not been consistent for students with LD in that goal setting has not always been effective. Within the goal orientation paradigm, however, the goals to master the material or outperform others have been consistently associated with positive academic gains for both typical students and those with LD (e.g., Eckert et al., 2000; Pintrich et al., 1994).

12. *Evaluation:* Both public posting of performance and personal best paradigms have been associated with positive academic gains for both typical students and those with LD (e.g., Greenwood, Terry, Arreaga-Mayer, & Finney, 1992).

13. *Mood/Affect:* An environment that promotes positive affectivity has been associated with increased academic gains, regardless of the source of affectivity. For example, Bryan, Mathur, and Sullivan (1996) induced positive

mood, and that induction had a positive effect on subsequent performance for both typical students and students with LD. Unfortunately, environments that result in heightened negative affect (i.e., when students fail to meet goals) are conducive to low achievement or even the presence of depression (e.g., Sideridis in press-b).

Conclusions and Recommendations for Future Research

The purpose of the present chapter was to present research evidence concerning the contribution of motivation on the achievement of students with and without LD. Using the achievement goal theory framework I described how our knowledge of goal orientations can be used toward modifying classroom environments to be conducive to learning. It is concluded that the pursuit of mastery goals is certainly adaptive for students' regulation of their behavior and their achievement. Also, pursuing performance goals proved to be adaptive, particularly for students with LD, in some studies but not all. Thus, the empirical literature regarding the adaptiveness of various goal orientations is inconclusive. Furthermore, recent theoretical propositions state that teachers have a powerful effect on the classroom climate they create because they are the "purpose" behind students' engagement in academic behaviors. Based on this thesis, several researchers attempted to evaluate classroom environments based on their "motivational" structure. Researchers' observations of specific teacher behaviors and their link to specific goal patterns were correlated with student behaviors and achievement. Preliminary empirical evidence suggests that creating mastery-oriented environments is adaptive for learning purposes. Regarding the adaptiveness of performance-oriented environments, findings have been inconclusive, suggesting the need for further research. Our lack of knowledge on what teaching structures work or don't work is partly based on our inability to: (a) have a clear theory of the taxonomy of goal structures, and (b) have a clear understanding of what behaviors represent those goal structures. In this chapter I attempted to combine all that knowledge and created my own taxonomy of what mastery and performance goal structures entail. The specific recommendations of the elements of goal structures were based on a synthesis of the literature and were not exhaustive. Other teacher behaviors, student-teacher interactions, and classroom settings may also be adaptive for learning purposes and need to be explored. Also, moving away from the classic mastery-performance dichotomy may help us motivate students in additional ways as the combination of the two orientations may result in enriched classroom environments (Linnenbrink, 2004). This line of research is promising and hopefully, we will understand the conditions under which students with and without LD will learn more efficiently.

ACKNOWLEDGMENTS

I would like to thank the teachers and students from Greece who participated in the studies reported herein. Also, I am indebted to Moira Munns for her careful editing of this chapter, which resulted in a much improved product.

Address correspondence for this chapter to Georgios, D. Sideridis, Ph.D., University of Crete, Department of Psychology, Rethimno, 74100, Crete, Greece. E-mail: sideridis@psy.soc.uoc.gr

REFERENCES

Adelman, H. S., & Taylor, L. (1983). Enhancing motivation for overcoming learning and behavior problems. *Journal of Learning Disabilities, 7,* 384–392.

Ames, C. (1992). Classrooms: Goals, structures, and student motivation. *Journal of Educational Psychology, 84,* 261–271.

Barron, K. E., & Harackiewicz, J. M. (2001). Achievement goals and optimal motivation: Testing multiple goal models. *Journal of Personality and Social Psychology, 80,* 706–722.

Barron, K. E., & Harackiewicz, J. M. (2003). Revisiting the benefits of performance-approach goals in the college classroom: Exploring the role of goals in advanced college courses. *International Journal of Educational Research, 39,* 357–374.

Barron, K. E., Schwab, C., & Harackiewicz, J. M. (1999, May). *Achievement goals and classroom context: A comparison of different learning environments.* Paper presented at the meeting of the Midwestern Psychological Association, Chicago, IL.

Beckman, P. (2001). *Access to the general education curriculum for students with disabilities.* ERIC Clearinghouse on Disabilities and Gifted Education. Arlington, VA: CEC.

Bonfiglio, C. M., Daly, E. J. I., Martens, B. K., Lin, L. H. R., & Corsaut, S. (2004). An experimental analysis of reading interventions: Generalization across instructional strategies. *Journal of Applied Behavior Analysis, 37,* 111–114.

Botsas, G., & Padeliadu, S. (2003). Goal orientation and reading comprehension strategy use among students with and without reading difficulties. *International Journal of Educational Research, 34,* 477–495.

Bouffard, T., & Couture, N. (2003). Motivational profile and academic achievement among students enrolled in different schooling tracks. *Educational Studies, 29,* 19–38.

Bryan, T., Mathur, S., & Sullivan, K. (1996). The impact of positive mood on learning. *Learning Disability Quarterly, 19,* 153–162.

Bryk, A. S., & Raudenbush, S. W. (1992). *Hierarchical linear models.* Newbury Park, CA: Sage Publications.

Butler, R. (1992). What young people want to know when: Effects of mastery and ability goals on interest in different kinds of social comparisons. *Journal of Personality and Social Psychology, 62,* 934–943.

Butler, R. (1993). Effects of task- and ego-achievement goals on information seeking during task engagement. *Journal of Personality and Social Psychology, 65,* 18–31.

Carlson, C. L., Booth, J. E., Shin, M., & Canu, W. H. (2002). Parent-, teacher-, and self-rated motivational styles in ADHD subtypes. *Journal of Learning Disabilities, 35,* 104–113.

Chapman, J. (1988). Cognitive-motivational characteristics and academic achievement of learning disabled children: Individual differences and their implications for treatment. In J. Torgesen & B. Wong (Eds.), *Psychological and educational perspectives on learning disabilities* (pp. 225–255). New York: Academic Press.

Chapman, J. W., & Tunmer, W. E. (1995). Development of young children's reading self-concepts: An examination of emerging sub components and their relation with reading achievement. *Journal of Educational Psychology, 87,* 154–167.

Church, M. A., Elliot, A. J., & Gable, S. L. (2001). Perceptions of classroom environment, achievement goals, and achievement outcomes. *Journal of Educational Psychology, 93,* 43–54.

Colbert, P., Newman, B., Ney, P., & Young J. (1982). Learning disabilities as a symptom of depression in children. *Journal of Learning Disabilities, 15,* 333–336.

Dalley, M. B., & Bolocofsky, D. N. (1992). Depressive symptomatology, attributional style, dysfunctional attitude, and social competency in adolescents with and without learning disabilities. *School Psychology Review, 21,* 444–459.

Daly, E. J. I., Martens, B. K., Dool, E. J., & Hintze, J. M. (1998). Using brief functional analysis to select interventions for oral reading. *Journal of Behavioral Education, 8,* 203–218.

Daly, E. J. I., Martens, B. K., Hamler, K. R., Dool, E. J., & Eckert, T. L. (1999). A brief experimental analysis for identifying instructional components needed to improve oral reading fluency. *Journal of Applied Behavior Analysis, 32,* 83–94.

Daly, E. J. I., Martens, B. K., Kilmer, A., & Massie, D. R. (1996). The effects of instructional match and content overlap on generalized reading performance. *Journal of Applied Behavior Analysis, 29,* 507–518.

Deci, E. L., Hodges, R., Pierson, L., & Tomassone, J. (1992). Autonomy and competence as motivational factors in students with learning disabilities and emotional handicaps. *Journal of Learning Disabilities, 25,* 457–471.

Dunn, P. B., & Shapiro, S. K. (1999). Gender differences in the achievement goal orientations of ADHD children. *Cognitive Therapy and Research, 23,* 327–344.

Dweck, C. S., & Leggett, E. L. (1988). A social-cognitive approach to motivation and personality. *Psychological Review, 95,* 256–273.

Dykman, B. M. (1998). Integrating cognitive and motivational factors in depression: Initial tests of a goal-orientation approach. *Journal of Personality and Social Psychology, 74,* 139–158.

Eckert, T. L., Ardoin, S. P., Daisey, D. M., & Scarola, M. D. (2000). Empirically evaluating the effectiveness of reading interventions: The use of brief experimental analysis and single case designs. *Psychology in the Schools, 37,* 463–473.

Elliot, A. J. (1997). Integrating the 'classic' and 'contemporary' approaches to achievement motivation: A hierarchical model of approach and avoidance achievement motivation. In M. L. Maehr & P. R. Pintrich (Eds.), *Advances in motivation and achievement* (Vol. 10, pp. 143–179). Greenwich, CT: JAI Press.

Elliot, A. J., & Church, M. A. (1997). A hierarchical model of approach and avoidance achievement motivation. *Journal of Personality and Social Psychology, 72,* 218–232.

Elliot, A. J., & Harackiewicz, J. M. (1996). Approach and avoidance achievement goals and intrinsic motivation: A mediational analysis. *Journal of Personality and Social Psychology, 70,* 461–475.

Elliot, A. J., & McGregor, H. A. (1999). Test anxiety and the hierarchical model of approach and avoidance achievement motivation. *Journal of Personality and Social Psychology, 76,* 628–644.

Elliot, A. J., & McGregor, H. A. (2001). A 2 x 2 achievement goal framework. *Journal of Personality and Social Psychology, 80,* 501–519.

Elliot, A. J., McGregor, J. A., & Gable, S. (1999). Achievement goals, study strategies, and exam performance: A mediational analysis. *Journal of Educational Psychology, 91,* 549–563.

Engelmann, S., Becker, W., & Carnine, D. (1988). Direct instruction: A general case for teaching the general case. *Education and Treatment of Children, 11,* 303–317.

Fulk, B. M., Brigham, F. J., & Lohman, D. A. (1998). Motivation and self-regulation: A comparison of students with learning and behavior problems. *Remedial and Special Education, 19,* 300–309.

Gagne, M. (2003). The role of autonomy support and autonomy orientation in prosocial behavior engagement. *Motivation and Emotion, 27,* 199–223.

Gallop, R. J., Crits-Christoph, P., Muenz, L. R., & Tu, X. M. (2003). Determination and interpretation of the optimal operating point for ROC curves derived through generalized linear models. *Understanding Statistics, 2,* 219–242.

Greenway, P., & Milne, L. (1999). Relationship between psychopathology, learning disabilities, or both and WISC-III subtest scatter in adolescents. *Psychology in the Schools, 36,* 103–108.

Greenwood, C. R., Terry, B, Arreaga-Mayer, C., & Finney, R. (1992). The classwide peer tutoring program: Implementation factors moderating students' achievement. *Journal of Applied Behavior Analysis, 25,* 101–116.

Gregg, N., Hoy, C., King, M., Moreland, C., & Jagota, M. (1992). The MMPI-2 profile of adults with learning disabilities in university and rehabilitation settings. *Journal of Learning Disabilities, 25,* 386–395.

Grolnick, W. S., & Ryan, R. M. (1990). Self-perceptions, motivation, and adjustment in children with learning disabilities: A multiple group comparison study. *Journal of Learning Disabilities, 23,* 177–184.

Grolnick, W. S., Ryan, R. M., & Deci, E. L. (1991). The inner resources for school achievement: Motivational mediators of children's perceptions of their parents. *Journal of Educational Psychology, 83,* 508–517.

Harackiewicz, J. M., Barron, K. E., Carter, S. M., Lehto, A. T., & Elliot, A. J. (1997). Predictors and consequences of achievement goals in the college classroom: Maintaining interest and making the grade. *Journal of Personality and Social Psychology, 73,* 1284–1295.

Harackiewicz, J. M., Barron, K. E., & Elliot, A. J. (1998). Rethinking achievement goals: When are they adaptive for college students and why? *Educational Psychologist, 33,* 1–21.

Harackiewicz, J. M., Barron, K. E., Pintrich, P. R., Elliot, A. J., & Thrash, T. M. (2002). Revision of achievement goal theory: Necessary and illuminating. *Journal of Educational Psychology, 94,* 638–645.

Harackiewicz, J. M., Barron, K. E., Tauer, J. M., Carter, S. M., & Elliot, A. J. (2000). Short-term and long-term consequences of achievement goals: Predicting interest and performance over time. *Journal of Educational Psychology, 92,* 316–330.

Harackiewicz, J. M., Barrron, K. E., Tauer, J. M., & Elliot, A. J. (2002). Predicting success in college: A longitudinal study of achievement goals and ability measures as predictors of interest and performance from freshman year through graduation. *Journal of Educational Psychology, 94,* 638–645.

Heath, N. L., & Ross, S. (2000). Prevalence and expression of depressive symptomatology in students with and without learning disabilities. *Learning Disability Quarterly, 23,* 24–36.

Hitchcock, C. H., Prater, M. A., & Dowrick, P. W. (2004). Reading comprehension and fluency: Examining the effects of tutoring and video self-modeling. *Learning Disability Quarterly, 27,* 89–103.

Hoy, C., Gregg, N., Wisenbaker, J., Manglitz, E., King, M., & Moreland, C. (1997). Depression and anxiety in two groups of adults with learning disabilities. *Learning Disability Quarterly, 20,* 280–291.

Hsu, L. M. (2002). Diagnostic validity statistics and the MCMI-III. *Psychological Assessment, 14,* 410–422.

Kaplan, A., Gheen, M., & Midgley, C. (2002). Classroom goal structure and student disruptive behavior. *British Journal of Educational Psychology, 72,* 191–211.

Kaplan, A., & Middleton, M. J. (2002). Should childhood be a journey or a race? Response to Harackiewicz et al. (2002). *Journal of Educational Psychology, 94,* 646–648.

Kaplan, A., Middleton, M. J., Urdan, T., & Midgley, C. (2002). Achievement goals and goal structures. In C. Midgley (Ed.), *Goals, goal structures and patterns of adaptive learning* (pp. 21–53). Mahwah, NJ: Lawrence Erlbaum.

Kaplan, A., & Midgley, C. (1999). The relationship between perceptions of the classroom goal structure and early adolescents' affect in school: The mediating role of coping strategies. *Learning and Individual Differences, 11,* 187–212.

Karabenick, S. A. (2004). Perceived achievement goal structure and college student help seeking. *Journal of Educational Psychology, 96,* 569–581.

Kastner, J., Gottlieb, B. W., Gottlieb, J., & Kastner, S. (1995). Use of incentive structure in mainstream classes. *Journal of Educational Research, 89,* 52–57.

Levesque, C., Zeuhlke, N. A., Stanek, L. R., & Ryan, R. M. (2004). Autonomy and competence in German and American university students: A comparative study based on self-determination theory. *Journal of Educational Psychology, 96,* 68–64.

Linnenbrink, E. A. (2004). Person and context: Theoretical and practical concerns in achievement goal theory. In P. R. Pintrich & M. L., Maehr (Eds.), *Advances in motivation and achievement* (Vol. 13, pp. 159–184). Greenwich, CT: JAI Press.

Maehr, M. L., & Anderman, E. M. (1993). Reinventing schools for early adolescents: Emphasizing task goals. *Elementary School Journal, 93,* 593–610.

Masi, G., Brovedani, P., & Poli, P. (1998). School failure in early adolescence: the psychopathological risk. *Child Psychiatry and Human Development, 29,* 127–140.

Meece, J. L., & Miller, S. D. (1999). Changes in elementary school children's achievement goals for reading and writing: Results of a longitudinal and an intervention study. *Scientific Studies of Reading, 3,* 207–229.

Middleton, M. J., & Midgley, C. (1997). Avoiding the demonstration of lack of ability: An underexplored aspect of goal theory. *Journal of Educational Psychology, 89,* 710–718.

Midgley, C., Kaplan, A., & Middleton, M. (2001). Performance-approach goals: Good for what, for whom, under what circumstances, and at what cost? *Journal of Educational Psychology, 93,* 77–86.

Nicholls, J. G. (1984). Achievement motivation: Conceptions of ability, subjective experiences, task choice, and performance. *Psychological Review, 91,* 328–346.

Noell, G. H., Gansle, K. A., Witt, J. C., Whitmarsh, E. L., Freeland, J. T., & LaFleur, L. H. (1998). Effects of contingent reward and instruction on oral reading performance at differing levels of passage difficulty. *Journal of Applied Behavior Analysis, 31,* 659–663.

Olivier, M. A. J., & Steenkamp, D. S. (2004). Attention-deficit/hyperactivity disorder: Underlying deficits in achievement motivation. *International Journal for the Advancement of Counselling, 26,* 47–63.

Page-Voth, V., & Graham, S. (1999). Effects of goal setting and strategy use on the writing performance and self-efficacy of students with writing and learning problems. *Journal of Educational Psychology, 91,* 230–240.

Palladino, P., Poli, P., Masi, G., & Marcheschi, M. (2000). The relation between metacognition and depressive symptoms in preadolescents with learning disabilities: Data in support of Borkowski's model. *Learning Disabilities Research & Practice, 15,* 142–148.

Patrick, H. (2004). Re-examining classroom mastery goal structure. In P. R. Pintrich & M. L., Maehr (Eds.), *Advances in motivation and achievement* (Vol. 13, pp. 233–263). Greenwich, CT: JAI Press.

Pelletier, L. G., Fortier, M. S., Vallerand, R. J., & Briere, N. M. (2001). Associations among perceived autonomy support, forms of self-regulation, and persistence: A prospective study. *Motivation and Emotion, 25,* 279–306.

Pintrich, P. R., Anderman, E. M., & Klobucar, C. (1994). Intraindividual differences in motivation and cognition in students with and without learning disabilities. *Journal of Learning Disabilities, 27,* 360–370.

Pintrich, P. R., Conley, A. M., & Kempler, T. (2003). Current issues in achievement goal theory and research. *International Journal of Educational Research, 39,* 339–356.

Reeve, J., Jang, H.,Carrell, D., Jeon, S., & Barch, J. (2004). Enhancing students' engagement by increasing teachers' autonomy support. *Motivation and Emotion, 28,* 147–169.

Reeve, J., Jang, H., Hardre, P., & Omura, M. (2002). Providing a rationale in an autonomy-supportive way as a strategy to motivate others during an uninteresting activity. *Motivation and Emotion, 26,* 183–207.

Riddick, B., Sterling, C., Farmer, M., & Morgan, S. (1999). Self-esteem and anxiety in the educational histories of adult dyslexic students. *Dyslexia, 5,* 227–248.

Rodriguez, C. M., & Routh, D. K. (1989). Depression, anxiety, and attributional style in learning disabled and non-learning disabled children. *Journal of Clinical Child Psychology, 18,* 299– 304.

Rogers, H., & Saklofski, D. H. (1985). Self-concepts, locus of control and performance expectations of LD children. *Journal of Learning Disabilities, 18,* 273–277.

Sabatino, D. A. (1982). Research on achievement motivation with learning disabled populations. *Advances in Learning and Behavioral Disabilities, 1,* 75–116.

Sansone, C., Weir, C., Harpster, L., & Morgan, C. (1992). Once a boring task always a boring task? Interest as a self-regulatory mechanism. *Journal of Personality and Social Psychology, 63,* 379–390.

Sideridis, G. D. (2002). The motivational determinants of elementary school students at risk of having reading and spelling difficulties: An application of planned behavior theory with goal importance. *Journal of Learning Disabilities, 35,* 343–356.

Sideridis, G. D. (2003). On the origins of helpless behavior in students with learning disabilities: Avoidance motivation? *International Journal of Educational Research, 39,* 497–517.

Sideridis, G. D. (2005). Attitudes and motivation of poor and good spellers: Broadening planned behavior theory. *Reading and Writing Quarterly, 21,* 87–103.

Sideridis, G. D. (in press-a). Achievement goal orientations, oughts, and self-regulation in students with and without learning disabilities. *Learning Disability Quarterly.*

Sideridis, G. D. (in press-b). Goal orientation, academic achievement and depression: Evidence in favor of a revised goal theory framework. *Journal of Educational Psychology.*

Sideridis, G. D. (in press-c). Performance approach-avoidance motivation and planned behavior theory: Model stability with students with and without learning disabilities. *Reading and Writing Quarterly.*

Sideridis, G. D. (in press-d). Understanding low achievement and depression in the LD: A goal orientation approach. In H. Switzky (Ed.), Current perspectives on individual differences in personality and motivation in persons with mental retardation and other developmental disabilities. *International review of research in mental retardation.* San Diego: Academic Press.

Sideridis, G. D., & Kaplan, A. (2005). *Achievement goal orientations and persistence across tasks: The roles of failure and success.* Manuscript submitted for publication.

Sideridis, G. D., Morgan, P., Botsas, G., Padeliadu, S., & Fuchs, D. (in press). Prediction of students with LD based on metacognition, motivation, emotions, and psychopathology: A ROC analysis. *Journal of Learning Disabilities.*

Sideridis, G. D., & Padeliadu, S. (2001). The motivational determinants of elementary school students at risk of having reading difficulties: An application of planned behavior theory with goal importance. *Remedial and Special Education, 22,* 268–297.

Sideridis, G. D., & Tsorbatzoudis, Ch. (2003). Intra-group motivational analysis of students with learning disabilities: A goal orientation approach. *Learning Disabilities: A Contemporary Journal, 1,* 8–19.

Sideridis, G. D., Utley, C., Greenwood, C. R., Dawson, H., & Delquadri, J., (1998). An intervention strategy to enhance spelling performance, social interactions and decrease inappropriate behaviors of students with mild disabilities and typical peers in an inclusive instructional setting. *Research in Education, 59,* 169–186.

Sideridis, G. D., Utley, C., Greenwood, C. R., Dawson, H., Delquadri, J., & Palmer, P. (1997). Classwide peer tutoring and its effects on the spelling performance and social interactions of students with mild disabilities in an integrated setting. *Journal of Behavioral Education, 7,* 435–462.

Skaalvik, E. M. (1997). Self-enhancing and self-defeating ego orientation: Relations with task and avoidance orientation, achievement, self-perceptions, and anxiety. *Journal of Educational Psychology, 89,* 71–81.

Stanovich, P. J., Jordan, A., & Perot, J. (1998). Relative differences in academic self-concept and peer acceptance among students in inclusive classrooms. *Remedial and Special Education, 19,* 120–125.

Taylor, L., & Adelman, H. S. (1999). Personalizing classroom instruction to account for motivational and developmental differences. *Reading and Writing Quarterly, 15,* 255–276.

Thomas, A., (1979). Learned helplessness and expectancy factors: Implications for research in learning disabilities. *Review of Educational Research, 49,* 208–221.

Tobias, S., & Everson, H. (2000). Assessing metacognitive knowledge monitoring. In G. Schraw & J. Impara (Eds.), *Issues in the measurement of metacognition* (pp. 43–97). Lincoln, NE: Buros Institute of Mental Measurements.

Turner, J. C., Midgley, C., Meyer, D. K., Gheen, M., Anderman, E., Kang, Y., et al. (2002). The classroom environment and students' reports of avoidance strategies in mathematics: A multimethod study. *Journal of Educational Psychology, 94,* 88–106.

Turner, J. C., Thorpe, P. K., & Meyer, D. K. (1998). Students' reports of motivation and negative affect: A theoretical and empirical analysis. *Journal of Educational Psychology, 90,* 758–771.

Urdan, T. C. (2004). Predictors of academic self-handicapping and achievement: Examining achievement goals, classroom goal structures, and culture. *Journal of Educational Psychology, 96,* 251–264.

Valas, H. (1999). Students with learning disabilities and low achieving students: Peer acceptance, loneliness, self-esteem, and depression. *Social Psychology of Education, 3,* 173–192.

Valas, H. (2001). Learned helplessness and psychological adjustment II: Effects of learning disabilities and low achievement. *Scandinavian Journal of Educational Research, 45,* 101– 114.

Watkins, M. W. (1996). Diagnostic utility of the WISC-III developmental index as a predictor of learning disabilities. *Journal of Learning Disabilities, 29,* 305–312.

Wehby, J. H., Falk, K. B., Barton-Arwood, S., Lane, K. L., & Cooley, C. (2003). The impact of comprehensive reading instruction on the academic and social behavior of students with emotional and behavioral disorders. *Journal of Emotional and Behavioral Disorders, 11,* 225–238.